The New Labor Press

The New Labor Press

Journalism for a Changing Union Movement

Edited by Sam Pizzigati and Fred J. Solowey

ILR Press
Ithaca, New York

Library of Congress Cataloging-in-Publication Data

The New labor press : journalism for a changing union movement/
edited by Sam Pizzigati and Fred J. Solowey.
  p. cm.
Includes index.
ISBN 0-87546-189-1 (cloth). — ISBN 0-87546-190-5 (pbk.)
1. Press, Labor—United States—History—20th century.
2. Journalism, Labor—United States—History—20th century.
I. Pizzigati, Sam. II. Solowey, Fred J.
PN4888.L3N48 1992
070.4′ 49331′ 097309045—dc20   92-10352

Copies may be ordered through bookstores or directly from
ILR Press
School of Industrial and Labor Relations
Cornell University
Ithaca, NY 14853-3901

Printed on acid-free paper in the United States of America

5 4 3 2 1

Contents

Part Four: Labor and Community

Part Five: New Approaches

Concluding Thoughts

Foreword

Patrick J. Ziska

At last, someone has tried to corral the wild horse we call "the labor press."

That was my first reaction when I learned about this project. That remains my reaction now that the book is complete and ready for readers.

The labor press, considered by some the Peck's Bad Boy of the labor movement, by others a necessary evil imposed by tradition and existing by sufferance of labor's hierarchy, is finally getting its day in print.

The authors have done a job I often imagined undoable. They have put life into that nebulous label—labor press—and produced a document that should spark discussion and evoke improvement in this season of labor movement discontent.

This document does not solve the puzzle of the labor press. What it does do is gather all the pieces and place them in order and perspective. It is for the readers to finish the puzzle.

If you have read this far, you are interested in the trade union movement. That interest is either friendly or hostile. To friend and foe, I issue an invitation and, with it, a challenge, even a warning.

Let me direct my comments first to labor's friends. You might come to this book as an activist union member, a union officer, or even the editor of a labor publication. To you I say, read on. You will learn from

Patrick J. Ziska is the immediate past president of the International Labor Communications Association. A veteran daily newspaper reporter, Ziska served as president of The Newspaper Guild Local 35 in Rochester, New York, before joining the staff of the International Association of Machinists in Washington, D.C. Now a special assistant to the IAM president, Ziska previously worked as the associate editor of the union's monthly publication, the Machinist.

these pages. The pieces are here. With your help, the solution—a stronger, more vital labor press—cannot be far behind.

You may disagree with all or part of what you read here. I certainly am not in total agreement. I find some contributors overly optimistic, the assessments of others too grim.

To those of you who may disagree with any contributor, I issue you this challenge: The discussion has begun. Now let *your* views be known in every forum available—this book is only a beginning.

And my warning? I warn against continued complacency. The hour is late. The time for corrective measures by and in the labor press is overdue.

And to readers who consider the labor movement no friend, I also offer an invitation and a warning. I invite you to read on as well. You will learn that it is too early to start celebrating the demise of the labor press. The very fact that such a candidly critical book could be written—by labor press practitioners—should tell you something about the resilience and vitality of America's labor journalists.

Finally, I would like to invite our brother and sister journalists from the "straight"—the commercial—press to take a look at this book, even if you no longer cover labor.

I have worked both sides of the aisle. I was a daily press reporter long before I skated into the labor movement, and I'd like to ask my former colleagues in the commercial press a simple question: Can you imagine anybody who sups at corporate America's propaganda buffet writing this kind of book about the kept corporate press? Try passing this book along to your publisher and asking if you could do a similar self-critical probe on your paper's chain operation.

If you really want to pull your publisher's "chain," you might note that if your employer's publication had worked half as hard digging up socially useful information on savings and loan scoundrels as it did and does sniping at labor, we might not still be stuck in a "Gong Show" economy.

Is the labor press alive enough to serve as a source of enlightenment for union members? Hell, yes.

Can the labor press become better? Read on.

Introduction

Sam Pizzigati and Fred J. Solowey

In 1985, after more than two years of deliberations, a blue-ribbon panel of AFL-CIO leaders released a long-awaited report on revitalizing the labor movement in the United States. This landmark report, *The Changing Situation of Workers and Their Unions,* called improving how unions communicate to members and the public simply "imperative."

How could labor communicate more effectively? *The Changing Situation of Workers and Their Unions* offered a long list of recommendations. Buy advertising. Stage teleconferences. Produce videocassettes. Link up with cable TV.

A good list, except for one rather significant omission. The entire *Changing Situation* report carried not one word about the labor press—the newspapers, magazines, and newsletters published, at great cost, by America's unions.

How could this landmark report label communications "imperative" to labor's future yet totally ignore the labor press, the only vehicle for communications currently common to all unions? Just two explanations seem possible. Either the labor press is doing such a good job that labor leaders can think of no recommendation that could reasonably improve it, or, alternatively, the labor press has been so listless for so long that it has become institutional wallpaper, something seen every day but never really noticed. The labor leaders who prepared *The Changing Situation of Workers and Their Unions* never mentioned the labor press because they never give the labor press a second thought.

Which explanation better approximates reality? This is not, unfortunately, a difficult question to answer. If the first explanation were true, if the labor press *were* truly doing a wonderful job—informing, educating, and mobilizing readers—then the nation's top labor leaders would not have had to spend more than two years trying to figure out how unions can communicate effectively to members. If the labor press were succeeding, unions would *already* be communicating effectively to union members.

Just what do we mean by the labor press? The labor press encompasses any publication that targets an audience of working people and advocates on behalf of the labor movement. Today, the labor press is overwhelmingly a *trade union* press. With few exceptions, the only publications written for working people on behalf of trade unionism are the newspapers, magazines, and newsletters published by trade unions.

This was not always the case. In the labor movement's earliest days, union-published papers were the exception, not the rule. Far more common were the publications edited by independent, outspoken advocates for labor, printers and journalists who scraped out a living publishing papers that working people bought to find the information and the inspiration they could find nowhere else.

These early labor publications sometimes billed themselves as the "official newspaper" of a formal trade union body. The most noted labor paper of the Civil War era, for instance, proudly proclaimed itself the official newspaper of the Philadelphia Trades' Assembly. But the paper, *Fincher's Trades' Review,* was, in the modern sense, far more independent than official. The paper's editor and publisher, Jonathan Fincher, had no direct access to any union treasury. To survive, Fincher had to hustle subscriptions and contributions from union members.

Equally widespread, as the twentieth century neared, were the papers that sought to mobilize working people behind one or another political banner. Socialist and then communist parties have published scores of newspapers that delivered pro-union messages to working class audiences. Just after the turn of the century, the largest-circulation weekly newspaper in the United States was the *Appeal to Reason,* an unofficial Socialist party paper that circulated over 760,000 copies at its peak in 1913. During the Great Depression, the newspaper of the Communist Party USA, the *Daily Worker,* saw its paid circulation climb to 100,000.

Individual unions, of course, also subsidized their own publications through these years. But these union papers, mailed free to union members, were just one facet of a larger labor press. Only later, after labor-oriented left parties had largely collapsed and competition from mass-circulation journalism had squeezed out the last of the pro-labor independent publishers, did the labor press lose its variety—and perhaps vitality.

By 1950, labor press meant union press, and a fairly extensive one at that. In the early 1950s, the labor movement in the United States stood at a historic high-water mark. One out of every three working people in the United States was a union member, and all these union members received labor papers from a variety of union sources.

At the local level, central labor councils published papers in cities across the United States. Union locals usually produced their own papers as well, as did every union at the national level. These publications appeared frequently. Postal rates were low—official government policy still reflected the quaint idea that a democracy ought to underwrite the dissemination of reading matter—and some unions, like the Machinists, actually published on a weekly schedule.

But those salad days couldn't last, not in the face of postal rates that were rising and union memberships that were, everywhere except the public sector, falling. In the postwar years, unions failed to see the deindustrialization storm clouds ahead that would decimate core union membership. By the 1980s, most national unions had been forced to scale back their publication programs significantly. Weeklies became monthlies, monthlies moved to bimonthly or even quarterly frequency, and some papers, like the railway workers' *Labor,* simply died.

Few union members seemed to notice. Union publications simply could not compete with commercial newspapers and magazines for working people's attention, in part because economic and cultural forces had combined to obscure the role of class—and class consciousness—in American life. In one sense, trade unions were victims of their own success. Unions had helped raise the quality of life for union members and, in the process, had become less central to their lives.

Most union papers, unfortunately, published little that could help reconnect members to their unions. Too many labor publications, critics charged, had become little more than "in-house puffery sheets" for out-of-touch labor leaders.

"The feeble state of the labor press," Ralph Nader wrote in 1977, "means that thirty million union members are often left in the dark about some major issues, never review or discuss them, and cannot really come to grips with many of the problems that beset labor." Five years later, another analyst blasted union papers as "poorly designed and edited" publications that "tend to withhold news that workers desperately need in order to decide democratically about union policy, union officers, political endorsements, and proposed contracts."

How valid are these critiques today? Is the labor press making a contribution, meeting its obligations to the labor movement and working people? If not, do we even need a labor press?

In the pages that follow, a broad assortment of journalists from both inside and outside the labor movement offer their perspectives on these fundamentally important questions. You'll find no unanimity here. Some of the contributors, longtime labor movement insiders, are clearly optimistic about the prospects for America's labor press. Others see little hope unless a vast upsurge from below shakes the labor hierarchy.

Despite these conflicting perspectives, all the contributors you'll find in these pages do share one overriding conviction. A labor press, they believe, remains as desperately needed as ever. Maybe more than ever.

This conviction, at first glance, might strike readers as somewhat strange. After all, don't we live in an "Information Age"? Aren't we Americans already bombarded by enough messages? Don't we already kill enough trees to produce an endless stream of periodicals of every sort? Why do we need still more publications?

We don't need more. We need different. We need a press that reflects the lives of working people—their hopes, their fears, their troubles, their triumphs.

Union leaders often attack the mass media as anti-union. And they're right. Daily newspapers and TV news programs don't give unions a fair shake, as our first contributors, the Machinists union's Robert Kalaski and former *New York Times* labor reporter William Serrin, will explain. But the damage America's media inflict upon the labor movement, as Kalaski and Serrin also explain, goes far beyond a simple anti-union bias. Day after day, the mass media attack the very core of trade unionism, the simple notion that working people count, that their problems matter, that their dreams are worth struggling for.

The American mass media give us a world where working people— and the challenges working people face—barely exist. In the parade of celebrities that dominates America's front pages and television screens, few working people ever appear. We see the peccadillos of our politicians. We follow the careers of our stars. We seldom see ourselves. We draw the unspoken conclusion: we must not matter. If we did, we would see our image on TV. We would see ourselves in headlines.

Sometimes, of course, working people do make the news, most often as victims—as unemployed, as unable to afford health care or a house, even as alienated from work. The American media, to their credit, do not shirk from exposing the social ills that plague working people. Every day's news, every day's dramas, bring more information about the endless crises facing the nation, and that's just the problem. The crises—environmental destruction, AIDS, school cutbacks, bank failures—tumble out one after another, with no rhyme or reason connecting one to the other. Besieged by crises from every direction, we tune out. Why bother trying to solve what we can't explain? Maybe the experts can help us.

The labor movement, of course, isn't about experts. The labor movement is about empowering people, about tracing problems to common root causes, about helping people make sense out of the world. With understanding comes confidence—and a willingness to struggle for change.

All this, of course, places a tremendous burden on the newsletters, newspapers, and magazines of the labor press, a burden union leaders haven't always been willing to bear. Over the years, critics have often blamed the inadequacies of the labor press on labor leaders, and, indeed, far too many labor leaders have historically treated union publications as little more than vehicles for self-promotion. That might be changing. Some of America's top leaders now seem willing to consider nontraditional approaches to labor journalism. Fred Solowey, the co-editor of this volume, spoke with three of these leaders: American Federation of State, County and Municipal Employees president Gerald McEntee, United Mine Workers president Richard Trumka, and Amalgamated Clothing and Textile Workers president Jack Sheinkman.

Much of what these three labor leaders have to say gives reason for cheer. But labor journalists, contributor Matt Witt points out in his analysis of the *UMW Journal* experience, can't afford to pin their hopes for a quality labor press on the personal attitudes of labor leaders. Witt watched firsthand in the 1970s as the *UMW Journal,* once a pitiful "puff" sheet for the United Mine Worker hierarchy, became a tool for helping mine workers better understand—and change—their world. That one brief moment of journalistic brilliance was subsequently extinguished by a leadership change of heart. Only structural changes that foster the independence of labor journalists, argues Witt, can guarantee union members the labor press they need.

The labor press independence that Witt seeks is commonplace in other countries, most notably perhaps in Sweden, where labor journalists work as independent advocates for their unions and their labor movements. Is the Swedish model relevant to American labor? Gunilla Wettergren, chief editor of the seven-hundred-thousand-circulation newspaper of the Swedish Municipal Workers Union, describes what Swedish labor journalism has to offer.

Fortunately, Americans don't have to look only overseas to find models for what labor journalism ought to be. A new labor press is building in the United States, a labor press that respects readers—and, in turn, attracts their respect.

No national labor publication published today better typifies this spirit than *Solidarity*, the national United Auto Workers magazine. How has *Solidarity* avoided the dead-end journalism practiced by so many other labor papers? Editor Dave Elsila explains.

A new labor journalism is stirring at the local level, too, notes David Prosten, the editor of a news service for local union editors. Prosten's contribution notes the elements that make some local newsletters stand out—and dissects the obstacles that still stand in the way of labor press effectiveness at the local level.

The emerging new labor press, at both the national and the local levels, faces no obstacle more challenging than ethnic diversity. How can the labor press help build unity among working people when, in some cases, working people can't even understand the languages each other speak? Lou Siegel and Jeff Stansbury, labor journalists and organizers in southern California, have some ideas.

The continuing wave of immigrants to the United States, as Stansbury and Siegel point out, poses one challenge to labor unity and labor journalism. Gender and race differences pose two others. It was not too long ago, note Bakery Workers editor Carolyn Jacobson and United Food and Commercial Workers associate editor Susan Phillips, that union papers were still running cheesecake photos of women. Labor journalism, the two argue, truly has come a long way and, along that way, has helped integrate women into the union movement. The road forward has been rockier for labor journalists who try to build unity in the face of increasing racial tension. J. J. Johnson, an American Federation of State, County and Municipal Employees editor in New York City, traces the reasons why.

The men and women working to build a new labor press are using tools new and old. Mike Konopacki and Gary Huck, a duo who have become the labor movement's most popular cartoonists, are resurrecting a journalistic art form that goes back to the days of the American Revolution. Earl Dotter, the dean of labor photography, is working equally hard to rescue his specialty from the stereotypes of the past. Dotter and Deborah Stern offer alternatives to the stale photography that deadens so many labor papers.

Mary Ann Forbes is exploiting new technology to open new vistas for labor journalists. The former director of publications for the Association of Flight Attendants, Forbes maintains that the emergence of desktop publishing can empower labor journalists in ways hardly conceivable even five years ago.

Daniel Beagle, longtime editor of the *Dispatcher,* the newspaper of the International Longshoremen's and Warehousemen's Union, is another labor journalist who is experimenting with new technologies. Beagle helped launch "We Do the Work," a unique West Coast–based labor affairs series on public television. In an age of television, Beagle argues, labor journalists can't think print only.

Half a continent away, in Racine, Wisconsin, labor journalists are involved in an equally unique effort. *Racine Labor* is a community labor weekly now celebrating its first half-century of publication. Fifty years ago, weeklies like *Racine Labor* were commonplace. Yet today *Racine Labor* stands as an isolated survivor. Is *Racine Labor* a throwback to an era that can never be recreated or a living inspiration for a new era of community labor journalism? Former *Racine Labor* editor Richard Olson explores the history that can help answer that question.

A decade ago, Pittsburgh was home to an even more unconventional variety of community labor journalism: the iconoclastic *Mill Hunk Herald,* a paper that regularly outraged and delighted readers inside and outside the labor movement. Former editor Larry Evans tells the story of the *Mill Hunk Herald* and what happened when he took the *Mill Hunk* spirit into more standard labor journalist haunts.

We move next to a look into the future of the labor press. Ought that future include a more ambitious national labor presence? Could a national, mass-circulation labor newspaper make a contribution that would warrant the expense the effort would surely entail? Coeditor Sam Pizzigati makes the case for a transitional step, a weekly "trade press" for trade unions, and two labor journalists a coast apart, Jo-Ann Mort from the Amalgamated Clothing and Textile Workers in New York and Karen Keiser from the *Washington State Labor Council Reports* in Seattle, relate their reactions.

Finally, we close this collection with some parting thoughts about the dialogue this book attempts to begin. We offer no panacea to the complex problems that American labor faces. But we remain convinced that a resurgence for American labor is unthinkable without a revitalized labor press. May these pages encourage the thinking we all so sorely need.

Part One

Why We Need a Labor Press

The Media Mirror: What Do Working People See?

Robert Kalaski

For working people in the United States today, the media amount to a badly broken mirror, with many big pieces totally missing. Any examination of what American workers see on the commercial media, especially television, should begin by looking at what they don't see. They don't see themselves.

Television, the most powerful communications medium ever conceived, presents an incredibly distorted view of American society from the worker's perspective. If we were to judge the prevalence and importance of jobs in American society by what appears on television, nearly half of us would work in law enforcement. Most of the rest of us would be gangsters, lawyers, or doctors, with a smattering earning our livelihoods as waiters, waitresses, nurses, reporters, and secretaries.

Except for minor supporting roles, television portrays few maintenance workers or clerical employees—and virtually no production workers. In television, there have been and are no union representatives.

Let's take a quick quiz. How many television characters can you name, either in sitcoms or dramas, who worked in factories? If you go back to the mid-1970s, you might remember that Archie Bunker worked on a loading dock in "All in the Family." Laverne and Shirley

Robert Kalaski joined the staff of the International Association of Machinists and Aerospace Workers (IAM) in 1966 after four years as a commissioned U.S. Air Force officer. Kalaski was named the editor of the IAM newspaper, the Machinist, *in 1977, and, a year later, became the IAM director of communications. A three-term vice-president of the International Labor Press Association, Kalaski became the president of the organization, newly renamed the International Labor Communications Association, in 1983.*

talked about their jobs in the brewery, but we never actually saw them actually working. Karl Malden was a steelworker on "SKAG." Today, there are even fewer TV roles in manufacturing jobs.

What about TV's portrayal of unions? In television's heyday decades of the 1960s and 1970s, unions were almost totally missing from the TV screen. In retrospect, that absence might have been merciful. Virtually every time a union presence was written into a television script, that presence was negative. The union was powerful, obstructive, and violent. Union leaders were portrayed in gangster stereotypes, and union members appeared as mindless followers.

There was one exception. In the early 1980s, Ed Asner, fresh from his starring role on the "Mary Tyler Moore Show," became Lou Grant, the feisty newspaper editor on a show of the same name. The show prided itself on its realism, both in its portrayal of the lives of reporters and the situations they encountered. That realism extended into one "Lou Grant" episode on newspaper labor relations. The program accurately dramatized the process of collective bargaining, imperfect as it is, sensitively portraying the personal pain of workers and managers during a strike. The episode went on to show the compromises necessary to end a strike.

Unfortunately, "Lou Grant" has not been the television norm. The show owed its accuracy in no small part to its star, longtime labor activist Ed Asner, whose skills and tremendous popularity as an actor gave him a prominent role in script development. But even "Lou Grant" talked about unionism only in the context of a *breakdown* in the collective bargaining process, a strike. Never has television portrayed union members or union leaders doing what they do 99 percent of their time, and that is not striking. If a union appears in a television drama, a strike—and frequently violence—usually follows.

Television news follows the same pattern. There's an old adage that if you're a union representative wanting to get on TV news, all you have to do is put up a picket line. If you *really* want to get on the news, create a violent confrontation on the picket line.

Strikes are the end product of 1 percent of the collective bargaining that unions do. Yet strikes account for more than 90 percent of the news coverage of unions. Through the distorted eye of television, unions contribute little to society except strike turmoil. Labor's ongoing campaigns for fair taxes, job safety and health, and decent social services go unnoticed. Rarely do union leaders appear on the nightly network news.

This failure to cover labor leaders can no longer be explained away by arguing that union leaders are not literate or articulate. Most unions now train their national and local leaders how to present story ideas to the media and even how to appear effectively on television. Most unions, from their international offices to their smallest locals in the heartlands, seek out positive media exposure. "No comment" is no longer the byword of union leadership.

Over a decade ago, in 1979, the International Association of Machinists and Aerospace Workers (IAM) undertook a major effort to achieve what we called "parity on television." After training more than fifteen hundred members in forty-three states, the IAM launched a month-long, prime-time monitoring of commercial network entertainment programming and newscasts, both local and network. This massive project documented widespread disparity, imbalance, and unfairness in the coverage of workers' and union issues in entertainment and news. The IAM moved this documentation in three different directions.

First, the IAM requested and received personal meetings with top TV network executives in New York City to discuss the findings. Second, Machinists staff taught local union leaders how to present the monitoring information on local newscasts to local station managers. Third, the union visited with writers, producers, and directors in Hollywood to explain the entertainment monitoring results and sensitize the creative community to the problems uncovered by the monitors.

The New York meetings produced mixed results, depending on the network involved. At the time, CBS was the undisputed leader in entertainment broadcasting and network news. The network sent one vice-president to the IAM meeting. He listened and commented only that the union's findings were "interesting." At ABC, then the proverbial number two and eager to try anything to dethrone CBS, the IAM met with nine network staffers specifically assigned to research and develop "socially responsive" programming. NBC was so far in last place at the time that paranoia ruled supreme. NBC sent four attorneys to the meeting with the IAM.

Interestingly, the three networks, which allegedly never speak among themselves, had identical answers to some of the issues the IAM raised. All three emphatically insisted that commercial television aimed only to entertain and inform, but *not* to educate. All three stressed that commercial television merely *expressed* American values and did not set them. The Hollywood meetings produced more responsive reactions.

The creative community at least acknowledged that much could and probably should be done.

But the most tangible long-term results came from the dozens of follow-up meetings in cities and towns across the United States. Local IAM activists, frequently accompanied by local officers, examined stations' public files and opened dialogues on how to increase and improve coverage of union events. Not all the meetings were cordial. But when the union leaders persisted, they won results. To this day, more than a decade later, many local union leaders still maintain critical dialogues with station officials on key issues facing workers, both union and nonunion.

The IAM TV monitoring produced enough positive results to warrant a second round of national monitoring in 1981. In that round, two other unions, the Bakery, Confectionery and Tobacco Workers and the Operating Engineers, joined the IAM in preselected cities. In the years since then, soaring costs for training and monitoring, coupled with the deregulation of the television industry during the Reagan era, have preempted any further union monitoring of commercial television.

But the campaign to achieve labor parity on television continues. The latest target is public broadcasting. American workers might expect to fare somewhat better on public TV than on commercial TV, but they don't. In 1990, the Committee for Cultural Studies in the graduate school of the City University of New York published the results of a study entitled *PBS and the American Worker*. The study looked at PBS prime-time programming in 1988 and 1989. It found that "programming devoted to the lives and concerns of the business and social elite is on average ten times more prevalent than programming devoted to workers." PBS programming about workers was found to make up less than one-half of 1 percent of the network's total prime-time schedule—and much of that almost insignificant amount was about British rather than American workers.

In 1990, the nonprofit media watchdog called FAIR—Fairness and Accuracy in Reporting—also concluded a broader study that examined the coverage, or lack of it, of workers and unions by all segments of the media. The study was conducted by Jonathan Tasini, a journalist who has covered labor issues for the *New York Times*, *Business Week*, and other publications.

Among the study's varied findings were the following:

■ Nightly commercial network news programs in 1989 devoted only 1.2 percent of their time to news about unions, and, if the 1989 Eastern Airlines strike hadn't taken place, union news would have been virtually undetectable. Additionally, the networks allotted only about 2.3 percent of their coverage to issues of general interest to workers such as child care, the minimum wage, and workplace safety.

■ TV coverage of workers and their issues may be declining, or at least not growing, but regular corporate-oriented business programming is increasing dramatically on PBS and cable news networks like CNN and CNBC. None of these outlets has a regular labor or worker show.

■ The "labor beat" is disappearing at many daily newspapers. In its place are "workplace" reporters who come from the business desk and usually know little or nothing about workers' problems or unions.

Despite all this gloom and doom, despite the almost total absence of a meaningful relationship between American trade unions and the media and the media and the American worker, there are some hopeful signs.

The AFL-CIO has recognized that a continuing presence on commercial television is not just desirable but necessary. The AFL-CIO Labor Institute of Public Affairs (LIPA) has made impressive strides in producing professional presentations on critical issues. The federation and its affiliated unions have backed LIPA with a TV budget that no union could possibly sustain over any period of time.

Individual unions have admitted that at least part of their problem with the media has been their fault. Many of them have significantly improved the training in media activism they offer national and local officers. The results have been impressive.

The union monitoring programs and studies of the 1980s and 1990s have indeed made the commercial media more aware of working people. Dramas and sitcoms alike are presenting situations that involve workers and unions more frequently and more fairly.

Last year, the CBS "Murphy Brown" series aired two episodes about strikes at the TV station. The episodes met the series' high standards for humor. The programs also accurately and fairly presented the skills and professionalism of union workers. More recently, a new CBS series, "WIOU," another program about a TV station and reporters, expanded the strike situation by including a dialogue about replacement workers.

In news, the quality, if not the quantity, of labor news coverage by commercial TV has improved somewhat. During the heat of the Eastern Airlines strike, media coverage was accurate and fair. Well-trained union leaders found a media willing to listen, at least for a while. But most of the media, both print and electronic, abandoned coverage when they decided the strike was over. Unfortunately, the media concluded the strike long before the striking workers did.

Pressure is also producing some positive changes in the Public Broadcasting System. PBS stations, though still not originating or actively pursuing labor- or worker-oriented programming, are beginning to respond to the call for more such programs, as Dan Beagle explains later in this volume.

But all this activity, unfortunately, doesn't amount to even a small step forward. It's barely a shuffle. Unions, individually and collectively, still need to increase their media awareness dramatically. They must learn how and when to work with the media. Since massive ad budgets are not and will not be part of labor's financial planning for the future, unions simply must become more aggressive in telling their stories.

In its early years, the AFL-CIO Labor Institute of Public Affairs operated under a banner that proclaimed, appropriately, "The Greatest Stories Never Told." In the turbulent years leading into the twenty-first century, there will be many more such stories, greater than ever, that will need to be told, more than ever.

Labor and the Mainstream Press: The Vanishing Labor Beat

William Serrin

When I was offered the position of labor writer at the *New York Times*, I said I didn't want it. I wasn't maneuvering for more money. Not only didn't I want the job, but I figured that the offer meant I was somehow regarded as a second-stringer. Most of the labor writers I had known were hacks, old-timers spending a last few years on the paper before retirement. Labor writing may have been better than the police beat, but it wasn't much of a job.

Most editors I knew didn't know or care about labor reporting. It was just something you had to have in the paper, like obits. Labor writers wrote about union presidents and strikes but not much more, and, unless the story was something big—like a union president caught embezzling from the pension fund or a major strike—the editors always dumped labor stories inside.

Most of my journalism until the time I was offered the labor job at the *Times* wasn't labor writing at all. For the most part, I had written features and urban affairs. My qualifications for the labor job seemed to be that I was from Detroit, a blue-collar town, and that I had written a book, *The Company and the Union*, a study of the relationship between General Motors and the United Automobile Workers.

The editor who made me the offer—we were sitting in an expensive northern Italian restaurant on Central Park South in New York City—

William Serrin, associate professor of journalism at New York University, is the author of Homestead: The Glory and Tragedy of an American Steel Town, *an examination of what happens to people and their institutions when an industry collapses, to be published by Random House/Times Books in 1992. He is a former labor and workplace correspondent for the* New York Times.

explained that the *Times* was interested in something different in labor reporting. The newspaper, he said, didn't want to cover just unions and the AFL-CIO, that is, do what labor reporters historically had done. I would cover unions, the editor said, but the newspaper also wanted to cover work: what Americans did at their jobs, what they thought about their work and their bosses, what trends existed in the American workplace.

This changed everything. An offer to write about work, about workers, was an offer to write about almost anything. No journalist, if the journalist were bright, could resist such an offer. If you had that job, you just had to get the word "work" in every piece, probably no later than the fifth paragraph. I told the editor I might be interested in such a job. A week or so later, the job was formally offered to me, and I accepted. I didn't ask about the money.

Thus it was that I arrived at the *New York Times* and was given a desk and a word processor, shown where the cabinet for pens and notebooks was, and began my years as the *New York Times* labor and workplace correspondent. In many ways, it was a wonderful job, one of the best I ever had.

I was able, as I was promised, to write about almost anything. Unions. Union people—regulars and dissidents, hard workers and piecarders. I did stories on everything from the first known woman killed in an underground coal mine to two young men, the last of their kind, who worked as cowboys on a ranch in Wyoming. I wrote about the life of union organizers, the troubles with working on word processors, on experiments, usually unsuccessful, in workplace cooperation. That and much more.

Unlike some other papers at which I had been employed, the *Times* had money and wasn't afraid to spend it on news. For me, the son of working class parents—a baker and a housewife—this was terrific. I would go to an editor and say I thought I should go to Arizona to cover a copper strike, then Las Vegas for the Teamster convention (always one of my favorite stories), then to Denver where I would rent a car and go to Wyoming to pick up the piece on cowboys. Maybe I'd stop in West Virginia on the way back to do a piece on coal miners.

"Fine," the editor would say. "How much of an advance do you want?"

"Oh, I guess $2,000," I would say. The editor would grab an advance slip, scribble $2,000 and his name on it, and I would go to the cashier's office to pick up the $2,000. The cashier was a sad-looking, long-faced man, and you knew that, as he looked over your advance slip, he was thinking how unfair life was. Here he was standing behind a steel cage giving large sums of money to whippersnappers who were getting $2,000 of the stockholders' money to blow on wine, women, and song. The cashier always gave you the dough, usually in $20 bills, but he never smiled. I would stuff the money in my billfold—the wad was so thick I could hardly close the billfold—and be on my way. Pretty good, I would think. I believe that $2,000 was about half the largest wages my father ever received in that hot, demanding bakery, putting tray after tray of bread into the oven.

Yet, as fun and exciting as it was, the job had many problems, and, I think, these go to the heart of what is wrong with labor journalism and the labor movement and, to a substantial extent, all American journalism. I was hopelessly overcommitted. I was supposed to cover all labor—New York labor, the national labor movement, the workplace. It couldn't be done by one person.

Other departments had far greater resources. The business section had forty or fifty reporters. Labor had me, plus a guy in Washington. He was supposed to cover the labor movement in Washington one-half of his time, the environment the other half. But he had once covered the White House and considered labor a dreadful comedown. He would call and ask if I could handle the annual AFL-CIO Bal Harbor meeting because he had a story to do about beavers.

Another problem was strike coverage. I had been told when I came to the *Times* that I would not, for the most part, cover strikes. Each reporter was to cover the strikes on his or her beat. I was just supposed to help out on strikes, give advice, maybe weigh in occasionally on an important strike with an analysis piece.

It didn't work out that way. Editors, naturally, wanted what, wisely or unwisely, they regarded as my expertise, and when they had a labor idea or thought a strike needed me, I was called. Most important, a number of editors were stuck in the past (in journalism, most people are). Labor writers, they felt, should cover strikes. The editors hadn't heard that the labor writer was supposed to write primarily about work.

Then there were the turf wars, for which the *Times* is deservedly well noted. The national editor wanted me. So did the metropolitan editor and the business editor. It was easier—and cheaper—for them to tap me for pieces than to add a reporter or two with labor expertise—or just intelligence and an interest in labor—to their staffs.

That wasn't the biggest problem. The *Times* would rather have good reporters and good writers than bad reporters and bad writers. Yet I always felt that much of what I wrote, though generally regarded, I think, of high quality, was often regarded as not important. A story exploring what union organizers do, a piece on old labor people such as H. L. Mitchell of the sharecroppers union of the 1930s, or Harry Bridges of the West Coast longshoremen, or Florence Reece, the author of the words to the great labor anthem, "Which Side Are You On?," could easily be held when other news occurred or, as all of these pieces were, be dumped inside.

A turning point came when I did a piece on Don Stazak, then the president of Local 65, the big steelworkers local in South Chicago. Stazak was a moderate man, in much turmoil over whether to grant concessions to his employer, the USX Corporation. After much reflection, Stazak had lobbied for concessions, thinking they would save jobs at his plant, the South Works. (Some somewhat radical labor people I knew condemned me for writing the story and asked me why I was wasting time on a sellout like Stazak.)

USX eventually reneged on its promises to build a new rail mill at South Works and provide new jobs. Stazak was outraged, then depressed. Then he quit, weary of the stress, wondering whether he had been taken in by the corporation, whether he had sold out his members. Some labor radicals have no understanding of personal quandaries like Stazak's.

The piece I did discussed the difficulties facing Stazak and noted that the problems he faced were typical of those that faced many local presidents. The story was held four months, then dumped inside.

Not long after, I did a story on Ralph Fasanella, the working class painter. I kept after my editor for weeks to do the story, finally got an okay, and flew to New Bedford, Massachusetts, where Fasanella was working with a United Electrical Workers local, to spend a day with him. I wrote the story up, handed it in, and assigned the art. The story sat for weeks and then was buried in the second section on a Sunday— in the truss ads, as they used to say.

There was another problem, of my own making. I had gone to the *Times*, in large part, to write about work. But the more I did my job, the more I felt I had to do more on unions and the labor movement. I wanted to be responsible. I figured that unions had as much right as other institutions to be written about. And, I suppose, as the decline of unions and the labor movement continued through the 1980s, the more I felt sorry for the sad bozos who led the movement and the workers who belonged to the unions that the bozos led. I wanted to chronicle what was happening to unions, and why, and what was happening to the people who ran them. I thought this was important.

The problem was that most editors disagreed. They saw the labor movement as passé, even dead. Why waste time on the labor movement, editors thought. Write about the workplace, they said, and economic trends.

This is not to say that I was soft on the labor movement. Many of the labor skates, unused to hard coverage, hated me, although the truth was, by reporting on labor, in a tough but hopefully responsible manner, I was one of the best friends that the labor movement had. At least I put labor in the paper.

The labor people never understood this. Once at an AFL-CIO convention, a top assistant, a man with nice suits who never smiled, came up to me and said, "I think your story this morning was shit." Clever public relations, I thought.

The truth was, the movement, particularly at its top levels, had no life, no excitement, and it has little of either today. Labor often was not, in the parlance of journalism, a good story. I knew that, as did a number of my colleagues. I can recall several of us sitting at the press table at an AFL-CIO convention. We noticed that leaders of the union that some of us belonged to but had never had much involvement in, the Newspaper Guild, were sitting next to members of the horseshoers' union. Appropriate, we said. That night, we got to talking and someone said that in covering labor he often felt like a paleontologist in Utah digging up dinosaur bones. Well said, we said; that, we said, was how we felt, too.

Truth be told, the American labor movement in large part deserves the paltry coverage it receives. The movement, for the most part, is about as creative and militant as the Rotary Club. Unions represent 12 percent of the private sector work force—16 percent of the private and public work force—about the percent that labor represented at the time of the passage of the Wagner Act in 1935.

These numbers merely hint at the problems facing the labor movement, for the movement is probably about as weak, as lacking in ideas, as the hapless, ossified labor movement, made up mostly of craft workers, of the early 1920s. That's what Michael Harrington said to me not long before he died.

Serving as a union officer is, for most labor leaders, a business, a profession, a way to get out of the shop and make something of yourself. This is the loam and compost from which germinate the demands for loyalty, solidarity, the company line, that characterize unions as much as most other institutions in American life.

The rules are usually unwritten, but they are as codified, as strictly enforced, as the rules of the church or the mob. Suffocating bureaucracies discourage new ideas and methods; the men and the few women at the top exercise tight, uncompromising control and hang on forever. The best people, meanwhile, are repeatedly beaten down, blocked. Young members know that to rise, you must imitate your predecessors. Ardent anticommunism and commitment to a strong military remain a litmus test even at a time when communism is busting apart.

It has always struck me how easily labor leaders are seduced by the notion that they will be accepted as equals by businessmen and that by working with business and the government they can settle labor's problems without consulting their members or the religious leaders, the feminists, and the environmentalists who should be among labor's dearest and most valuable friends.

Labor, management, and government working together—it's a recurrent theme. Labor history makes clear that such cooperation, such a civilized arrangement, is not possible. Labor and management and government cooperated, in large part, during World War I and World War II. Then, when each crisis was over, management and government turned against labor. But labor leaders are for the most part as ignorant of labor history as most Americans—most historians, for that matter.

The "corporate unionism" that developed during and after World War II and saw labor, business, and government work together was useful in a sense. This corporate unionism delivered increased wages and benefits. Industry was willing to help labor leaders deliver wages and benefits, even help them sell the agreements at the bargaining table to the rank and file, because this kept unions and workers quiet. But, importantly, this relationship also sapped the spirit of unions and workers, made those who spoke out look like uncontrolled militants, and made labor leaders more powerful.

The labor press is a part of this. I probably have a bias when I say that. When I was a child, my father belonged to the dairy and bakery workers union, and for years the union paper came to our house every month. I can still see it: small, crowded type; pictures of union officers, the same guys again and again; then maybe, in the back, tips on bass fishing or how to cut Christmas decorations from shoebox cardboard. Today, for the most part, labor papers still print what the union president and the other top union executives want printed, but not much more.

In seven years at the *Times*, I found one story idea out of the labor press. Only a handful of labor press editors attempted to get together with me and discuss difficulties they believed faced their unions (at least they didn't swear at me at AFL-CIO conventions). I once remarked at a gathering of labor editors and publicity people that, in several years at the *Times*, I had never received a call from the AFL-CIO press department suggesting a story. I said I didn't need any story ideas; I probably always had fifty or more stories that I wanted to do. But, I said, I thought the union movement was shortchanging itself by not suggesting stories to what is probably the nation's most important newspaper.

A few days later, I got a call from a man in the AFL-CIO press office. He said he had heard what I said and was distressed. It would, he said, be unprofessional to suggest story ideas to a reporter. I said I appreciated his call and had not meant any personal criticism. But I thought if a public relations man feels it is beneath him to suggest stories to a reporter, he should probably consider entering another profession.

Today, with economic and political conditions so changed, after a decade of Republican administrations and a conservative Congress, corporate unionism cannot deliver. All that remains of the older order is a helpless leadership, feckless unions, and a tamed and bored rank and file. The movement cannot go on the offensive, cannot organize, cannot lead its members.

Still, the coverage that labor and the workplace receive is not fair—and not good journalism.

Within journalism, it used to be, you frequently met journalists who wanted to right wrongs, to fry capitalists (those who deserved frying), to get out of the city room and do down-and-dirty stories. It's hard to meet journalists like that today.

It also used to be that, in journalism, you made the story. That is, you hit upon an idea, reported and wrote it, made it into a story. Now, I think, many journalists just want to get in on the big story, want to be part of the journalism herd, not make their own stories. It is more fashionable this way.

It used to be, too, that reporters and editors often came from working class backgrounds. Some brought working class concerns to their journalism. No more. Today, many reporters and editors regard unions and the working classes as beneath them. They want to rise, want to write glitzy page 1 or magazine cover pieces, want to get the glamour beats—political campaigns, the State Department, the Defense Department, the White House, a foreign bureau—not to muck around in decaying industrial towns or crummy local union halls.

Journalists, I suspect, ape the corporation people they cover, just, as I have always thought, labor people ape the corporation people with whom they bargain. As a result of this, and more, labor journalists are, for the most part, nearly an extinct species, like the black-footed ferret, the Everglades puma, and the California condor.

The *New York Times*, the *Washington Post*, the *Chicago Tribune*, the *Los Angeles Times*, the *Wall Street Journal*, the *Boston Globe*—these newspapers and others are giving much less space and importance to the labor movement and the workplace than they have in the past. Many American newspapers and magazines give almost no coverage to labor. Television is worse.

Today, some publications, including the *New York Times*, are, in halting fashion, attempting to cover the workplace. They should be commended for this. The irony is that reporters—including friends of mine in journalism—are using this coverage of the workplace as an excuse for not covering unions. I suspect it somehow sounds better to say "I cover the workplace" than "I cover labor."

Not long ago, a person I knew in the labor movement called me up with a good labor story. I said I had no newspaper to put it in and suggested he call a former colleague. He did and soon called back.

"The guy told me he didn't want to do it," he said. "He told me he covered the workplace, not labor."

I know another journalist who was asked if he would like to cover labor. He immediately assumed his career at his newspaper was at an end and quickly found another job at a newsmagazine. He went on to get a gig as a panelist on a television weekend news interview show. I sometimes see this journalist on Sunday morning TV, talking about what's going on inside the Beltway. I guess he feels he saved himself.

I once watched a colleague getting congratulated on her assignment to the Washington bureau. She was asked what she would be covering. She said she had been promised that she would write feature pieces, then be assigned to the White House.

"I know one thing," she said. "I'm not going to be covering any of those dreary regulatory agencies."

Of course, those "dreary regulatory agencies"—the Department of Labor, the Occupational Safety and Health Administration, the Environmental Protection Agency, and the Bureau of Labor Statistics—are where some of the best stories in the nation are.

So, too, is the labor movement, and that is another reason, maybe the most important one from the point of view of American journalism, why the dismal labor journalism practiced in America is unfortunate. Papers are missing good stories.

I can think of hundreds of stories not being done. Death and injury in the workplace. Problems in the white-collar work force. How unemployment statistics understate unemployment. The difficulties facing labor organizers. How labor laws have been altered in the last fifty years to subvert the promises of the Wagner Act and make it often almost impossible for unions to organize and win contracts. How the American labor movement might reenergize itself. The large number of talented, dedicated local officers and staff members you meet in the labor movement and how, for the most part, they almost never communicate with one another. The alliances that unions, like construction unions, make with business. How characteristics of assembly line work have been implanted in the white-collar work force. The great demands that working class people face, day in, day out, and how, against all odds, they persevere, endure. But these stories and others are, sadly, not done or are done badly.

It's like the *Times* editor—the man who had hired me seven years before—said to me on the Ralph Fasanella piece: "Goddamit. I don't want any more goddamned labor culture pieces. I want front-page trend stories."

For these reasons and more, I left. The irony is that I miss it all immensely, labor reporting for a newspaper, newspapering itself.

Maybe I should have stayed. Most people treated me well. If nothing more, they put my stories in the paper, and I was proud of the stories and proud to work there. Once, after I left, I was speaking at a university and a student asked, "Didn't you think it was your responsibility to stay?" I thought she made an excellent point. She may have been correct.

But there is another point, the tyranny in journalism that, after a time, compels many writers to leave newspapers and do books. Writing books seems, somehow, more fulfilling, more important. Right or wrong, that was what I wanted to do, and that is what I did.

I met many people in the labor movement I admired immensely:

workers, local officers, staff members, a handful of national presidents and AFL-CIO people. I was allowed to go, at someone else's expense, to fascinating places: coal patches in the Appalachians, western mining camps, farming communities, auto and steel towns. As I said, not bad for the son of a baker and a housewife in Saginaw, Michigan.

I miss those strange and wonderful places, and I also miss the newsroom—the noise, the excitement of deadlines, the talented people (and the newspaper characters), even the office politics.

I was talking once with a labor organizer, a creative and dedicated woman who was disillusioned with the disarray and hopelessness she found in the movement and getting ready to find something else to do, which she did.

"Nowhere," she said, "is there any room for me."

That's the way I sometimes feel about labor journalism. And the rest of newspapering, too.

Part Two

The Contemporary Scene

A View from the Top:
A Conversation with
Three Union Presidents

Writing in the Metal Worker *in 1904, Eugene Victor Debs offered a provocative view of the role of the labor editor: "The editor of a labor paper is of far more importance to the union and the movement than the president or any other officer of the union. He [sic] ought to be chosen with special reference to his knowledge upon the labor question and his fitness to advocate and defend the economic interests of the class he represents."*

It is important to remember that Debs—though a union president himself for some years—was no longer head of a union when he offered this observation, which has become something of a secretly sacred inspirational motto for many harried editors of union publications.

When Fred J. Solowey, the coeditor of this book and then associate editor of the American Federation of State, County and Municipal Employees (AFSCME) national magazine, sat down with the president of his union, Gerald (Jerry) W. McEntee, United Mine Workers (UMW) president Richard (Rich) Trumka, and Amalgamated Clothing and Textile Workers Union (ACTWU) president Jack Sheinkman, he knew better than to ask their opinions of the Debs quote. Solowey did, however, ask them a wide assortment of questions about the labor press that national labor leaders seldom get asked—and seldom consider. He met with the three presidents April 24, 1991, in Washington, D.C.

Solowey: Let me start with you, President McEntee. All American labor unions, large and small, are facing budget crunches. National labor publications are very expensive to publish and postage rates are going crazy. Why have a national union publication? Why spend all that money on it?

McEntee: Well, to put out the *Public Employee*, our magazine that goes to 1.25 million people, costs the union, without staff cost, about $2.5 million. We see the *Public Employee* as the basic avenue of communication between the national union and the individual member. We have three thousand local unions, we have over seventy district councils, and communicating with people is extremely difficult, especially because of the way we are structured. Our national union does not negotiate any contracts for individual members. We do a lot of assisting. But since the basic service mechanism in AFSCME is the district council, we think it's critical that we have a mechanism at the national level that can communicate with the individual member. That's really the reason we have the *Public Employee*.

We poll our members every two years on all kinds of issues and also on the *Public Employee*. Forty percent of the people, according to the latest poll, read the *Public Employee* well. This is an increase of readership over the last few polls. But some members see the magazine as a propaganda piece for the leadership of the union. It's important to know and important to be honest about these things.

Solowey: President Trumka, as President McEntee noted, a union publication is something that all members get but many don't read. The union publication comes in the mail like the American Automobile Association magazine. Members don't have to subscribe, and some people throw it in the trash. What do you think makes a difference and convinces people to read a union publication?

Trumka: First of all, the members have to find the union publication relevant. We do polls also. When my administration first took over, readership was lower than 40 percent. The reason members didn't read the publication was because it wasn't relevant to them. We try to make the *UMW Journal* the members' publication. We print letters to the editor, some very critical, as is. Our magazine does a lot of how-to's: how to build local support, how to deal with the press. We also feature articles on topics of interest.

I don't exert any editorship over the *Journal*. I try to address it pretty much like an outside publication, and I appear very infrequently in it. I probably don't appear frequently enough.

The membership has begun to consider the *UMW Journal* more and more their publication. It's become more accepted and read. We have also put more educational things in the journal. We do, in fact, have a lot of face-to-face contact with the rank and file out across the country. But still our membership is so spread out that you have to have a means—not only to communicate—but to educate and train.

Solowey: President Sheinkman, it could be said that there are perhaps four groups of potential readers: people who identify with the union; people who are apathetic and don't see the union as a very important part of who they are; people somewhat in the middle; and family members. Who do you pitch to the most and can you get to them all?

Sheinkman: Obviously, as presidents of unions, we can't get to everybody. Our newspapers are the one opportunity we have to reach people. We have gone through several transformations. Originally, at one point, there were too many pictures of the officers. Now, basically the only time I'll appear is in my column, where I try to get a viewpoint across concerning something the union is trying to do. We use our publication as a political arm. People need to know what the issues are that are coming up legislatively and politically, and we try to deal with issues in terms of what rank-and-file members are doing, how they are involved in politics. We have members in Canada, and we see the newspaper as an opportunity—the only opportunity really—to get an international perspective on all the things we're doing.

One of the things that we've been zeroing in on is the role of members in organizing. We give that a play and that enables us to get more membership involvement. The big problem we have is mechanical—the turnover. We have a problem getting our mailing lists accurate and up-to-date. And that's a perennial problem.

Solowey: President Sheinkman mentioned political action. Political action is very, very important to the labor movement. The polls I've seen seem to show that members don't seem to be very interested in what the union has to say about who to vote for. But we're always telling them anyway. What do you have to say about how the labor press deals with politics and candidates? Do people get turned off by the hard sell?

Sheinkman: We don't really push that hard. We try to push for what the candidate stands for. Obviously, we have all gone about things a little differently in recent years on presidential elections, as a result of the AFL-CIO procedure. We now get a lot more local input before making a presidential endorsement, which has made a big difference. People can't say we're imposing a candidate. But nowadays, we have a new problem. Suppose my union supports candidate X, Rich's candidate Y, and Jerry's candidate Z. We go through the AFL-CIO endorsement process, and it turns out to be candidate B. How do we then go to our membership? That's an added burden for the union and the publication. We want to have unity, but that's one of the negative aspects of it, and we have to bear that cross.

Trumka: We separate out the legislative stuff and the political action. We have some of the political in the *Journal*, but we also have a special communication that deals with political action. With Dukakis, we did postelection polls. Better than 90 percent of our members voted for Mike Dukakis and, in Pennsylvania, where we endorsed a split ticket, about 80 percent of our people voted for Republican senator Arlen Specter while 90 percent of them voted for Dukakis. I'm sort of blessed along these lines. Our members really do look to the Mine Workers to see which of the candidates will deal with our issues. Now we have, like everybody else, some one-issue members. The only thing they look at is the stand on abortion or guns. If you're right on the issue, they vote for you, and if you're wrong, they don't. But even some of them tell us "we couldn't support that candidate, but we didn't have it in us to go against the union's candidate, so we didn't vote."

Solowey: President McEntee, you have a more politically diverse membership. When you do a big push in the magazine for a candidate or on behalf of the ticket, are you trying to mobilize the loyal troops who are out there, or trying to reach the people in the middle? Do you try to reach the folks who don't want to listen to the union anyway?

McEntee: I think we're trying to do all of those things. We attempt to use the magazine both to educate our people and tell them how candidates voted. We tell them, after the input process, where the union is going and why the union is endorsing a person. But I think it's true in a lot of unions—maybe not yours, Rich, and I should say you're blessed—that the average voter and the average union member has changed so much. It used to be in the past, twenty years ago, if the union was for "Charlie Jones," very, very real consideration was given to Charlie Jones, and not so much concern was expressed over particular issues, whether they might be abortion, or choice, or life, or whatever. It was much more important to the average union member where the union was in those days. Today, we have about 25 percent of our members who are registered Republicans. We then have probably 20 percent who would consider themselves independents, and the rest are Democrats.

We get flak from our Republican members that we are always dressed as Democrats. So we go to great lengths to show that we are supporting Republicans as well as Democrats. When we support Republicans like Governor Kean in New Jersey or Governor Thompson in Illinois, we make it a big story in our publications. Also, our PAC pays all expenses for members elected as delegates to the party conventions. The last time around we sent 217 people to the Democratic National Convention. We sent two to the Republican National Convention. We tried to make a story out of that, but it's not much of a story. But trying to, as least, shows the people that we do politics with a degree of fairness. But it is not an easy thing to do. A lot of our members, if they had their druthers, would prefer that we not be in the political arena because we have a large degree of cynicism in our membership concerning politicans.

Sheinkman: What do you mean by cynicism, Jerry?

McEntee: In terms of where our members work, dealing with mayors, and governors, and state legislators. They see patronage and political favoritism. It's like whether your members would vote for factory owners. A lot of our folks—including many of our activists—would like to see us divorced from the political process. It's sort of "shame on both of your houses."

Sheinkman: We've gotten away from running those "right-wrong" voting lists in our national publication because nobody ever read them. You need a set of glasses thicker than mine to read them. We just try to pick a few key races in each region in terms of important issues to our members—like imports—and see how the candidates stand on them. Our members don't have to be educated on these issues. If they don't have the sense to vote their own self-interest, it doesn't matter what we do in the newspaper.

Trumka: Just look at the American public. In the presidential election, fewer than 50 percent of the eligible voters voted. I refuse to believe that 50 percent of the public out there are dummies or don't care about democracy. I think they look at it real simply, just as some members do. They say, what difference does it make? If I vote for this one or that one, I get the same results. I take it on the chin. That's a function of the Democratic party drifting further and further to the right, to the point where I don't believe we have a two-party system.

Sheinkman: This relates to the problem we have with politics in the labor press. The problem with politics is not a problem of the publications. I go around the country talking to members. There's a lot of feeling that the problems are the candidates.

Trumka: I don't think you can say to labor unions that "you failed because more of your people didn't vote for this candidate." I can sell ice to the Eskimos, but I bet I can sell more to the people in Florida. If you want people to vote, you have to be able to say, "Here's the difference between the candidates." We can't fabricate stuff. You lose credibility if readers think an article is a propaganda piece or if we say something about a candidate that isn't so. If a publication lacks credibility, it's dead.

Solowey: A good transition to the next couple of questions. President Sheinkman, in looking over one of your recent issues, I saw something that I haven't seen too often in the labor press—an article discussing why you lost in an organizing drive. That's fairly unusual. The labor press tends only to cover victories. Now that you have covered that defeat, would you tend to cover another?

Sheinkman: As I noted earlier, we're using members more and more in our organizing drives. They've got to look at the upside and the downside. Both Jerry and Rich made the point about using the publication for education. We're trying to use coverage of defeats as an educational device. Why did we lose and what are the problems we face? This gives our people a realistic picture of the world. I think it's another aspect of the credibility that Rich was talking about. We report on our negotiations even when we sometimes don't get very good contracts. There are times when we have reported in the newspaper that in some negotiations we got big bucks and in some contracts we didn't do as well. Then someone said, "Why do you report about the big bucks? You're only creating a problem for the guys who get the small bucks." But that's the reality and the nature of the industry we are in. Members have to realize this. A Xerox worker in our union makes six or seven bucks an hour more than a power worker. That's the reality.

Solowey: President Trumka, let me ask you a hypothetical question. A district contract has been negotiated. It's not very good. The members won a 2 percent raise, but they also have to pay $100 more a month in health insurance, and that increase has more than wiped out the raise. A district union leader wants the contract touted and would like a very positive story in the *United Mine Workers Journal*. On the other hand, the covered members are going to know what the contract was like. How do you handle that?

Trumka: It's real simple. In my case, I don't have to handle that because we don't negotiate on the district level.

Solowey: Hypothetically.

Trumka: We have a rank-and-file ratification. Before any of our members work under a contract, it has to be ratified by the membership. We publish. We don't editorialize. We put the basic facts out. Here are the wages, here's the vote on it. I don't care if my dad came to me and said, "Editorialize on the contract." I won't do it. My predecessors used to take out radio ads and television ads and go around the country "trying to sell a contract." I refuse to do that. I insist that our leaders who explain the contract do it honestly. Don't understate it, don't overstate it. You could only get away with what you asked about once. You write in your article that a contract is something that it isn't, then there's no second bite of that apple. It spills over not only there but in the rest of your leadership capabilities. I have to tell you something: leadership is the same thing as the credibility of your newspaper. You lead when the membership trusts you. If you squander that trust, then you lose the ability to lead.

Solowey: President McEntee, you might face more of this kind of problem situation because there are many district contracts that get negotiated in AFSCME. So let me ask you the same question. A contract has all these givebacks in it. The leader who negotiated the agreement wants to put a more positive spin on the contract. How do you handle that in the publication?

McEntee: First of all, our people are negotiating contracts every day. When I was in Pennsylvania, we negotiated about three hundred contracts alone. So we literally negotiate thousands and thousands of contracts. Most contracts don't get written about in the *Public Employee*. We do run stories on the contracts negotiated by large affiliates. And we run stories if there's been a ground-breaking contract, like the first Harvard clerical worker agreement, or if there's a major contract innovation on something like child care. But I can say that no one who has negotiated a contract has ever called me and said, "Put a different spin on the contract than what really happened." I don't suspect that I'll even get that kind of call. I have to say that in a city or state with financial problems, where our union may have had to give back or take a zero raise, I think it's certainly fair to report the facts of the situation and what they were up against. What's fair is fair.

Sheinkman: I would second that. I've never been asked to put a different spin on a contract story, and I've been a general officer for almost twenty years.

McEntee: Of course, we may have some contracts that our people just don't tell us about.

Sheinkman: People may not tell us either. We're sort of a mix between Rich and Jerry. We have some national agreements covering seventy thousand members. These national agreements are always reportable. Jerry touched on a point about local agreements. I don't go into each area and ask how many contracts have you negotiated. They don't usually send in a story. So I think in a sense, the question is a little academic.

Solowey: Let's talk about letters to the editor. President Trumka mentioned them. They're a very regular feature in the *UMW Journal.* Now they appear sometimes in the *Public Employee.*

Sheinkman: We're looking at running letters to the editor now. In fact, what we're doing is checking around to see how many unions publish letters. We've never printed them in the past. This discussion is helpful.

McEntee: We do it. But we just started. How long ago did we start, Fred?

Solowey: A couple of years ago, but they've been in and out. One of the problems I hear about from many editors is that when there is a letters columns, sometimes there's a tendency to manage it, as opposed to leaving it open. They don't want letters on this topic or don't want to take a blast on that.

Sheinkman: How would you get them in? You're an editor. May I ask you the question?

Solowey: Absolutely.

Sheinkman: I'm a good rabbi, I'll answer your question with a question. You get fifteen or twenty letters on a variety of subjects. How do you pick which ones you're going to publish? Some positive, some negative.

Solowey: Same way a newspaper editor does.

Sheinkman: That's what I'm saying. You've got to make a judgment. You have some idea of what the policies of the union are. There's going to be some negative stuff. How do you handle it?

McEntee: I'd let the editor handle it.

Solowey: If it were left to me, I'd choose representative ones, and I'd print everything.

Sheinkman: You can't print them all.

Solowey: No, I don't mean I'd print every letter, but I wouldn't restrict the topic. We got one letter about the Martin Luther King, Jr., holiday issue in Arizona from a retiree who said it was just an excuse for another holiday, among other things. Or someone might write that pay equity is terrible, and men should get more. I'd run these letters.

McEntee: Do you know any we haven't run?

Solowey: Yes.

Sheinkman: What kind?

Solowey: For example, letters that are considered to be crank letters or ones on topics that we want to leave behind. You do get those, too.

Trumka: That's fair. Why would you run a crank letter?

Solowey: We don't, of course, want to run real crank letters. But labeling something a crank letter can be used to do filtering out of topics that people don't want to get into—gun control, for instance, or complaints about contracts.

Trumka: But it's legitimate for an editor to decide that a letter is dated, that it talks about something that's six months or seven years old. Or to decide that the stuff stated in the letter is just so erroneous that it shouldn't run—because printing it would give it a credibility it doesn't deserve. Editors in every newspaper in every city and town make those decisions every day, and it's never considered a violation of the free press. So there's nothing different about unions. Some letters won't make it, and legitimately so. Some letters shouldn't.

Sheinkman: I concur with that.

Solowey: On the question of president's columns: if letters to the editor make a publication more the members' publication, officers' columns tend to project the national leadership. Now, as far as I know, the *Public Employee* has always had a president's column. President Sheinkman, a president's column is something I believe you've instituted in *Labor Unity*. I understand that President Trumka thought about starting one and then thought better of it.

Trumka: We thought about it when I first came into office, and I was faced with a choice at the time. I had a magazine that had very little credibility with the rank and file because it was considered just an internal tool. Of course, if you publish something and it costs you a lot of money and nobody reads it, it's essentially a waste of money. So I opted to say, "No, we won't have a president's column." However, on some occasions, when something important comes up, I do have a column addressing a specific issue. I found out that whenever I do have a column, it seems to be read more because it's not something that's there all the time. Members say, "Trumka wrote something because he had something to say."

McEntee: We've always had the officer columns. This goes back to something said earlier about the magazine not only being a communications tool, but an educational tool as well. That's what we use the president's column for: to educate on topics like revenue sharing, state layoffs, antirecession measures, and all those kinds of things.

Trumka: Compare this to the *Washington Post*. Every day in every issue they have a president's column. It's called an editorial.

Sheinkman: That's the point. The column shouldn't be abused as an election tool, that's unfair, but as long as you understand that, it's fine. Jerry, in his editorials doesn't say, "I did this, I did that." In our next issue my column is going to be on occupational safety and health because of Workers Memorial Day. It's going to be talking about the issues. It won't be talking about McEntee, or Trumka, or Sheinkman. It's not a puff piece. It's an editorial. It just happens to be the editorial noted as a president's column.

McEntee: I'll say this as well. I had the hardest time when I first got here. I remember looking at one issue of *Public Employee* and there were nine pictures of me—action pictures from a convention. I was new and was all over the place at the convention. I'd look at every column and say, "Jesus Christ, we really don't need that many pictures of me or [Secretary-Treasurer William] Lucy either." We're always on our own people's backs about running too many photos of officers.

Trumka: There's also another reason for the president's column. I think a lot of our membership, particularly the local union leadership, want to know where the leadership of the union stands. And, at times, I've been criticized for not having a president's column, and it's legitimate criticism. The members ought to know what my positions are on various issues. When I stand for reelection, if they don't like my positions, and somebody else has positions they do like, they ought to be able to vote me out.

Solowey: President McEntee just mentioned pictures of officers. This topic is the subject of many jokes among labor editors. There was one AFSCME council publication where there were more than twenty pictures of the president in a sixteen-page paper. I counted them. One AFL-CIO union ran seven pages of photos of the union president shaking hands with each member of the national board. I've looked very carefully over all of your papers and none of you do that very much. But you expressed a worry, President McEntee. Why were you concerned that there were too many pictures?

McEntee: Because I think that there's a tendency on the part of members and activists to see the union paper as a propaganda piece on behalf of the national leadership. If there are going to be nine pictures of the president at these various functions, they may not even know when the president is running for reelection, but they'll see those photos as being about getting elected—and the magazine as being an obviously political piece.

Trumka: Let's face it, we run for election and we stand before the membership and some people think that running lots of pictures of yourself is the best way to get elected. I personally think that running so many pictures lessens your chances of getting reelected. If you have a legitimate newspaper, you have a better chance.

Solowey: Let me play devil's advocate. President Susan Bianchi-Sands of the Association of Flight Attendants, who was originally to be part of this discussion, couldn't be here because of an emergency meeting on the United Airlines contract struggle. She's facing a tough reelection battle [editors' note: which she lost]. One of the questions I would have asked her is this: In such a situation, a few months before your election, isn't there a pull to make yourself more visible in the publication—to show the members how much you're doing for them?

McEntee: I wouldn't do it, and I don't think that Susan, or Jack, or Rich would do it either. Just as a very basic concept of fairness. First, by our union constitution, anybody in opposition would have an equal access to the magazine. Second, it would be the dumbest political thing to ever even try. What you're implying by your question is that our members and activists wouldn't see through it. If there are usually one or two pictures of you in the magazine and all of a sudden before an election there are six or seven, those activists would see through it, then they figure you're about the biggest —— in the world.

Solowey: Before a union convention, should there be debates on convention issues in the union publication?

McEntee: Resolutions can be all over the place. We get over three hundred resolutions submitted to a convention, and they have a wide range. They run from pro-life to pro-choice and back again, to gun control, to El Salvador and Nicaragua. So I don't know which ones we'd pick to debate in our magazine. It would be somewhat hard to pick.

Solowey: Let me follow up on that. President McEntee, you mentioned a number of issues, including abortion rights. *Flight Log*, the magazine of the Association of Flight Attendants—which has a predominantly female membership—ran a debate on whether the AFL-CIO should take a position on abortion rights, and you were one of the two union presidents who participated in this debate. But this is an issue you haven't written about in the *Public Employee*. What goes into the kind of balancing you do to decide when—and where—you'll take up a particular issue?

McEntee: I think that depends on discussions that go on all the time with members of the international executive board, with people in the field, our legislative people, and the directors of various departments. I mean if the women's department comes to me and says that the Family and Medical Leave Act is on its way to a vote in the House of Representatives on such and such a date and we think it should be featured in the *Public Employee,* we'd do it. That's basically how issues find their way through. Plus the staff covers all of the activities of the union and what happens out in the field.

Solowey: But you were a leader in raising the questions about abortion rights at the AFL-CIO. Would it have been excessively divisive to do so in the *Public Employee,* given the diversity of the membership? Is that potential divisiveness something that would have been in your mind?

McEntee: No. Susan asked me to write that article, so I did. I would not have had any problems doing something in the *Public Employee* about abortion. The issue just didn't find its way into the paper. But I wouldn't have had a problem with that. As a matter of fact, this union has been on record for choice for probably about ten to twelve years by virtue of convention action. As you well know, at our last convention, which took place during the height of the abortion debate, our delegates were overwhelmingly pro-choice. And let me note this: in AFSCME, and I think this is true of all unions, our activists on many issues are a little to the left of the membership.

Trumka: I just want to comment on something, because your question implied something. The only people who are afraid to say something anywhere that they're ready to say somewhere are people who don't really know who they are. Jerry McEntee knows who he is. So does Jack Sheinkman. They're probably two of the best examples I could give you.

Sheinkman: You're not so bad yourself.

Solowey: No inference intended. But I remember the late AFSCME president Jerry Wurf insisting that we not write about guns or abortion rights because the issues were too divisive.

Trumka: There may be strategic reasons not to. Let's assume that you're about to go into major contract negotiations where you need everybody just swinging together. You don't need a sideshow. You don't need a diversion. So there are strategic reasons not to handle an issue at a particular time.

McEntee: You don't want to commit suicide. We're not here to commit suicide.

Trumka: That's right.

Sheinkman: Six years ago I got attacked from the convention floor for going to El Salvador. Members wanted to know what I was doing in El Salvador. I took flak and stood my position.

Solowey: President Sheinkman, earlier in the interview you touched on the ethnic diversity of your membership. Looking at your publication, I see stories in three languages, and I understand that your members speak at least twenty different languages. What problems does this ethnic and cultural diversity pose for your newspaper?

Sheinkman: Historically, we used to have our paper printed in English, Italian, Yiddish, Polish, and we still have that diversity. Up in Montreal, for example, there are publications in French, Greek, and Italian. The issues are no different than they were fifty years ago in terms of what you're fighting for. It's just that you had different ethnic groups involved. But workers today are facing the same kind of problems that their predecessors faced. It's just in a different mode and a different era.

Solowey: Another matter of diversity that both Presidents Trumka and Sheinkman face is having members in Canada. President Sheinkman brought up this topic earlier. Are there particular problems each of you faces in making sure that the publication addresses Canadian needs, and are there stories and issues that might divide your Canadian and U.S. members?

Trumka: We are better able to reconcile an issue that has, in some instances, adverse affects on members in different areas than some outside agency or third party. The issues that miners face are the same in the United States as they are in Canada. The health care issue is different. We used the health care system in Canada as an example of what should exist in the United States. There will be specific issues that affect one side and not the other. What you can't do and what we don't let happen is to have us pigeonholed. They are not U.S. members or Canadian members. They are mine workers. Just like a mine worker in Colorado might have a different isssue than a mine worker in Tennessee or in southern West Virginia, a member in Alberta or Nova Scotia may have a different concern. But first and foremost, they are mine workers.

Sheinkman: I have to disagree, though I agree with your general concept. Given the size of the United States and the presence of nationalism in Canada, there's a lot of pressure. A lot of people say, Why do you send the dues to New York?

Solowey: Now, President McEntee, you face diversity questions, too. Your members are mostly government workers, but they're everything from social workers to corrections officers, from people who change bed pans to professionals. Certain types of questions—like policy on AIDS—become very difficult ones for a union like AFSCME. To cite another example, you have some members who want more prisons built and some people who want prisons torn down, with the money put into jobs programs. All of this makes communications and guiding the magazine more complicated, doesn't it?

McEntee: It makes it more interesting. Members of AFSCME have varying opinions on all kinds of things out there. We have a committee on just about everything you can imagine. We have a gay and lesbian committee. We have a correctional officer committee. I remember a gay and lesbian rights resolution at the convention. A guy got up by the name of Marty Beall, who is a parole officer as tough and as big and as hard and aggressive as anybody in this union. I said to myself, "Jesus Christ." But he spoke 100 percent in favor of gay and lesbian rights. Is there a lot of diversity? There certainly is. Who is best able to handle that diversity? It's the institutional mechanism itself, and the magazine is part of that. Do you satisfy every member in the union? The answer is no.

Solowey: In terms of how these things do and don't take expression in the publication, I've seen controversial things of one sort or another, not the same ones necessarily, in all of your publications. Did any of you ever see an article slated for publication and think, I'm going to get hell on this, but I'm letting it go in anyway?

Trumka: I'll be honest with you. I see the publication after it's printed. I don't see it before it's printed.

McEntee: I do, and I'll tell you why. First of all, I don't have anything to do with writing the stories. I rarely have anything to do with where the staff is going or what they're doing. But we're a big, diverse union, and we've had situations that have led me to look at the stories and pictures. I have the best political feel for this union. If I didn't, I shouldn't be here. I don't want anybody to be embarrassed in any shape or form. When I first got here, we had a march for Martin Luther King, Jr., down in Memphis. We march every April 4. Marching was one of our council officials with his girlfriend, and the staff—without knowing the situation—was planning to run a picture that included them. It would have been a disaster for this guy. There are other issues, too. We are a diverse union, and I don't want all the pictures to be of whites or Blacks. The staff is working down there on their own stories and not paying any attention to this. I'll pick up the paper and I'll pick up the pictures and, depending on the story, 85 percent or 90 percent of the people are Black. I'm very sensitive to that thing. We need to have a measure of balance. That's the kind of stuff I look for in terms of the paper. There also is, once in a while, an article on gun control or something like that, and I know we're having a representation election for a group of correctional officers soon. Something like that is a red flag and a big whistle. We can run it next month, but you don't have to run it now. We're not going to go in there and have the Teamsters or somebody else putting that edition on every bulletin board. That's suicide.

Sheinkman: I'll do a little of what Jerry does after the fact. I found that in a couple of issues we were running 95 percent pictures of Black people.

Trumka: So you corrected it in subsequent issues?

Sheinkman: Yes. I told the editor we're a diverse union.

Solowey: On that question about knowing that you'd catch hell for something about to appear, President Sheinkman, was that the case for you on opposition to U.S. policy in Central America?

Sheinkman: I've had no trouble with that. First of all, it's no secret. I take an open position. I feel, for example, that the paper should have international stuff but not overwhelmingly. What we try to do is take issues that affect the union internationally, like South Africa, where we have relationships and strong events. It's got to be balanced in the paper. It's not different from what faces a news editor about what goes in and what doesn't. I try to tell the editor about some of the political problems that Jerry was talking about. You know that it's a question of using judgment.

Solowey: President Trumka, what about you?

Trumka: I can't think of anything offhand. A lot of people have come up to me and said, "Why did you print that critical letter?" Sometimes I ask why we did print it.

Solowey: Why do you print it?

Trumka: I don't handle any kind of editorial problem. There have been things that we've caught flak over. The way I try to handle the process is to let the editors—who know the issues and what we're dealing with—handle it. I imagine that if they were way over there, if the union was over here, I'd probably do something about it. I just haven't had to.

Solowey: A sensitive topic concerns the issues of racism and sexism within the union. How do you deal with the existence of these problems within the union in your publication?

Sheinkman: We had a issue, for example, on sexual harassment on the job and on how women should cope with it.

Trumka: You hit it head-on. If you have women members who are being sexually harassed, or members in your own organization who are being racist—hit it head-on. I don't care what it costs me, I'll stand up and tell somebody. First of all, you're being stupid if you help an employer discriminate against a Black man and you're a white man—because if he can discriminate against a Black, he'll discriminate against you. You call discrimination for what it is. You condemn it and you point out that it divides workers, and it's bad for all of us. When women came into the coal industry, they faced a tough time. Mining wasn't just male dominated. It was male exclusive. All kinds of myths and lore grew up that if a women went into a mine, the mine would explode. And some of my own members gave the first women a hard time. We hit that thing head-on. The best thing that ever happened to the Mine Workers was when we brought women in. They gave us an injection of new ideas. And that's not hype.

Solowey: Most union members don't see themselves primarily as union members. There's their family, there's church, their ball team. When I went to Sweden with a group of labor editors, we were struck by how much the Swedish union publications were writing about things of general interest. In terms of all the competition we face to get the members to read union publications, should the labor press be dealing with more non-work-related things—sports and music, for instance—to get readership up?

McEntee: I don't think so. I think we do have a measure of success, and we can improve upon that. I think the average member of a union gets enough of those things already, whether from *People* magazine, *Life*, or *Reader's Digest*, or whatever. They look to that kind of magazine for that kind of entertainment and information. And it's not going to make them read the union publication any more often, or get any more out of it, because you have a page in there about entertainment, or about popular news. That's my judgment.

Sheinkman: I couldn't agree with you more.

Trumka: Again it comes back to credibility. What credibility do I have talking about rock music? *Rolling Stone* has credibility. What credibility do I have talking about race cars? Members look at us and say we have credibility on worker issues. That's what we are. We represent workers.

Sheinkman: We're not a general paper. If you have a union sports team that's won a championship in a league, that's different. But a general issue of who is winning the pennant race, no. Now, we do have a column from time to time that covers what's happening in other unions or labor news of general interest.

McEntee: Rich, we have stuff in there about your union—like about the Pittston strike. That's of interest to our members.

Trumka: I was really blessed by all of that. We were the recipients of tremendous help.

Solowey: I've never seen as much writing about another union's strike as I did in the labor press about Pittston.

Trumka: I really believe that it's important that we don't get pigeon-holed. I don't want my members to think they're only mine workers. And I'm sure Jerry and Jack don't want their people to think they are only AFSCME or ACTWU. First and foremost, we're all workers. And we have to keep our members interested and let them know that something that affects Jack's union affects us, and that something that affects a South African worker affects a white worker in Alabama. That's what's important.

Mobilizing an Informed Membership: The Mine Workers Experience

Matt Witt

Miner John Martin said the experiment had the potential to improve working conditions and safety practices. But co-worker Vic Potkalesky called it simply a management ploy to undermine workers' rights. These were some of the sharply differing opinions offered by United Mine Workers members in Osceola Mills, Pennsylvania, about a local experiment in labor-management cooperation.

Under an agreement between the company and the union, the Osceola Mills workers were supposed to have an unprecedented opportunity to suggest ways to improve both mine efficiency and the quality of work life. In return, the company would gain new flexibility in assigning work.

Whether the UMW should take part in such experiments was a controversial subject. To make an informed judgment, the national membership needed the facts about the Pennsylvania miners' experience.

The union magazine, the *United Mine Workers Journal*, helped fill that need. A *Journal* reporter and photographer went to Osceola Mills to do an in-depth story. Miners who saw the experiment as a way to relieve boredom and open up opportunities for younger miners were given their say. Those who charged that management only accepted suggestions that would increase productivity—and who worried that

Matt Witt was the managing editor of the United Mine Workers Journal *from 1973 to 1975 and then editor until November 1977. In 1976, the* Journal *became the only labor publication ever to win the National Magazine Award as the top U.S. publication in the field of specialized journalism. In February 1992, Witt became the communications director of the International Brotherhood of Teamsters after Ron Carey's election as the union's president.*

competition between union members would replace solidarity—were also quoted.

Honest analysis and open debate exemplified the *UMW Journal* of the mid-1970s at its best. The *Journal* of that era was the product of a successful rank-and-file movement for democracy within the union. The magazine's strengths—and its failure at times to live up to the reform movement's ideals—suggest lessons for those who seek to make the labor press as effective as possible.

An Activist, Democratic Journal

Until 1973, the *Journal* was almost exclusively a heavy-handed mouthpiece for union president W. A. "Tony" Boyle. His strategy for survival in office was simple: make no move to mobilize the membership to fight for its interests. Instead, Boyle allied himself with mine companies and government officials. The *Journal* reflected this strategy, carrying ritualistic statements "calling on" the companies or politicians to respect miners' concerns but rarely providing the information or inspiration that members needed to act.

The Miners for Democracy movement advocated a different vision of unionism, and thousands of UMW members came to support it. The union dues these miners paid made them part owners of the *Journal*. Yet these Miners for Democracy advocates had no access to their own publication.

During the successful campaign to defeat Boyle in late 1972, Miners for Democracy supporters made the abuse of the *Journal* a political issue. As a result, the editors appointed by the new UMW president, Arnold Miller, had a strong mandate to implement four major reforms. The new *Journal* began

- promoting more open discussion of important workplace, union, and political issues;

- focusing coverage on union members who were actually organizing to challenge corporate power, instead of on empty pronouncements by top union officials;

- providing specific, practical information about how to use contract rights, mobilize members, challenge politicians, insist on safe working conditions, and take other actions; and

- publishing investigative reports about the activities of the companies and government officials.

39

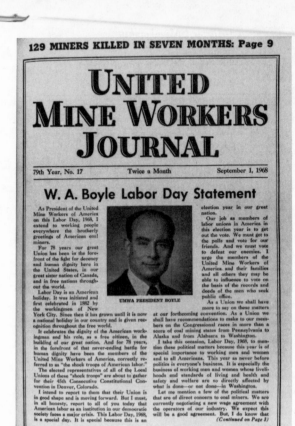

129 MINERS KILLED IN SEVEN MONTHS: Page 9

UNITED
MINE WORKERS
JOURNAL

| 79th Year, No. 17 | Twice a Month | September 1, 1968 |

W. A. Boyle Labor Day Statement

As President of the United Mine Workers of America on this Labor Day, 1968, I extend to working people everywhere the brotherly greetings of American coal miners.

For 78 years our great Union has been in the forefront of the fight for decency and human dignity here in the United States, in our great sister nation of Canada, and in free nations throughout the world.

Labor Day is an American holiday. It was initiated and first celebrated in 1882 by the workingmen of New York City. Since then it has grown until it is now a national holiday in our country and is given recognition throughout the free world.

It celebrates the dignity of the American workingman and his role, as a free citizen, in the building of our great nation. And for 78 years, in the forefront of that never-ending battle for human dignity have been the members of the United Mine Workers of America, correctly referred to as "the shock troops of American labor."

The elected representatives of all of the Local Unions of these "shock troops" are about to gather for their 45th Consecutive Constitutional Convention in Denver, Colorado.

I intend to report to them that their Union is in good shape and is moving forward. But I must, in all honesty, report to all of you today that American labor as an institution in our democratic society faces a major crisis. This Labor Day, 1968, is a special day. It is special because this is an

UMWA PRESIDENT BOYLE

election year in our great nation.

Our job as members of labor unions in America in this election year is to get out the vote. We must get to the polls and vote for our friends. And we must vote to defeat our enemies. I urge the members of the United Mine Workers of America and their families and all others they may be able to influence to vote on the basis of the records and deeds of the men who seek public office.

As a Union we shall have more to say on these matters at our forthcoming convention. As a Union we shall have recommendations to make to our members on the Congressional races in more than a score of coal mining states from Pennsylvania to Alaska and from Alabama to Washington.

I take this occasion, Labor Day, 1968, to mention these political matters because this year is of special importance to working men and women and to all Americans. This year as never before politics is everyone's business. It is especially the business of working men and women whose livelihoods and standards of living and health and safety and welfare are so directly affected by what is done—or not done—in Washington.

Let me mention a few of the political matters that are of direct concern to coal miners. We are currently negotiating a new wage agreement with the operators of our industry. We expect this will be a good agreement. But, I do know that *(Continued on Page 8)*

(Continued on Page 8)

These two United Mine Workers Journal covers, one from before the union's internal reform struggles and the other after, reflect the union's shift from a top-down to a member-oriented labor journalism.

None of these reforms was implemented with total success, but, to the extent they were put in place, the reforms did contribute significantly to the strength and democracy of the union and, as a side effect, the political popularity of top union leaders.

Democratic Debate

An attempt to stimulate a freer flow of information and opinions was fundamental to reform of the *Journal* for two reasons, one a matter of principle, the other of pragmatism.

The right to express yourself—and hear what others have to say—is an essential prerequisite for democracy. By the same token, the capacity to acknowledge problems, unmet goals, and differing points of view is an essential prerequisite for credibility, without which a union publication is useless because it won't be read. If, for instance, a union journal presents a controversial new contract only as a great victory won by a dedicated leadership team, workers critical of the agreement

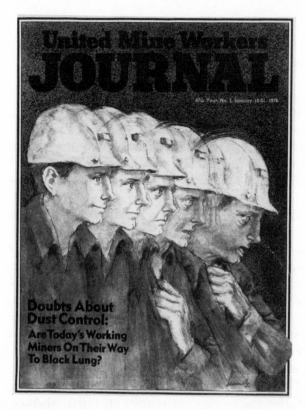

will inevitably reject the magazine as a publication that doesn't present the full story.

At the new *UMW Journal*, a first step toward more open discussion was a letters-to-the-editor column, with space for comment on corporate, government, and union policies, as well as on the *Journal* itself. In this letters section, a letter calling the 1974 national coal contract "the best that has been written" would be balanced by another arguing that, "in comparing profits with wages, I am inclined to say that the miner came out on the short end of the deal." Letter writers could—and did—freely debate the UMW's political action strategy of virtually always endorsing Democratic candidates, with some contending that the labor movement and its allies should put more emphasis on running their own candidates and others claiming the union would have more leverage if it endorsed more Republicans.

Since miners, like most people, rarely write letters to distant institutions, even if they are concerned about an issue, a second addition to the *Journal* was a column called "The Rank & File Speaks." Each *Journal* issue ran interviews with members on a particular theme, accompanied by photos of all persons interviewed. The *Journal* staff deliberately chose interviewees to represent variety in viewpoint, geographical area, age, gender, and race.

To maintain reader interest, it was important that these interviews address substance and not become just a way to reward administration allies mouthing support for official policies. The interviews asked questions that mattered: What did miners consider the strengths and weaknesses of their current contact with the coal companies? What rights and benefits did they want to see in their next agreement? What were the root causes of wildcat strikes? How well was the union's system for contract enforcement working, and how could this system be improved?

A third change in the new *Journal* was more balanced coverage of union conventions, elections, contract talks, and other major union events and activities. After the 1976 UMW convention, for instance, the *Journal* excerpted several key debates and published seven pages of frank interviews with delegates from all factions. The interviews helped give readers an accurate picture of how delegates felt about the top convention issues, everything from priorities for upcoming contract negotiations to the conflict over whether union field staff ought to be elected or appointed. The delegates interviewed also commented on the convention itself—how committees operated, whether the debate had been democratic, how rulings by the chair had affected the outcome.

In the six months before the 1977 elections for top union offices, coverage of the competing candidates, including the incumbents, was eliminated from the *Journal*'s news section. Instead, in keeping with the union constitution enacted as part of Miners for Democracy's reforms, each competing slate was given more than thirty pages, spread across four editions, to use as it saw fit.

Before the 1974 coal industry contract negotiations, the *Journal* published a special issue that highlighted all the demands presented to the companies. The magazine also shared much of the information available to union negotiators on corporate profits, stockpiles, and management's likely demands and arguments. With this as background, the members who would later vote on whether to accept the contract could evaluate the gains won and compromises made. Open bargaining also put pressure on the coal companies, who knew they were negotiating not just with a handful of leaders but with an informed rank and file.

Featuring Members in Action

Miners for Democracy came to power with the expressed goal of encouraging members to get involved in all aspects of union activity, rather than sit back and wait for their leaders to single-handedly put everything right. The growing number of nonunion mines could not be organized by UMW staff alone. Members needed to help tell unorganized miners how they had benefited from the union. Safe and healthful working conditions could be won only if the rank and file at each mine insisted on its rights. Union legislative lobbying would be effective only if politicians saw that UMW members were informed and mobilized. Success in contract negotiations depended on the reports corporate executives received from line supervisors about workers' determination and priorities.

The new *Journal* squarely faced the question of how best to involve members. Frequent messages from the president simply exhorting people to participate would obviously be ineffective. Exhortations don't address the reasons why people don't get involved. Union members often either don't believe that they're capable of making a contribution or don't know how to get started. They need role models, examples, and practical guidance.

The axiom that "the medium is the message" applies here: union journals that constantly run quotes from and photos of top officers send members the message that the officers are the union, regardless of what the quotes say. To encourage members' involvement in union action, the *Journal* avoided this approach. Instead, the *Journal* featured stories and photos that showed members taking an active part in addressing on-the-job and community problems. One feature, for instance, reported on West Virginia miners who elected one UMW member to the state legislature and another to the post of county constable. The article showed how the new legislator was raising environmental, tax, education, and mine safety issues that his predecessor had ignored and how the new constable was forcing coal companies to start obeying water quality ordinances.

Another *Journal* article described a project at a coalfield high school where UMW members visited classes and explained the importance of unions in community life. The article described what the miners discussed and why they thought their school visits were valuable. Still other *Journal* stories profiled miners and their families who were attacking the health care crisis by demanding seats on hospital boards and even organizing their own clinics. Reading these features, a UMW member could say, "These people are like me. I could do what they did."

Practical Information

To act effectively, union members need information and advice about how to proceed. In most unions, some information along these lines is distributed to local officers or committees. But many locals simply don't have effective education programs that involve more than a handful of activists. The information distributed to local leaders may never reach rank-and-file members who might be motivated to put it to good use.

The *Journal*, as the only publication reaching every UMW member, regularly ran columns on such subjects as how to keep the coal companies from cutting corners on job safety and health and how to use contract rights. Sidebars accompanying feature stories frequently described, in checklist format, the steps readers could take to do something about the problems the article described. The *Journal* didn't just expose company and government failure to protect miners from dust and noise. It told miners how to use their legal rights to fight back.

Investigative Reporting

To help fulfill the reform movement's pledge to confront the anti-worker policies of corporations and government officials, the *Journal* engaged in persistent investigative reporting, often in collaboration with other union departments or coalfield organizations. Such reporting often stimulated action at various levels of the union, as well as follow-up reports in the commercial news media.

One example: When deaths in western Kentucky mines jumped from one in 1974 to thirteen in 1975, most of the Kentucky media, quoting government officials, attributed the deaths to "freak accidents" or "human error." By working with union safety experts, the *Journal* was able to show that most of the deaths were caused by company violations of safety laws or by weak enforcement by government inspection agencies. The *Journal* investigation helped generate a UMW safety alert in western Kentucky that included special union inspections and educational programs about workers' rights.

In Tennessee, a *Journal* exposé prodded the commercial media to cover a conflict of interest involving then U.S. Senator Howard Baker, Jr. In West Virginia, the state Human Rights Commission took action against racial discrimination in the state's coal industry after a *Journal* series made the issue a subject of controversy in the general press.

Investigative reporting, along with the letters column, rank-and-file interviews, feature writing, top-quality photos, how-to advice, and a space for poems and cartoons by miners and family members all combined to attract readers both within the union and among interested community organizations, journalists, and politicians. The *Journal* could compete for attention with the regular news media, in at least a modest way, because it was no longer seen as a mere house organ. By applying some of the techniques of commercial journalism, the *Journal* had become more unpredictable—and more interesting. Readers never knew when they opened a given edition what scandals, debate-provoking interviews, or practical guides to solving everyday problems they would find.

The *Journal*'s popularity among members, not surprisingly, rose significantly. A 1976 UMW research department poll showed that miners considered the *Journal* one of the union's most important services. More than 70 percent of local union leaders said they made direct use of its educational material.

That popularity reflected well on the union's top leaders, which is one reason an activist *Journal* survived for four years. Union president Miller frequently reported after trips to the coalfields that members had praised him not only for the openness and informativeness of the *Journal* but for the aggressive, democratic unionism it portrayed and encouraged.

The Internal Politics Obstacle

Not everyone in the union bureaucracy was completely pleased with the reformed *UMW Journal*. Some officials with roots in Miners for Democracy raised legitimate concerns. A few organizers, for example, complained that employers were using the member criticism the *Journal* published *against* the union during organizing campaigns. Most of the organizing staff, however, learned to turn this issue to their advantage by pointing out that the publication of dissent in the *Journal* showed that the union was a democratic, rank-and-file organization and not the dictatorship the bosses described.

Some other union officials protested that open discussion meant "hanging our dirty laundry where the coal operators can see it." A union is a fighting organization with powerful enemies, they argued, not a debating society. To win, the union must present a unified front. "There is such a thing as too much democracy," said one UMW executive board member.

Such concerns obviously had to limit, to some extent, what could be printed in a public forum. But a majority of the union's democratic forces believed that open discussion builds, not undermines, unity. The coal companies would know about divisions within the union in any case, they argued. The union would be stronger if it tried to resolve those divisions rather than pretend they didn't exist.

Other complaints against the *Journal* came from those elected officials and staff who were concerned with preserving their own jobs. They complained that the *Journal*

■ didn't do enough to promote incumbent officials. "How come you never put my picture in the *Journal?*" some would ask out of frustration when they saw so much space devoted to the thoughts and actions of mere rank and filers. Worse yet, from this point of view, was the possibility that an interview in the *Journal* might lead members to become even more involved, perhaps to the point of running for union office themselves someday. Some district officials went so far as to argue that they should have control over which workers from their districts were allowed to speak out in the magazine's pages.

■ let members see what their officials were or were not doing. Conservative officials—many of them former Boyle supporters—became furious, for example, when the *Journal* began printing their votes on important issues.

■ caused members to expect leaders to challenge the companies and the government. Most UMW officials saw an informed and mobilized membership as an essential asset in their battles with industry and government leaders, but some weren't interested in that battle in the first place. They preferred to socialize with their industry and government counterparts as "responsible" labor statesmen, rather than take on the difficult task of leading a workers' movement for social change. If the *Journal* would stop publicizing problems, they reasoned, the membership would be less likely to demand solutions.

"Why don't you people lay off the government and the [coal] operators for a while and let the leadership take care of [dealing with] them?" one executive board member admonished the *Journal* editor.

The UMW's chief contract administrator—a holdover from the Boyle era—urged Miller not to allow the *Journal* to print columns about members' contract rights.

"You put this kind of stuff in," he complained, "and all of a sudden we're going to have a stack of grievances this thick!"

For the most part, Miller resisted pressures to censor the *Journal*, but not always. Miller, for example, never allowed the *Journal* to apply the principle of democratic debate to the issue of strip mining. A growing percentage of the union's members were strip miners who were strongly opposed to any government regulation that could affect their job security. Tens of thousands of other members lived in Appalachian hollows where strip mining tortured the land, poisoned the water, and created mud slides that destroyed families' homes. Yet the *Journal* ran no interviews in "The Rank & File Speaks" for or against abolition or regulation of strip mining. There were no photos of destroyed homes, no dramatic feature stories and profiles of the kind the *Journal* produced on the victims of black lung disease or unsafe mining conditions. The best the magazine could do was to provide occasional dry accounts of congressional testimony or executive board resolutions on strip mine legislation, and even those were sometimes vetoed.

Inevitably, the biases of the staff also played a role in the *Journal's* imperfections. In 1976, when executive board members tried to use budget cuts to cripple activist union programs in organizing, safety, political action, and other areas, the *Journal* devoted most of five pages to presenting the Miller administration's point of view and only a few paragraphs to the board's. At the time, it seemed that one goal—a democratic magazine—had to be sacrificed momentarily for a higher goal—that of preserving vital union programs, including the *Journal* itself. Looking back, it's hard to justify not having given the two sides equal space. If the proposed cuts were wrong, presumably members would have reached that conclusion. Limiting debate to preserve the key programs of a democratic administration sounds in retrospect dangerously like U.S. generals' claims in Vietnam that they had to "destroy the village in order to save it."

Nor should the *Journal's* honesty and openness be overstated. The magazine was still a house organ, even if an unconventional one, and the staff made countless compromises to protect itself politically. As in most labor publications, for example, friendly union officials were routinely worked into stories in ways that made them seem to be actively representing members' interests, even in cases when they personally were doing little or nothing to contribute to the initiative the story described. Every organizing victory was reported as a major triumph, while losses were not mentioned, much less analyzed.

Information to which members were entitled was sometimes withheld if it would call union policy into question. In the 1976 presidential campaign, when Jimmy Carter's aides told the *Journal* that they could not make any specific commitments to coal miners for publication because "he plans to wait until he is elected and then review these issues," that revealing quote never appeared in the *Journal* because it might have undermined readers' enthusiasm for the union-endorsed candidate.

The Members' Right to Know

There are plenty of reasons for top union leaders to encourage more open, activist labor journalism. A popular publication that is read and helps mobilize members can do a great deal to help leaders achieve their goals and maintain their own popularity.

But the experience of the *UMW Journal* over the past two decades suggests that the members' right to know about corporate, government, and union developments should not depend on whether top leaders share that enlightened view.

Most leaders, no matter how well intentioned, will tend to become more cautious and more closed when they feel threatened. The *Journal* was allowed to become open and activist because a rank-and-file movement demanded that kind of union publication. When the momentum of reform slowed, the UMW magazine was one of the first casualties.

In the 1977 UMW presidential elections, the candidate of the old Boyle forces received only a third of the vote. But Miller and another member of the original Miners for Democracy team split the remaining ballots so that Miller only narrowly won reelection. His top aide, a former Boyle supporter, convinced Miller that the best way to reassert his power was to return to the strong-arm tactics of prereform administrations. The aide began to censor letters to the editor and ordered publication of a photograph and puff piece promoting a pro-Miller executive board member facing a tough reelection fight. In the 1977 contract negotiations, instead of details about union demands, company profits, and industry strategy, the *Journal* offered material prepared by an outside public relations firm that emphasized the qualifications of union negotiators and featured photographs of Miller on the average of one per page.

The *Journal* wasn't to recover its vitality until the reform pendulum swung back and Richard Trumka was elected UMW president in 1982. The Trumka campaign highlighted the abuse of the *Journal*, and his victory was a clear mandate for change. The new UMW leadership brought in and trained miners with a talent for writing and a commitment to militant unionism. Once again, the *Journal* began exposing coal company and government wrongdoing and offering union members specific information about how to fight back. The interview feature, "The Rank & File Speaks," and an open letters column were reinstated after an absence of five years.

Is there no way to institutionalize members' right to democratic debate and aggressive unionism in labor publications so that that right does not depend on the ebbs and flows of union politics?

Would vesting editorial control in a group—such as an editorial board or the union executive board—instead of the union president make a difference? The *UMW Journal* experience suggests the limits of this sort of structural change. In 1975, after the UMW executive board set up a committee to oversee the *Journal*, an article was prepared describing how Governor George Wallace had failed to help unions on the "right to work" issue in Alabama. The union executive board member from that state, in his capacity as *Journal* review commission member, protested that publication of the article could affect his own political standing with miners back home. Wallace was "popular in Alabama and some of our members won't like to see him criticized," the board member said. The story's facts were not in dispute, but UMW president Miller agreed to have the references to Wallace removed. Realizing how further such incidents could undermine his own authority, Miller later told the board that the commission had abused its review power, and he dissolved it.

The solution, then, lies not so much in changing who runs labor publications as in spelling out clearly in union constitutions both the obligations of those overseers and the membership's right to know. Union constitutions ought to require, for example, that membership publications

■ provide information about activities, plans, finances, and strategies of employers and government agencies that affect the membership;

■ provide clear explanations of members' contract and union rights;

■ advise members how they can take part in actions to improve conditions on the job and in their communities;

- include a letters column of a specified minimum length that accurately reflects mail received;

- provide campaign space to candidates in union elections;

- objectively describe debates at union meetings and conventions; and

- provide a specified amount of space to any group of a specified number of members that submits a petition indicating its desire to raise a particular issue with the membership.

Like many rights in a democratic society, some of the rights noted here would be open to interpretation. How each union carries out its obligations to the member's right to know would depend in part on the resources available. But the formalization of these rights and duties would establish specific standards for union leaders to measure themselves by and, when necessary, for members to enforce through organized pressure, internal appeals, and legal challenges.

Union Leaders and Union Papers: The View from Abroad

Gunilla Wettergren

In Sweden, a nation of 8 million people, trade union newspapers reach 85 percent of the wage-earning population. Almost every union has its own newspaper, which is mailed to members in their homes.

Some two million industrial and service sector workers in Sweden, both public and private, belong to the LO unions. The white-collar workers and academics are organized in the TCO unions and SACO, with roughly 500,000 and 330,000 members each.

Union newspapers in Sweden are financed from member dues, the main source of income for unions. Some extra income is earned from advertising. The union national executives appoint the editors and are, in most cases, the publishers. In practice, the editors are responsible for the content and style of their papers. Compared with other countries, the Swedish union press is relatively independent.

This independence has its roots in the 1930s, the early days of the modern Swedish labor press. The LO newspapers of that time established a high degree of journalistic integrity and a tradition of promoting open debate on trade union and cultural questions. Throughout the 1930s, the LO newspapers provided a platform for proletarian writers, publishing short stories and articles that criticized social conditions and even dared to criticize the actions of unions as well.

But this vitality didn't last. Unions increasingly chose their editors

Gunilla Wettergren worked as the "leaderwriter" for the Aftonbladet, *the newspaper owned by the Swedish LO union federation, for eleven years. In 1983, she became the editor of* Kommunalarbetaren, *the newspaper of the Swedish Municipal Workers Union. This article was translated by Patrick Breslin.*

from the ranks of national full-time union officers, and the editorial desk of most labor papers became an integral part of the national union, which tightly controlled the contents. This didn't leave much room for real journalism, and labor papers became little more than a means of passing information to union members. These papers, or "members' information sheets" as they were called, met with little respect from commercial editorial desks.

Over the past thirty years, this situation has turned around. The Swedish labor press has seen a slow but dominant trend toward greater professionalism. Unions have recruited more and more professional journalists and provided them with greater editorial resources. The resulting changes were especially noticeable in the 1980s, when many papers adopted modern techniques, both in layout and journalism.

Cases of old-syle authoritarian control over trade union editorial desks still linger. But what's different today is that such authoritarianism leads to direct confrontation between editors and national union executives. In 1990, for instance, the dismissal of two trade union editors because of their critical approach to reporting led to a heated labor movement debate on the role of union newspapers.

Overall, Swedish trade unions over the past ten to twenty years have clearly reached a stronger understanding of the value of a relatively independent and vital trade union press. This understanding has helped establish the credibility of Swedish labor journalism.

Union newspapers in Sweden, once instruments used by union leaders, have become instruments in the hands of members. Communication in the Swedish labor press is now two-way: reporting on members' working conditions provides the union leadership with important information on the views and interests of members.

Today, with the commercial media in Sweden often uncritically accepting the views held by the business community, the Swedish labor press is more important than ever. Swedish commercial newspapers do very little critical investigative reporting on business activities and working conditions. Swedish business leaders generally enjoy the admiration of court journalists, who subject trade union and political leaders to a far tougher scrutiny.

Into this investigative void have come Swedish trade union newspapers, particularly those owned by the LO unions. Union papers, despite their limited resources, have become important national forces for investigative journalism and political and economic reform.

To meet this investigative responsibility, union newspapers need more money and larger editorial staffs. Union papers have become somewhat larger over recent years, thanks primarily to the structural changes now under way in the Swedish labor movement. The amalgamation of smaller unions into larger unions has been accompanied by the fusion of smaller newspapers into bigger ones.

Discussions are presently under way on the formation of two large unions to replace the twenty unions that now make up the LO. The food workers, garment workers, and factory workers would amalgamate to form BELIFA, a union with some two hundred thousand members. The state employees, transport workers, and seamen's unions are involved in discussions to form a communications workers union with around three hundred thousand members. Six trade union papers would merge to form two.

This introduction is a necessary backdrop to the story of my work at *Kommunalarbetaren*, the biggest trade union newspaper in northern Europe, with seven hundred thousand copies published twice a month.

I took over the editorship of *Kommunalarbetaren* (The Municipal Worker) in 1983, with a battery of ideas on what the newspaper should look like, the principles to be followed by journalists working under me, and how I would tackle the business of renewal and change. With eighteen years of work on a daily newspaper behind me, I found the move to join a trade union paper both exciting and daunting.

I must confess to the feeling of trepidation with which I accepted the post as editor in chief of *Kommunalarbetaren*. Like many of my colleagues in the daily press at the time, I found the trade union press somewhat boring and off-putting. The union newspapers had a definite amateurish style. In many cases, they were badly edited. Worse still, some of them were hopelessly old-fashioned and quite simply unengaging. The contents gave the impression of routine thinking and a general lack of editorial planning, as if the contents had been left to chance. I was only too aware that most of the LO newspapers were published on a shoestring budget, on unreliable presses, and with a good measure of tight control exercised by the owners/unions. At the *Aftonbladet*, the newspaper I worked for, my colleagues and I agreed that union newspapers could and should be better. They didn't have to meet our worst expectations.

I came to the *Kommunalarbetaren* offices with a firm promise of more hard cash to work with, and I saw an opportunity to help develop a new type of trade union newspaper, a paper that could play a more active part in shaping public debate, that could get close to the nerves of our members' working lives, and, above all, that could compete with the commercial press.

Trade union newspapers, my colleagues and I believed, had fallen into a rut, unaffected by changes in their readers' expectations of media products. The media market offers a wide choice of products, and the competition to win over media consumers is tough. Readers expect quality.

Trade unions need to deliver this quality. The LO unions, for instance, reach the homes of some 2.2 million readers/members. This is no small market. Spending millions of dollars on newspapers that people don't read is not just stupid—it is utterly unjustifiable.

Unlike commercial newspapers, trade union newspapers have a guaranteed circulation. But this guaranteed circulation does not guarantee readership. For union journalists, the key challenge is getting a paper read.

The distinction between circulation and readership is important in my view, and I have always maintained that the journalistic challenge facing the commercial press—to sell copies—is basically the same challenge we face. Instead of selling copies, we must win readers.

This challenge for all of us in the Swedish labor press has taken on a new urgency since the September 1991 electoral defeat of the Social Democratic party. The right-wing government now in power is seeking to destroy many of the gains made by our unions through decades of struggle. The need to reach, educate, and mobilize our membership through union publications is greater than ever. But it is not automatic that union members will turn to their union publications to explain the situation and point the way to the solution.

Labor journalists still face several significant obstacles. One is the almost total lack of understanding of journalism and newspapers often displayed by union leadership. As long as the newspapers roll off the presses on time, many union officials regard the problem as solved. They tend to forget that the most important step in the process still has to be cleared: how to get members to open their union papers and read them. No message, no matter how important it may be, will have any effect whatsoever until the union member has read it, grasped its meaning, and been influenced by it.

I have often wondered about the rather peculiar view of the union member held in some quarters. This view considers the union member a mere consumer of services. But union members are not vacuum cleaners for information, ever eager to scoop up any informational crumbs that drop their way. The members of the Swedish LO are normal people who have normal levels of interest—and disinterest—in newspapers.

It is something of a myth that people must deliberately buy or subscribe to a newspaper if they are to want to read it. The decisive factor is the content of the newspaper, how that content is presented, and how attractive the newspaper is to the reader.

Union newspapers are in a unique position to deliver an attractive content that addresses the interests of union members. Unlike family-owned commercial newspapers or papers controlled by political parties, trade union newspapers are, after all, owned by the organized working people.

Union papers may be owned by members, some might add, but they are managed by union executives. But this is no excuse for publishing boring newspapers aimed at a small niche. Nor is it an argument for regarding the reader of a labor paper as simply a union member with interests limited to the union. This view, the not uncommon view held by many full-time union officials, is a major reason for the narrow perspective that some union newspapers still maintain. Full-time officials no longer control union newspapers, but, despite the influx of professional journalists, the weight of tradition still plays a role in some boardrooms.

At *Kommunalarbetaren*, I was able to win support for a new editorial policy based on the recognition that union members have a wide range of interests. We combined this new editorial approach with a modern, effective layout. The changeover to color in every issue was our most expensive innovation. I wanted to escape from that very Swedish view that a serious product calls for a strict, dull layout. A serious article, I believe, calls for a stimulating and attractive layout to capture the reader's attention.

Our *Kommunalarbetaren* has taken a holistic view. We see our member/readers as more than amalgams of incompatible roles: the unionist, the consumer, the producer, the citizen, the voter. LO members may well be all of these things, but they are also something more. They are wage earners with skills, union members, taxpayers, commuters, mothers and fathers, patients (sometimes), cultured and educated consumers of arts—in short, everything imaginable.

Sweden's many workplaces, where millions of people spend most of their daily lives, provide a relatively unexamined arena for journalists interested in drama and conflict. The general public sees only a fraction of what goes on at a workplace. Workplace reporting calls for a fresh approach, and we have adopted a more "insight" type of journalism, with a stronger emphasis on relationships between employees. We have emphasized the psychosocial dimension—how people feel about their working situations, the content and value of their jobs, measured by more than just money. *Kommunalarbetaren* runs a regular column on these issues under the headline "Our Jobs."

Another column has the headline "If it were left to me, I'd. . . ." This column gives ordinary members the chance to present the changes they would like to introduce into their jobs or into society at large. Our ambition is to provide a platform for people who are normally silenced, whose voices are not heard because they lack money and power. Our readers may lack power, but that does not mean that they lack opinions or the desire to implement change.

People play different roles and have different interests, depending on their personalities. Newspapers cannot specialize to such a degree that they concentrate on only one or two of these human traits. Specialized newspapers appeal to a limited readership. Trade union newspapers must broaden the scope of their articles if their readership is to match their circulation.

One further factor of central importance for us is that 80 percent of our members are women. The very real differences between male and female readers cannot be ignored. Our newspaper is, to all intents and purposes, a women's newspaper. We must interest half a million women and 150,000 men.

Every issue of our paper offers articles of general public interest: consumer information, answers to everyday questions, articles on housing, schooling, leisure-time activities, living together, and specific women's questions as well. We write about local municipalities and take up questions that interest our readers, both as employees of municipalities and as citizens. We have also introduced more international issues and cultural questions.

Innovations are not always welcome, and full-time officials in the union have at times openly demonstrated their disapproval. The newspaper has been criticized for looking like "any other weekly magazine" or, even worse, a "rag for bitches."

I like to point out that the borderline between what is a trade union issue and what is not a trade union issue is no longer so clear or easy to define. Trade unions have, after all, widened the scope of their activities in the past ten to twenty years.

Above all, as labor journalists, we must never forget that we work for our members. For them, the newspaper has a very special role to play. For many members, the newspaper is the only direct link with the union. When their newspaper succeeds in representing the lives and jobs of ordinary members in a vital and vibrant style, it becomes a key link in the chain of solidarity between different groups.

Market research has demonstrated that many Swedish union members now view their union newspapers as a source of knowledge, a means of broadening their perspective. This is just what we as labor journalists must seek to accomplish. No one has a better opportunity than we do to strengthen members' self-confidence and promote their active participation in both union and social affairs.

Part Three

Building a New Labor Press

Taking Readers Seriously:
UAW *Solidarity*

Dave Elsila

In most cases members of a union are forced, willy-nilly, to subscribe to their official paper since the subscription is included in their dues. But this does not imply that they read it. Neither is this neglect wholly the fault of the union member. A worker coming home at night, pooped out by his day's occupation of putting nut three hundred and eighty-six into hole seven hundred and seventy-seven is not exactly in the mood to read fulsome accounts of the junketings of his union officials, adorned with flattering pictures of these same officials and their families enjoying themselves at the expense of the local union treasury. . . .

Is it any wonder . . . that the weary worker hands the labor paper over to his wife for shelf lining or other more intimate uses and turns to the pulp magazines or the sports pages of the local capitalist "kept press"? Is it any wonder that the weird journalistic offerings of William Randolph Hearst, labor-baiter and yellow reactionary that he is, are still the favorite reading matter of millions of American workmen?

Some fifty years ago, a veteran labor journalist used those words to describe the trade union press in the United States. The author of this critique, Oscar Ameringer, perhaps best known as editor of the respected radical weekly, the *American Guardian*, had spent a lifetime in the labor and socialist movements. For more than nine years, he also

Dave Elsila is the editor of Solidarity, *the magazine published by the United Auto Workers. The son of an autoworker, Elsila grew up in Detroit and broke into labor journalism as the editor of the* Michigan Teacher, *a publication he edited while still a classroom teacher in Livonia. He later edited the publications of the American Federation of Teachers before joining the UAW staff in 1976. In 1989, after three terms as vice-president, Elsila served two years as secretary-treasurer of the International Labor Communications Association.*

edited the *Illinois Miner*, regarded by some critics as "the most readable labor paper in the U.S." That paper's appeal, Ameringer said, "lay in the fact that we wrote rank-and-file pieces for rank-and-file readers. I don't mean 'writing down,' either. No people in this country are quicker to understand when they are being patronized than the coal diggers. Inter-larding miner stories with tough talk, the use of slang where slang was not called for, and the baby babble all too frequently resorted to by labor writers who never bother to keep in touch with the rank and file, was as verboten on our paper as the Marxian dialectic."

Ever since a friend gave me a copy of Ameringer's autobiography, *If You Don't Weaken*, in which these words appear, I've been intrigued by his comments and have returned to them many times. Those of us who help produce today's labor press are painfully aware that, a half-century later, too many union officials still measure a labor paper's value by how many times it runs their photo and whether it prints their columns on page 1. Overall, however, the labor press of the 1990s does not seem nearly as one-dimensional as the labor press described by Ameringer in decades past. There may be constraints on what can be printed (as there are in most organizational publications), but more labor papers are paying closer attention to their readers, in both content and style. Dramatic, illustrated stories on health and safety, strikes and lockouts, AIDS, and international solidarity are supplanting dry accounts of conferences and officers' speeches. There is a slow but steady growth in letters-to-the-editor pages. You can even find, in some labor papers, equal space for opposing candidates for union office. Still, even in the best of today's trade union press, there's a long way to go.

In the United Auto Workers (UAW), our journey began in 1976, when the UAW publication *Solidarity* underwent a fundamental change. Under the editorship of Don Stillman, who had helped revitalize the *United Mine Workers Journal*, our old, standard-format tabloid newspaper was redesigned as a magazine and given a new editorial approach that emphasized human interest stories, investigative reporting, and the generous use of photos and illustrations. The magazine's staff sought out and wrote stories about workplace dangers, organizing drives in the South, bitter strikes, and other topics. A letters-to-the-editor column was expanded, supplemented by "Solidarity Soapbox"— a section on interviews with members. Talented photojournalists were hired to document workplaces and workers. With television and more specialty magazines competing for members' attention, the new approach, it was hoped, would attract and inform UAW families about their union's concerns and programs. By focusing on human interest features—through articles, for instance, on the victims of workplace poisons—we sought to connect abstract issues like health and safety legislation with the lives of our readers. We also hoped that, redesigned as a magazine, *Solidarity* wouldn't get tossed out with the papers, but would sit around members' homes longer.

New writers—including one with a background in environmental writing—were hired. The magazine began an internship program to attract journalism students and members who wanted to learn journalism skills. Imaginative free-lance artists and graphic designers were sought out, and a full-time staff person was brought on to upgrade and coordinate the local union press. The long hours and the demands of writing, editing, and dealing with printers and mailers on a tight triweekly schedule seemed worth all the aggravation because many of us on the staff felt we were opening a new chapter in labor journalism. The fact that no officer read and marked up the magazine's page proofs enhanced our sense of creative freedom. We wanted to do the best possible job to advance the interests of the labor movement, and we were given the responsibility to do so.

Our staff felt then—and still does—that the job of labor journalists is to listen to workers and, by reporting their concerns, to help build a movement to improve their lives. Our challenge is constantly to search out fresh approaches to writing, editing, illustration, and design. Why not do a special issue on a day in the life of the union? Turn over part of the publication to members' original writing? Use eye-catching art—even comic-book style on occasion—on the cover? Plan an issue about the union by and for children? Feature the art and music of members? Those are some of the nontraditional approaches we have used or hope to use.

Taking on such creative tasks, however, means understanding that a labor publication is not just another narrow house organ but an advocacy journal. Conditioned as we all are to operating in bureaucracies in our society, that's not always so easy. A new (or old) editor can be intimidated into thinking that a union publication must reflect all the traditional organizational trappings and emphasize official reports of union meetings, columns by officers, triumphalist press releases, and grip-and-grin photos or smiling head-and-shoulder portraits. A labor journalist who never ventures outside these narrow confines may enjoy a certain level of job security but is probably destined for a life of unrewarding work and unresponsive readers.

But if we instead take the broader view that union publications constitute the country's most potentially powerful advocacy press—the only mass media that defend workers and advance the causes of social justice and economic democracy—our job takes on a new dimension. Labor journalists need to think less like bureaucrats and more like the idealists who helped create and build the trade union movement. We also need to help more of our leaders understand that creative labor journalism can be effective in building the movement.

To do our job, we must also learn to view the labor press through the eyes of our audiences—the new, younger workers who've never before been exposed to the labor movement, as well as the older members and retirees. We need to visualize the women and minorities among our readers, as well as the family members who see our publications when they arrive in the mail at home. For all these readers, we have the chance to provide an information alternative to what they get from the dailies, from television, from radio, and from schools and textbooks. We can give them a new perspective on the economy, on politics, and on workplace issues that they won't find elsewhere—and we can also entertain and inform them about cultural issues, with reviews and commentary on music, films, the media, even sports, from a working class point of view.

With such an approach, our work becomes a calling, our job is more fun, and our product is, we hope, more effective. What follows, in no particular order, are some of the things we do with *Solidarity* magazine to try to meet these goals, as well as a description of how we listen to readers and continue to change.

The Personal Touch

The typical union calendar is filled with conferences and educational meetings on subjects that range from political campaigning to skill building for stewards. A traditional labor press mind set would have us "cover" such meetings by sitting, taking notes, and writing a story quoting the "experts."

At *Solidarity*, we don't cover meetings and conferences in this traditional style. We search out personal examples that dramatize the issues. One example: At a recent legislative conference that highlighted the anti-scab legislation now before Congress, we identified a delegate from a local union whose company had replaced strikers with scabs. We accompanied the delegate around Capitol Hill as he lobbied for the anti-scab bill, and, later, we followed the delegate home to Mobile, Alabama, where for two days our reporter and photographer listened to local union members talk about their struggle. The resulting article vividly dramatized the need for a federal law to prohibit the hiring of permanent replacements during strikes. We opened the article with a two-page photograph of southern flowers framing an old plantation house, with an inset photo of a striker and picket sign, and a headline describing the "storm beneath the calm of a quiet Southern city."

Another *Solidarity* cover story focused on the role of a union steward. Instead of distilling abstract information from UAW publications about the duties of a steward, we asked regional union officials to find us a couple of outstanding stewards. They led us to one steward in a traditional industrial plant and another in a college local union. With notebook and camera, we followed these two stewards as they made their rounds, meeting with workers, discussing their grievances, and challenging management. The resulting story, a day in the life of the two stewards, mixed dialogue and description to show how a good steward defends workers' rights on the workplace floor. By focusing on outstanding stewards, the story also helped our readers everywhere know what they have a right to expect from their own stewards or committeepersons.

As labor editors, our challenge is to bring to life the nuts and bolts of trade unionism—collective bargaining, organizing, grievance handling, and so on. Human interest features like the two noted above—whether done in person or via telephone interviews—can accomplish this goal by telling the story through experiences that our readers understand.

Investigative Reporting

Investigative reporting. The phrase conjures up glitzy television shows like "20/20" or "Exposé." The labor press does not, of course, have the same resources as the TV networks, but there are things we can do, through investigation and research, to expose anti-worker practices. Whenever possible, we've used our own *Solidarity* staff to investigate and document stories that might not be seen by our members if they had to depend on the commercial press.

One simple yet effective investigation can help show union members who their employers are backing for political office. Starting several months before each November's general elections, we buy from the

Federal Elections Commission copies of financial reports from Senate and House candidates and go over these reports to find out which candidates are raking in contributions from corporate political action committees and the owners of companies where UAW members work. We then chart these contributions in *Solidarity*, sometimes illustrating the contributions with company logos. This kind of story underscores the "them and us" nature of so many political campaigns and helps readers understand why their union takes an interest in politics.

Another example: Working from leads supplied by union sources, we sent a reporter to a nonunion plant in Indiana to investigate the deaths of five young workers overcome by toxic fumes. The five, with no safety equipment or training, had entered a holding tank where they were overcome by deadly hydrogen cyanide fumes. Four died almost instantly; the fifth held on for two more days. The company was fined a paltry $41,700—the equivalent of about $8,000 for each life. The subsequent publicity our story helped generate sparked a campaign to improve Indiana's health and safety laws.

We have also investigated and exposed the growing phenomenon of corporate "alter-ego" tactics. More and more companies today are closing down, taking on new names, and reopening with new, nonunion work forces. Our reporters have traveled to several workplaces to get firsthand interviews from workers directly affected by these alter-ego "name games," and their stories have helped alert other local unions to what they need to know to fight back effectively.

At other times, we've tracked down UAW members who had been illegally spied upon by federal agents for participating in anti-war activities. We ran a cover story that linked this illegal surveillance to FBI and "red squad" efforts against labor leaders such as former UAW president Walter Reuther. Some time later, as a follow-up, we interviewed a retired UAW staff member who had just received her "red squad" files. She described for readers how, during the McCarthy period, she had been followed, fired, and, with union help, reinstated.

In-plant alternatives to striking have captured the attention of much of the labor movement, as a direct response to employers who force strikes and then hire permanent replacements. In the early 1980s, *Solidarity* sent a reporter to talk with workers who used such strategies successfully at the Moog Company in St. Louis. Workers described a wide variety of imaginative tactics—from filing grievances en masse, to holding union meetings on the shop floor, to organizing a solidarity committee to confront management. These tactics, first publicized in

Solidarity, subsequently became a widely publicized model for many other unions.

In 1988, with the world's attention focused on the Olympics in Seoul, we sent a photojournalist to South Korea to investigate the working and living conditions of South Korean autoworkers. The result, a photo essay entitled "Behind the Olympic Curtain," described South Korea's fifty-four-hour workweek, sky-high workplace accident rate, and incredibly low wages—just $1.40 an hour building cars for export to the United States.

One of our investigations even brought legendary labor martyr Joe Hill into the act. Acting on a tip from a Washington, D.C.–based union staffer, a *Solidarity* intern investigated and wrote a story on how a packet of Joe Hill's ashes had been seized by the government during World War I and stored in the National Archives for over seventy years. Our story helped win the release of the ashes to Joe Hill's union, the Industrial Workers of the World, which has been scattering them in various locations as a memorial to Hill's work.

All these stories may not have been investigative pieces in the purest sense of the word—that is, they didn't lead to criminal charges or new legislation or to the discovery of a new workplace poison—but these articles did require research and legwork and commitment. They reflect a creative journalism that gives workers valuable information and ammunition that they won't get from the commercial media.

Are there investigations that we haven't pursued? Yes. We would like, for instance, to do an in-depth story exploring racism among union members. Why have some members voted for David Duke? Why are others directly involved with the Ku Klux Klan? These are difficult questions to ask. Some trade unionists argue that we shouldn't even acknowledge the existence of racist union members, much less interview them.

We've also wanted to do an in-depth story on overtime. Many workers agree in principle with the idea that overtime should not be accepted at a time when union brothers and sisters are unemployed. But some of these same workers like the extra money in their paychecks.

How should labor journalists approach issues like these? Should we write stories that quote members who express racist or selfish, nonsolidaristic points of view? Should we open our pages to views that don't coincide with accepted union or liberal canon—all the time hoping that, by doing so, we can help readers reach a clear, more educated understanding? Is this a risk worth taking?

A Swedish union magazine recently took a different sort of risk. The magazine carried a cover story interview with the head of the Swedish equivalent of the National Association of Manufacturers here in the United States. What would happen if we ran Lee Iacocca's photo on the cover of *Solidarity* and an interview with him inside? We might well be criticized for giving "them" a voice in the magazine designed for "us." But if we had the opportunity to do a no-holds-barred interview with a corporate leader, couldn't such a story stimulate debate that sharpens readers' understanding of corporate economic and political prescriptions?

From the Ground Up: Letters and Stories from Members

People are sometimes amazed to find that *Solidarity* has never published a regular column written by the UAW president or any other union officer. Indeed, there are entire issues in which the president's photo does not appear. Is this heresy? Hardly. UAW officers understand that effective union education and communication mean using as much available space as possible to reflect the experiences and voices of the union membership. Obviously, we also report on the stewardship of union officials, normally in the context of their efforts on behalf of members, testifying before Congress on legislation, representing members on fact-finding missions abroad, or speaking out at a press conference on union concerns. But there's no quota on photos or mentions of officers' names.

At the same time, *Solidarity* encourages readers to use their magazine in a variety of ways. Every *Solidarity* issue carries a page and a half of letters to the editor up front. These letters are probably the best-read part of the magazine. Readers often write in about workplace problems and political issues. We've even had a couple of letters debating whether or not there's a union in heaven. Critical letters come most frequently from the right end of the political spectrum—from members who chastise us for criticizing Republican party policies, or who object to the union's support of Nelson Mandela. We get far more letters than we can use and, after editing them for length, try to make sure we balance comments fairly. Sometimes, when a letter criticizes the union, we'll append an editor's note explaining or clarifying the union's position.

Interestingly, we seldom if ever receive letters on internal union political disputes—perhaps because such issues are usually hashed out in leaflets and caucus newsletters distributed at local union levels. Once in a while, a local union official may ask us why we've printed a letter

NEVERMORE

Science Fiction by John M. Blankenship

Art by Susan Kramer

The warehouse on the outskirts of town waited in the night, filled with the hollow volumes of dimness and darkness. Within the thick walls resided the storage bins and shelves of lime-colored metals, tall racks, and wide platforms fastened to the concrete floors, replete with all manner of packaged tubings, titanium skins, and alloy bones. Huge crates lay about unsealed, the aerodynamic artistry within undisturbed like fine Kings in their pine sarcophaguses.

In all, Building 201 was like any other warehouse of the Flying Aces Aircraft Company on this holiday. Except, of course, for the ghost.

Soon after midnight, a dark figure entered through a side door, closed and locked it, then wove through the gulfs of quietness to stand at the steel staircase and gaze up into the darkness. Mr. Phipps, Supply Manager, brother of the Company Manager, touched the banister and found it unpleasantly cold.

His face, resembling a cherubic Monty Hall, glistened with cool perspiration. The taste of champagne, still on his lips, was the only reminder of the party where the clinking of glasses followed the toast of "To the most successful company ever," as the sweet wine flowed and the music played.

The phone had rung, hadn't it! Phipps answered, uncertain. The voice in the handpiece was familiar, wasn't it! Begging excuses, Phipps slipped out of the party to motor through the liquid darkness, now to stand unnerved in the chilly warehouse where machines slumbered and things went bump in the shadow night. Swallowing, Phipps climbed the stairs to the second-floor platform and. . .what! The ghost! Yes, the ghost! That haunting tremble of 201 that revealed itself, spouting sermon and Revelation all in the same icy breath.

Phipps found him sitting, as always, at the empty desk.

"Day care, Mr. Phipps. . . ."

"What!"

"For the working soon-to-be mothers and wifeless fathers and the husbandless wives of the coming year. Day care, Mr. Phipps, and another Cost of Living Allowance would be in order. . . ."

Phipps angered, his courage hammering in his chest. In the long years past, the demands had been for safety! Wage increases! Increased medical benefits!

Intimidated and unnerved, Phipps had complied with these demands, carrying them like a messenger bird to the Board without question. But now. . . .

"That's right, Phipps. There will be new children. New parents facing new challenges. I want you to see to their unique needs."

The ghost watched Phipps closely.

"Yes, Phipps!"

"I've had about enough!" Phipps said, his voice echoing. "And why me, Poe!"

Silence fell in on them, for this was the first time his name had been spoken above a whisper since the accident.

Poe. Alfred Edwards Poe, having taken a fancy to his dark namesake, had spent a lifetime collecting the black-bound volumes of poem and sorrowful tale of the one named E.A. Poe.

Alfred Poe, working the late shift, had met his death head-on: And having no family to cherish his possessions, watched in sadness as his collections were trundled off to the Goodwill. He had lived in those books, pawing the covers off their raw backs, gouging the words off the pages to make Amotillado soups for cold suppers. As tidbits and snacks, he had taken them to bed, dreaming fitfully on their crumbs that itched him to sleep with the Premature Burial and the Tell-Tale Heart. His was the only such collection in the town of Longwood.

Again Phipps asked, "Why me!"

"You know the answer, Phipps. Deep inside. You were responsible for my livelihood as well as my death. . . ."

"But I wasn't even in the building—"

"The brakes on that forklift were bad and yet you took no action. My words fell upon your ears as smoke into the night. I died because of you, Phipps."

A heartbeat drummed in Phipps' ears. Was it his own!

"And this warehouse. It is very old." Poe turned his pale face about, searching the rafters as if feeling the age in his tattered soul. "The sprinklers are corroded, the system substandard, and I just recently discovered the forged papers. . . ."

Phipps breathed nervously.

"It's all over, Poe!" he laughed. "Ha! Over! No more bleedings. No more compensations. I'm going to burn this place to the ground, Poe. To the ground! Everything is taken care of. The insurance will pay off handsomely!"

Moth-like, Poe wavered as he stood, leaning his feather lightness on the desk.

"What's wrong, Poe! Can't I deal with it! Frightened! No more discussions, ever. And this time tomorrow, no more 201, Poe!"

Phipps patted the matchbook in his blazer pocket and thought of all the plastics and fluids that would make the burning easy. Phipps turned, intent on his deed when—

"One last request, Phipps. A change in management is long overdue. I regret this choice you have made and that you will be with us. . . ."

The shapes that Phipps saw as he turned loomed from the shadows and, as in a dream, no, nightmare, he disbelieved up to the last moments that lifeless things could move their alloy skeletons, rising from their graves, suddenly finding flesh in the shadows, ebbing, flowing in founts of black blood from the cabinets and the bins to slither up and touch his polished shoe. There may have been a silent scream.

". . .Nevermore." finished A.E. Poe.

John M. Blankenship is a member of UAW Local 148 and an expediter at the McDonnell Douglas aerospace plant in Long Beach, California. "Working second shift, the shadows and things-that-go-bump-in-the-night work hand-in-hand with an overactive imagination," he says. Solidarity magazine welcomes your short stories, essays, and poems. Write us at 8000 E. Jefferson, Detroit, MI 48214.

15

Solidarity's "On the Line" page features original writing by UAW members on everything from directly work-related issues to childhood recollections and science fiction.

from a "known dissident." We've explained in response that there's no way to screen letters according to the writer's political tendency and, even if we could, members have a right to express their views in their union publication.

"On the Line" is a *Solidarity* page devoted to original writing by UAW active or retired members or members of their families. It's a place where readers can share their own short stories, essays, or poetry with other members. Many of the contributions focus on work-related issues, but a good share of other material also arrives: childhood recollections, science fiction, and family stories. We hope to use more member-contributed artwork to illustrate these pieces.

We run "Solidarity Soapbox" as an occasional feature. At our last legislative conference, we photographed around forty delegates—industrial workers, white collar, men, women, young, old, Black, white, Hispanic, Asian—from throughout the country. From time to time, we telephone four or five of these delegates and ask them to respond to a question. We pull their photos from the file and run them with their responses.

Expanding Horizons:
Reporting on Friends at Home and Abroad

In 1981, Solidarity Day brought a half million people to Washington, D.C., to protest the direction of the new Reagan administration. President Ronald Reagan's firing of PATCO members had led to a labor boycott of the airlines, and most of us traveled to Washington by car, train, or bus. Our *Solidarity* reporter and photographer boarded a train that had originated on the West Coast three days earlier. That experience put us in contact with workers from different unions from many states, and it taught us a valuable lesson: we shouldn't cover events like Solidarity Day parochially and interview and photograph only UAW members. We're a part of a larger labor movement, and by interviewing and photographing members of other unions—and telling their stories—we can build a sense of unity that helps us all. That's why an issue of *Solidarity* is as likely to lead off with a story about another union as an article about the UAW. Here are some examples:

In April 1989, our lead story focused on the battle by the Machinists, Pilots, and Flight Attendants against Eastern Airlines boss Frank Lorenzo. Their fight was critical to all workers and deserved the full support of all our readers.

In July 1990, we led off with a huge photo showing police beating Service Employees activists in Los Angeles. The story was a way to call attention to the need for legislation to defend all workers' rights.

In July 1990, when the postal workers' contract fight reached an impasse, we ran a back-cover photo of a letter carrier delivering *Solidarity,* accompanied by copy explaining the postal workers' plight. The photo drew appreciative letters not only from readers but from dozens of postal service employees—one of whom wrote that all work stopped in the mail sorting room when *Solidarity* came through to give postal workers a chance to read the *Solidarity* coverage.

Every issue of *Solidarity* includes a two-page photo of a worker on the job—sometimes a UAW member, sometimes a member of another union, perhaps even a nonunion worker. The accompanying text tells our readers something about the worker's job and union. We've featured tugboat captains, lobstermen, utility repairmen, zookeepers, bakers, and more. These features help build a sense of solidarity and community among all workers.

By running stories on how civil rights legislation benefits *all* workers and doing features on women in the union, we try to break down old prejudices and attitudes.

Our magazine also tries to promote alliances between labor and other social movements. When the twentieth anniversary of Earth Day was observed in March 1990, *Solidarity* devoted a cover and lead story to environmental themes and highlighted union members who have built community coalitions around the issue of toxic waste dumps.

Solidarity consciously tries to cover non-UAW members who are victims of government policies—both to build a sense of solidarity with them and to show how union organizing can create a better life. The issue of national health care is a good example. Most union members have good contractual health insurance, but 37 million Americans are uninsured. They need our help. When *Solidarity* did a story on health care, we interviewed and photographed for the cover not a UAW member but a woman who had lost her baby because the nearest hospital was closed to the noninsured like herself. Some traditionalists might say that a union journal shouldn't place on its cover a person who has no union connection. But how better to tell this kind of story than through the eyes of a victim? Unless we build unity between nonunion and union members, we'll never be able to build the strength necessary to overcome society's problems.

Normally, you wouldn't expect to find *Rocky* reviewed in a union publication, or read a story about baseball players. But union members don't just work or march on picket lines. They go to movies, play baseball, listen to records, and read books. *Solidarity*'s "Workers of the World, Relax!" page offers reviews of music, TV, movies, and other popular and labor culture. A Ford worker who interns on our staff reviewed *Rocky V.* Another staff member reviewed the TV show "Roseanne." A movie buff wrote capsule reviews of favorite video rentals. A baseball fan wrote a feature story, illustrated with original baseball card parodies, on the dispute between major league players and owners. Our reviews usually try to relate popular culture to basic worker issues—but we try not to be heavy-handed or preachy when we write them.

Expanding our horizons also means looking overseas. Just as multinational corporations are spreading their influence across borders, workers, too, need to build global ties, to prevent the companies from playing us off against each other in the name of competitiveness. On three occasions, we've sent staff members to the U.S.-Mexican border to report on the *maquiladoras* that are siphoning jobs from the United States to low-wage plants in Mexico that pay workers $5 a day—the same wage Henry Ford promised Detroit workers in 1913. When twenty UAW members went to El Salvador in a demonstration of solidarity with the beleaguered FENASTRAS labor federation, we hired an on-site photographer, then interviewed delegates on their return and published a three-page spread.

The successful fight for the thirty-five-hour workweek in Germany is another overseas story that has import for U.S. workers. On a recent vacation trip, I took the opportunity to interview workers in Bremen about the shorter workweek campaign and to attend the first joint May Day celebration in Berlin in over forty years, which ended up as a *Solidarity* story. Another story, based on an International Metalworkers Federation editors' tour of Hungary and Czechoslovakia, looked at the challenges facing Eastern European workers by the impending invasion of Western multinationals.

The Style of the Substance

Style and format are also important elements that can help eliminate the dull and the ordinary in the labor press. Among the steps *Solidarity* has tried are the following:

■ Using comic-strip characters on the cover to illustrate a story on housing and using dialogue in the characters' "bubbles" to communicate statistics, in place of traditional charts and graphs.

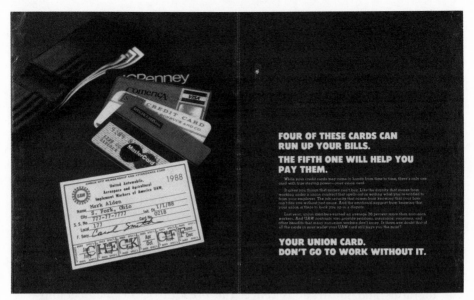

Why write a whole page of dull text on the importance of union membership when a mass media ad format can get your message across far more effectively? UAW's Solidarity *magazine devotes several pages per issue to "ads" that communicate ideas and market social causes.*

■ Stapling inside the magazine preaddressed tear-out postcards to Congress on free trade and antistrikebreaker laws. On another occasion, we stapled in envelopes from Citizens for Tax Justice and urged readers to use the envelopes to mail in crumbs to Congress. The mailings, we noted, would help protest proposed tax changes that would have given breaks to the wealthy and left "crumbs" for the rest of us.

■ Developing an annual "Humbugs and Heroes" cartoon feature, patterned loosely after *Esquire*'s Dubious Achievements Awards, that lampoons the high-and-mighty and honors labor heroes and heroines.

■ Using mass media-type advertising on the back cover and pages 2–3 of each issue to sell ideas and support for social causes. Why write a whole page of dull text on the importance of union membership, when you can have fun creating an ad selling the same notion? For example, we ran an illustration of four credit cards and a union membership card. Copy: "Four of these cards can run up your bills. The fifth one will help you pay them." These ads can be effective when done well, but they're often the hardest thing in the magazine to conceive—which probably explains why advertising agencies and copywriters are so well paid.

■ Trying to eliminate old labor jargon. There are too many terms that bureaucrats and ideologues toss around that, when they appear in print, seem self-righteous. We guard against using phrases like "sweat equity" or "ruling class" or even "rank and file" (readers have told us they are members, they are workers, but "rank and file" sounds patronizing to them). We use the dialogue we hear in the workplace or in interviews. "At the end of the day, don't [just] go over what happened, [but] live it again," the great Minnesota labor writer Meridel LeSueur once wrote, "hear everything Charlie said in that row he had with the boss . . . that's history. Write it down just as you would say it."

Finally, and this goes almost without saying, we make sure that photographs and illustrations reflect the breadth of the membership—men, women, all racial groups, blue collar, white collar, young, and old. This sensitivity helps all members understand that the union represents everyone and also helps all readers understand who their sisters and brothers are.

Making Changes

In 1988, twelve years after making the change from a tabloid to a magazine format, we took another hit at redesigning *Solidarity*. The magazine had evolved over those years—adding slick-paper covers, trimming to eliminate ragged edges and permit bleeding, and using some four-color process printing—but we felt it was time for more. Our stories were long and crowding our twenty-four-page format. We hadn't made any fundamental changes for a long time, and we worried about getting stale. We wanted a fresh, new design with more white space, more illustrations, and more emphasis on features.

The hardest thing to do once you've decided to make changes is to find the time to institute them. The pressure of regular deadlines doesn't leave much time to step back and look at things from a new perspective. It took us a long time, but eventually we began by putting together some "focus groups," made up of random members attending union conferences. Meeting with them, we asked them questions about the magazine and recorded their responses, trying to find out what kinds of stories they liked, what they didn't read, and what changes they'd like to see. We asked professional labor writers for feedback. We studied union magazines from Europe, where popular labor journalism seems more advanced—especially in Sweden, Finland, Germany, and Austria (one Swedish metalworking publication, in particular, stood out: it featured a cover photo of a young worker surrounded by rock music posters with the headline "What Today's Young Workers Want").

Digesting all this, we sketched out a prototype dummy in a blank book and contacted several graphic designers to come up with proposals for redesigning the magazine. At the same time, we began surveying printers to find out what sizes, papers, and printing processes were available and affordable. We found that by switching from twelve issues to ten a year, our postage savings would pay for an oversize page format with coated paper throughout and let us increase the number of pages in each issue from 24 to 32. We were cutting two issues, but we were actually going from 288 pages a year to 320. We also found that a rotogravure process would save us the cost of replating during the press run and would give us better photo reproduction.

Making a change is never easy—you have to unlearn old traditions—and a sharp disagreement emerged over the cover of our first redesigned issue. The cover needed to illustrate our story on workers in South Korea, "Behind the Olympic Curtain." Should the cover feature a grim worker, symbolizing oppression? Or should we use an Olympic swimmer? The first choice would have been the traditional approach, but the second, our department director argued, would make readers sit up and take notice: what's a swimmer doing on the cover of a union magazine? This second approach—slightly modified to show a torn curtain revealing a workers' slum in the lower right corner of the page—won out and has helped us set a tone for trying to find nontraditional cover ideas ever since.

The new *Solidarity* format—with its emphasis on white space and big illustrations—forces us to write shorter pieces, to concentrate on fewer features for each issue, and to search out strong photos and illustrations. We usually open each issue with a five- to seven-page major story, which leaves us room for two or three double-page feature spreads, plus our regular sections of letters to the editor, members' fiction or poetry, a "Frontlines" section on economic and political news, and culture reviews. Spot union news is folded into a four-page section called "The Union This Month." We try to balance our features editorially. If we're profiling a strike or organizing drive, we try to find a "softer" story—perhaps an interview with a union blues musician. By doing so, we feel that we're responding to the wide range of interests that union members share—and perhaps enticing some people into reading the magazine who wouldn't normally read a publication that was only about strikes and struggles or hard economic and political issues.

The magazine is largely written and edited by two full-time staff members and a full-time intern, with the help of a free-lance designer and the contributions of free-lance photographers and illustrators. In the three years since our format change, we've redesigned some sections, and we continue to look for ways to fine-tune the publication and to search out new approaches to covering labor and socially relevant topics.

There are, of course, problems and annoyances that continue to plague us—as they do most labor journalists. There's never enough time to do the job you'd like to do to achieve a "perfect" publication. Good ideas for stories flow in from staff and members around the country, and the dilemma of having to pick priorities is frustrating to them and to us. Once in a while, someone will say to us that we shouldn't use a particular photo or quote a particular person because that person is a "troublemaker"—an occupational nuisance, of course, that plagues editors in any publication, organizational or commercial.

Yet other sources of frustration for the labor editor have ebbed considerably. Views that might once have been excluded from the union press—particularly on foreign policy issues—are now much more widely circulated. During and before the Gulf War, for example, a number of national and local union publications carried pro and con comments, a sharp contrast to the virtual unanimity of opinion in the labor press over the Vietnam War years. Stories critical of U.S. policy in Latin America get wide circulation within labor papers, without the red-baiting against their writers or the censorship against the articles themselves that would have been expected a couple of decades ago.

With a combined circulation in the tens of millions, and with the new emphasis on video production as well, the labor media remain the strongest potential alternative provider of information for America's workers. Since the early 1980s, our job has become even more critical, as government and business have attacked the labor movement with everything from permanent replacements to economic policies that send work overseas and leave workers back home jobless. But the pendulum has started to swing: labor solidarity defeated Lorenzo, the Tribune Company backed down from union-busting at the *New York Daily News,* the Pittston coal miners were victorious, the Colt firearms workers successfully blocked company takeaways. In each of these struggles, the labor press played an important role in informing workers and building solidarity. We have a responsibility to continue our efforts and make them even more effective.

Nothing describes our goal better than Meridel LeSueur's words from a guide for union writing first published in the 1930s and still used in classes for union journalists today: "We are facing hunger, want, thousands are unemployed. There is the struggle to unionize, meeting with strong and violent opposition. More and more, we need words to write and express the true history of the past and to create the true history of the future. . . . Who is to record the true history of our lives? You live it. You make it. You write it."

From the Bottom Up: Resuscitating the Local Union Press

David Prosten

The local union press in North America reflects the very best and the very worst the labor movement has to offer. Local union publications are at once a symptom of organized labor's decline as a force for social change and a potential source for labor's renewal.

In the hands of committed unionists who have a sense of labor's mission, the local union newsletter can be a rallying force beyond compare: exciting, provocative, inclusive, a tool to build the union, to secure and maintain equity and justice in the workplace and in the community.

But in the hands of the insecure, those leaders afraid of "making waves" that may increase their work load or endanger their political prospects, the local union newsletter can be a stultifying bore, an insult to the membership, a waste of money. In fact, in these situations, a local newsletter can actually weaken a union, reinforcing whatever negative attitudes and cynicism that may already exist about unionism in a work force that has, in all too many cases, received little in the way of labor education in recent decades.

Nearly every national and international union offers its members a periodical publication that invariably serves as the primary vehicle for communicating with members on policy, politics, and news that affect wages, hours, and working conditions. As a rule, until recent years

A former daily newspaper reporter, David Prosten has held staff writing, public relations, and organizing positions with several national unions. Since 1980 he has operated a Washington, D.C., company that provides a variety of communications services to subscribing local unions across the United States and Canada. Prosten is a member of The Newspaper Guild.

these newspapers and magazines were distributed monthly. Some still are, but, with rising postal costs, the trend has been toward semi-monthly and even quarterly frequency. The result? Both the amount and the timeliness of information flowing to union members from national union headquarters have been on the decline.

This decline makes local union publications all the more important, but few internationals have acted to bolster or even encourage their locals' abilities to publish and fill the communications gap. Few internationals have recognized the strategic ability of local publications to help rally members around vital national issues and directly affect the political and economic lives of their communities.

Local union editors need support. These editors face the same difficulties, demands on their time, and competing interests as do the volunteers for other union projects, but they tend to get less in the way of help and more in the way of negative feedback. Stewards can generally count on receiving at least a basic how-to primer, an introductory skills program, some form of continuing education, and a step up the ladder, if desired, toward higher union office. Social committee volunteers encounter (at least occasionally) fun tasks. Election committee members can look forward to a relatively brief, finite period of service. Bargaining committee members have the satisfaction of having an indisputably direct say in the determination of their wages, hours, and working conditions.

But newsletter editors can generally only count on never-ending deadlines, Monday morning quarterbacking and fault-finding from local leaders who ought to be cooperating more with them, and little in the way of resources, either human or financial. As so aptly phrased in a poster distributed to editors of member publications by the Canadian Association of Labour Media, and then to U.S. editors by the International Labor Communications Association (ILCA): "There are two times in life when you are totally alone: Just before you die. And just before you do a newsletter."

Surrounded by and supported by professional staff, far removed from the daily grind of rank-and-file life, international union leaders often lose sight of the difficulties faced by their local union editors—if such concern even occurs to them. The frequency and quality of local union publications are not high on the union national headquarters agenda. They should be.

If presented with a regular, reasonably attractive publication that acknowledges their existence and addresses issues that concern them, local union members will read their newsletters and respond. They will learn more about their union, they will understand its function better, and they will participate more in union life.

Despite the institutional value of a strong local union press, the overwhelming majority of national unions do nothing—quite literally nothing—to encourage local union publishing efforts. Some, in their own way, actually discourage an active local press. One currently sitting national union president, approached soon after his election about starting an association for his union's local editors, dismissed the proposal with the remark that he didn't want to create a potential independent political force in the union that he couldn't control. To his credit, albeit after a couple of reelections, he did agree to the dissemination of packets of news and cartoons, although he continued to reject the idea of a full-fledged local editors' organization within the union.

In fact, only perhaps a dozen of the one hundred U.S.-based national and international unions today offer their local unions concrete assistance in the form of regular—some more, some less—packets of news and graphics, occasionally accompanied by how-to counsel. For a nominal annual fee, or no fee at all, services of varying quality and quantity are offered by the Auto Workers, the State, County and Municipal Employees, the Communications Workers, the National Education Association, the Service Employees, the Teamsters, the Food and Commercial Workers, the Postal Workers, the Steelworkers, the federal Government Employees, and the Bricklayers and Allied Craftsmen.

Some union services, like the pace-setting UAW Local Union Press Association (LUPA), offer a broad range of reproduction-quality news and feature articles, cartoons, and fillers. One LUPA package is tailored for more costly offset publications, another for the less expensive mimeographed variety. LUPA also sponsors week-long retreats for its local union editors roughly every eighteen months. The retreats bring in professional labor journalists to help upgrade editorial skills.

Other services, like the Service Employees' comprehensive and high-quality graphics packet, concentrate heavily on visual aids. Some services are markedly better than others: the Postal Workers service offers advice on production techniques, but little in the way of usable material. The Teamsters have for years pumped out volumes of material, but relatively little of it has had anything of substance to do with nuts-and-bolts union activity. But change appears to be coming. In 1992, soon after taking office, a new administration surveyed local editors, asking for suggestions on ways to improve the Teamsters service.

Of some seventy-five thousand local unions across the United States and Canada, barely fifteen thousand are large enough to own or even to rent office space. That means that much of labor's work is done on kitchen and dining room tables, usually on the volunteer's own time. These volunteers need all the help and encouragement they can get.

There are national organizations, both in the United States and Canada, that reach out to union editors and offer resources. The International Labor Communications Association in the United States issues a monthly newsletter that features news about member publications and hands-on advice, an increasingly healthy sprinkling of "pick-upable" labor news and artwork, and regular updates on postal rates and other advice. The Canadian Association of Labour Media issues a monthly packet of news and graphics to its members, along with frequent doses of hands-on advice and counsel.

Additionally, two U.S.-based private companies (one of which is operated by the author) market news and graphics packages to local unions, and several independent cartoonists sell their wares as well. These private ventures would be unlikely to succeed, however, and would have little reason to exist, if the international unions were doing all they should to aid their locals. Outside assistance—or lack of it—notwithstanding, some local union publications do a wonderful job of keeping their members up-to-date, rallying them to the union's cause, and involving them in its activities. When local union newsletters do succeed, the odds are great that the following factors are at work:

■ Local union leaders view the newsletter as a vital tool in fulfilling the union's mission, not as a threat or headache they are obligated to suffer.

■ The editor is enthused by the job, albeit most likely frustrated over its difficulties. The editor can count on the moral and financial support of the officers and the assistance of other rank and filers to get the task done.

■ The newsletter contains much more than "The President's Report" (you may substitute "Secretary-Treasurer," "Business Manager," and so on), sleep-inducing verbatim minutes, and a meeting notice. It's filled with news of local union activities and union members, with plenty of names and facts and, budget permitting, photos.

■ No matter how inexpensively it is produced, the newsletter makes an effort to be attractive and readable. Thought goes into layout and design. The newsletter uses cartoons, rules, boxes, and other inexpensive graphic devices.

■ The newsletter does not glorify the elected leadership. (A top-of-page-1 story in a recent issue of a large western state local union's tabloid offered a headline alerting the membership that the local's president was a "world-renowned labor statesman." The same officer is also listed as editor of the newsletter, which is generous with its photo coverage of the editor/president.)

The best local union editors and local union leaders have taken these points to heart. "We try to keep articles short and accurate, and we keep the propaganda to a minimum," says Dwight L. Wenham, an officer of the Union of Psychiatric Nurses in Coquitlam, B.C., a local that publishes a modest yet attractive semimonthly. "On the occasions there is bad news such as a union loss, we print it rather than having the employer or the rumour mill spread the word."

"It is our belief that everyone is important," notes Mary Gibson, the editor of International Brotherhood of Electrical Workers (IBEW) Local 111's award-winning newsletter in Denver. "Our emphasis is on the local, rather than the national or international labor scene. There are occasions when we use the national labor news, but we try to localize that as well. People most like to read about what's happening today to them right here."

Steelworkers Local 7619 in Logan Lake, B.C., offers a wonderful example of a quality publication on a limited budget. Produced with the aid of a personal computer, this attractive newsletter is packed with members' names and competes effectively with the slick employer magazine that's mailed to each member's home. "The company complains because our less expensive 'amateur' effort is better received," says editor Donna March.

One nice touch that both acknowledges a tight budget and puts the leadership in closer touch with the rank and file: Local 7619 Executive Committee volunteers personally hand out the newsletter at plant gates during shift changes.

The *Maine Stater,* the newspaper of the Service Employees–affiliated Maine State Employees Association, routinely uses the newsletter to rally members during contract fights. The *Maine Stater,* says editor Donald Matson, doesn't shy away from "hard-hitting articles" on sexual harassment, management incompetence, and controversial grievances, but it doesn't "flood the paper with them, either."

Comes the question: What can concerned unionists do to improve the local union labor press?

At the international union level, conscientious union leaders can lead by example, by giving appropriate priority, resources, and respect to their primary publication. This means not just getting the national union magazine or newspaper into members' hands on a regular basis but committing themselves to the modest design and printing investment necessary to make sure their publication looks good and can reasonably compete with the slick commercial publications that vie for readers' interest. Leading by example means treating the national union publication as a vehicle for informing and rallying the members, not just satisfying political constituencies or meeting constitutional requirements. Leading by example means establishing credibility by reporting at least some of the bad news along with the good.

Union officials at all levels must recognize the inconsistency inherent in, on one hand, complaining about lack of turnout at union meetings, while, on the other, offering members pap in union publications—or no publication at all. People respond and get involved when they have an understanding of what's going on and believe they have a reasonable chance to change things. Open discussion and reporting may mean controversy, but they also breed interest. Controversy need not be equated in leadership minds with problems. (The late George Hardy, as president of the Service Employees, rejected his editor's suggestion that the union newspaper print occasional letters to the editor with the response: "I didn't spend 40 years getting where I am so some sonofabitch could take potshots at me in my own newspaper!")

Unions also need to support and train local union editors on an ongoing basis, just as they support and train local union presidents and secretaries-treasurer. The UAW offers local editors both support and training through the union's LUPA conferences at UAW's Black Lake education center in Michigan and through a monthly news and graphics service. The Machinists do training at their own center as well, and other unions sponsor occasional sessions with professional labor journalists at the George Meany Center for Labor Studies outside Washington.

The UAW sets a particularly good example for training. Classes at Black Lake run for a week and cover everything from basic fact gathering and layout to advanced writing and desktop publishing. Every session brings together first-time editors as well as grizzled veterans— so veteran, in fact, that one 1991 session was titled, "Feel Like You're Getting Burned Out? How to Bounce Back."

Unions considering a training program for local editors should understand that virtually anything is better than nothing. Simply bringing editors together in a room for a few hours, giving them the opportunity to compare notes and learn from each other's experience, can be a tremendous aid.

Unfortunately, the majority of national unions don't just fail to offer support or encouragement to their local union press. Most national unions don't even know where local union publications exist. In the United States, with nearly fifty thousand local unions, fewer than 1 percent belong to the International Labor Communications Association. National unions should be surveying their own ranks to find out who's publishing, encourage those who aren't publishing to do so, and offer a onetime per capita rebate—enough to cover the cost of membership—to local officers who sign up with the ILCA.

At the local union level, elected officers must recognize the value of their newsletters and their unique capacity to rally the rank and file. Local union officers need to help local editors upgrade their skills through the Meany Center or local university labor education centers, and they also need to give financial support to the International Labor Communications Association in the United States and the Canadian Association of Labour Media in Canada.

Local officers should also be wary of the temptation to judge their union too small to justify a newsletter. A handful of workers employed at the same work site can be counted on to share information regularly, and an active leader in such a local can, with a little effort, keep everyone up-to-date. But once a union has members at more than one location, or when shift work keeps members from communicating with one another, or when work is so compartmentalized that people can't easily speak with one another, then a newsletter is needed, even if it's just a single typewritten sheet.

Local union editors, for their part, must talk to each other, both in their communities and their national unions, and they must talk to—and write for—their members. UAW Local 898's *Raw Facts,* published for members at a Ford plant in Rawsonville, Michigan, does a marvelous job of keeping the newsletter a membership vehicle rather than a leadership bulletin board. "Rather than featuring the President's Report," points out editor Anne Drake, "we are sure to have a report from the Benefits Rep. We have two rank-and-file members who contribute fairly regular columns. Standing committees are encouraged to report on their activities." Beyond that, *Raw Facts* is packed with news and feature articles, photos, and cartoons that touch on the work and home lives of Local 898's members.

Local officers, and editors, must reach into their own ranks to generate involvement in the newsletter. They need to seek out writers, cartoonists, and photographers and acknowledge them in print for the work they do. They need to be sure the publication doesn't become an insider's club. Just as the "regulars" tend to be the participants in union meetings, so too can a newsletter turn into a family album, with the same cast of characters—all too frequently, the officers and, if any, the union staff. For a union to be effective, the newsletter must reach out to and report on all constituencies: no race, no gender, no department, no job title, no area of the union's life can be ignored or minimized.

Local unions should consider providing their editors with a computer, or at least arranging for access to one, and help out in training if necessary. From the simplest one-sheet publication to the most comprehensive slick magazine, computers help ease the burden for those who can get comfortable with the technology—and it's getting easier and easier to get comfortable. The same machines also can be used to generate mailing labels and otherwise make the newsletter work load lighter. For those who really get into it, there are even labor-oriented computer "bulletin boards" that can provide everything from another editor's shoulder to cry on to hard-core labor news.

Well-written, attractive, and aggressive local union publications today appear across North America. They report the news of their unions, they rally the rank and file behind their negotiators, they report grievance victories—and defeats—and sometimes help win a favorable outcome in those fights by building workplace support for the cause.

These same newsletters report extensively on what takes place at local union meetings and help develop participation by reporting on what will be on the next meeting's agenda. They profile rank-and-file members; they report on workplace hazards and what the union is doing about them; they use their pages to acknowledge the efforts of unsung union heroes and heroines—the stewards, the committee activists, the retiree leaders. They use photos when they can afford to, and cartoons. They spell names correctly and try not to report the same names issue after issue.

The typical good local union paper is almost always published by a good, successful local. That's no coincidence. You'll rarely find one without finding the other.

Beyond English: The Labor Press in a Multicultural Environment

Lou Siegel and Jeff Stansbury

We will not dwell on the labor press past. We will say only this. In the 1920s and 1930s, when unions were central to the lives of immigrant workers, it would have been inconceivable for the garment workers not to have published their newspaper in Yiddish, the granite workers not to have published theirs in Italian, or the butchers not to have published in Polish.

Yet today, with millions of union members and potential members in the United States who have emigrated from Mexico, Central America, the Caribbean, Korea, China, Vietnam, the Philippines, India, and other countries, the newspapers and newsletters published by U.S. unions appear, with isolated exceptions, only in English. The American labor movement is doing a dismal job of communicating with immigrant workers through the labor press.

Yes, we hand out organizing leaflets in a babel of tongues and styles. We hold union meetings that are increasingly (though not adequately) multilingual. But the labor press should be our strongest unifying weapon. It isn't. Our failures leap boldly off the pages we publish.

As a former reporter for *Solidarity*, the UAW's imaginative and

Lou Siegel, a labor public relations specialist working out of Los Angeles, has produced newspapers for a variety of union locals. He also teaches labor communications for the Los Angeles Community College District and co-hosts a weekly radio program on issues that affect workers and unions. Jeff Stansbury is a community outreach coordinator for the Western Region of the Hotel Employees and Restaurant Employees International Union. He previously worked as the Western Region educational director for the International Ladies' Garment Workers' Union and as a reporter for Solidarity, *the United Auto Workers magazine.*

thoughtfully edited newspaper, coauthor Stansbury recalls an incident that exposed the gulf between this publication and the union's non-English-speaking members:

In 1980, I covered a contract strike by 400 Mexicans in Brownsville, Texas. Most strikers crossed the border from Matamoros each day. Others had lived in Brownsville a year or two or were using a friend's address to claim residency there.

I will never forget the moment I met them. Three picketers were slowly patrolling the main gate of the Eagle International custom bus plant. Another 40 or 50 had gathered around the corrugated shack that served as the strike headquarters. They were listening intently—joyously, in fact—to strike leader Humberto Garcia as he strummed an old guitar and crooned in an unbelievably high falsetto.

"What's he singing?" I asked in shameless Spanish. "A labor tune?"

"No, compañero, una canción." (Pause) "A love-song."

I took down a line of lyrics: ¡Este amor apasionado anda todo alborotado por volver! The words defy exact translation. "I miss you so much I'm crazy" comes close enough.

Humberto sang his love songs day after day, week after week, more buoyantly than "Solidarity Forever." His songs kept his co-workers' blood up until their strike was won.

I tried to convey their feelings in my Solidarity *story. Did I succeed? I don't know—I never heard from the Brownsville workers again. I'm sure they wondered about what I wrote, but they couldn't read a word of it. Neither could countless other Latino members who would have taken pride in the Brownsville victory. To this day the UAW's justly celebrated newspaper appears only in English.*

Over the 10 years I worked for Solidarity, *I ventured often into this wide gulf of language, experience, and tradition. I knew the paper had thousands of readers, or potential readers, whose preferred tongue was Spanish. A Latino reporter, someone both bilingual and bicultural, should be doing what I do, I told my colleagues. And we should put out a Spanish edition or at least a Spanish section of* Solidarity. *We made a few vain efforts to find the right people. Meanwhile, I reassured myself, it's better for someone to be writing about immigrant workers than not to do it at all.*

This reassurance did not solve the problem, of course. It did not even begin to address it.

Solidarity has always been good at covering the many sectors of its huge, multinational work force. You'll see more people of color on its pages than in most union newspapers—Asians, African-Americans, Latinos, new immigrants—in the same photos, on the same picket lines.

You'll see their faces, that is—not their bylines. How did this discrepancy, so characteristic of the best labor papers, arise?

Most of us know unions whose "old-boy" leaderships have belatedly recognized the need to hire female and African-American, Asian, or Latino organizers and reps. We can probably cite cases in which the "old boy" himself was ousted by an insurgent non-Anglo movement.

Five years ago in Los Angeles, for example, members of Local 11 of the Hotel Employees and Restaurant Employees International Union (HERE) threw out a longterm white incumbent president who, among other things, had gone to court to prevent union meetings from being simultaneously interpreted into Spanish. Four-fifths of his members were Latinos. Outraged, they elected a Latina, Maria Elena Durazo, as their new leader.

Even unions whose non-English-speaking members are still a minority have discovered the tremendous well of talent and enthusiasm these members are contributing to our movement. One example: the dramatic "Justice for Janitors" organizing victories in downtown Los Angeles and nearby Century City in 1990. Against a powerful multinational employer and a brutal Los Angeles Police Department (a year before the videotaped beating of Rodney King made LAPD thuggery a nationwide scandal), the SEIU-led janitors showed inspiring discipline, courage, and intelligence.

As a matter of survival, unions have begun to target Latino and other immigrant workers in organizing campaigns. Through carefully produced organizing leaflets, shop reports, letters from the president, radio spots, and election ballots, unions are showing they can effectively communicate with immigrant workers. At their best, these communications aren't mere translations from English. They're written in the immigrant idiom.

A Case of Cultural Jet Lag

The same cultural diversity already expressed in organizing leaflets and new local leaderships will eventually produce a multicultural labor press. In the meantime, the labor press continues to suffer from cultural jet lag. For airline travelers, jet lag is at worst a temporary malady. Travelers can adjust to change in a matter of days. But for the press, both commercial and labor, change can be far more debilitating. The press, in fact, is usually one of the last institutions to accept fundamental change—and do something about it.

Compounding this problem for the labor press is a serious case of bureaucratic inertia. Underfunded and understaffed, most national union papers can't afford to send many, or any, reporters into the field. The few reporters union papers do dispatch to the field often lack tough investigative skills (rare enough even in commercial journalism), mainly because most labor journalists, convinced that unions are right about the issues and clear-eyed about the devil, feel relieved of the need to investigate anything. The result? The editors of many national union newspapers find themselves isolated from their readers and potential readers, *particularly* those who speak no English.

At the local level, the situation isn't very different. You might expect the social distance between local union newspapers and their readers to be much shorter than between national unions and *their* members. Unfortunately, this often isn't the case.

The editor of a small union local paper usually has other union responsibilities to worry about, not to mention a full- or part-time job in the plant. The editor may also lack the time to keep up with an ethnically diverse and changing membership. In a large local, the editor is often an ally and instrument of the leadership caucus. If the caucus faithfully reflects a multicultural rank and file, so will the paper. If the leaders are out of touch, however, chances are the newspaper will be out of touch, too.

We have reached two additional conclusions about the newspaper staffs of ethnically diverse unions. First, most of them are whiter than their readerships. Second, at the local union level, very few editors recruit, train, and regularly use rank-and-file reporters, writers, artists, and photographers. Very few, that is, view their newspaper as a tool for *organizing* workers.

It's true that we haven't conducted a scientific survey on these points, but each of us has worked for and studied the labor press. Over the years we've known enough editors and read enough papers to confirm that people of color—especially recent immigrants—are severely underrepresented on union newspaper staffs. They are likely to remain underrepresented as long as editors resist recruiting and training rank and filers in the name of professionalism.

A final observation before we get down to specifics: the "English-only" movement may be led by professional demagogues, but it has deep roots in the native-born working class. Under Samuel Gompers, the AFL tenaciously fought to exclude Asians from our shores, and it didn't much like Latinos, either. Some of this racism carried over into the CIO, despite the latter's determination to organize unskilled workers, whatever their color or national origin. To this day the AFL-CIO favors excluding "illegal" immigrants from U.S. workplaces through employer sanctions that fall far more heavily on workers than employers.[1] Not all union newspaper staffs are immune to the xenophobia behind this position. And even when editors show respect and understanding for America's immigrant tradition, as many of them do, they may still have to contend with readers who resent the intrusion of bilingualism into their familiar monolingual world.

A Multilingual Labor Press Sampler

Many labor newspapers that should be reaching out to a multilingual work force in their own languages, our experience leads us to conclude, are failing to do so.[2] Meager union budgets and the technical roadblocks to bilingualism[3] play a role in this failure, but cultural my-

---

1. The AFL-CIO has held this position since well before employer sanctions were embedded in the Immigration Reform and Control Act of 1986. But individual unions and labor organizations are increasingly calling for the repeal of sanctions. Among them are the ATWU, HERE, ILGWU, the California Labor Federation, the Western Region of SEIU, and many local unions. These unions seek the full enforcement of protective labor laws and, above all, to organize *all* workers. The AFL-CIO, meanwhile, continues to support sanctions, though by the fall of 1991 change was clearly percolating within the federation.

2. Among the unions we surveyed with significant bilingual memberships whose newspapers lack regularly appearing second-language editions, pages, or sections are the United Auto Workers, the Service Employees, the International Union of Electrical Workers, the Carpenters, the United Steelworkers, the Machinists, and the United Food and Commercial Workers. The situation is not much better locally. In Los Angeles, where Latino participation in dozens of unions and in organizing drives is high, we found no regularly appearing Spanish sections in most newspapers or newsletters going to the whole local union membership. One UAW editor pointed out that most of the Latinos who make up 60 percent of his local membership speak English. His local, however, has also organized and represented many recent immigrants who do not.

3. In ethnically diverse unions with a majority of native-born members, for example, it may be difficult to target the non-English-speakers. You could identify key immigrant locals or work sites and bundle the appropriate editions to them, but this approach would fail to reach many non-English-speakers. Besides, national union papers generally mail direct to members' homes. Try-

opia is the underlying cause. Still, given the realities of this prevailing English-only climate, we're impressed by the growing number of national and local unions that do try to communicate with their foreign-born members. These unions are pace-setters for the rest of the labor movement, and they have much to teach us.

Let's look at some examples of how the labor press in these unions is fulfilling its role as informer, educator, and organizer.

We'll begin with HERE, the Hotel Employees and Restaurant Employees, a union with a high percentage of non-English-speaking, entry-level workers among its 350,000 members in the United States and Canada. In Los Angeles, the city we know best, three-quarters of HERE Local 11's members are women and people of color. Many recent immigrants work in back-of-the-house cleaning, delivering, and cooking jobs. In these jobs, English is a distinctly second language, when it is heard at all.

Catering Industry Employee (CIE) is HERE's monthly newspaper, an easy-to-read, twenty-two-page mix of slick and newspaper stock, color cover, feature centerfold, local news, and a recipe page called "Dining with Dekker." Page 3 is the standard "Message from the General President," Edward T. Hanley. Page 4 is a Spanish translation of Hanley's statement. Page 5 is a French translation.

CIE typifies the international union newspapers that have made an effort to communicate with their non-English members without fully succeeding. Most of these union papers merely translate a story or two. A few editors select articles for translation that have a special relevance for their audience—immigration reform, for instance, or the Mexico-Canada-U.S. free trade pact—but in *CIE*'s case Spanish-speakers may get only the president's message while French-speakers may get Hanley and just a page of Canadian news.

HERE has thirty thousand members in Canada, and the *CIE*'s French pages help make the paper more relevant to French-speaking Canadians. But there's a problem: President Hanley's message is often tailored for Americans. Hanley's column in the February 1991 issue, for example, discusses the permanent replacement of strikers—a routine practice in the United States—without noting that Quebec

---

ing to target a national readership of Latino, Asian, or other members by surname would be costly and unreliable. We recognize these problems but think they can be overcome once a union decides it *must* communicate with its foreign-born members.

law prohibits this form of scabbery. *CIE* editor Don Byers concedes that his publication is short on multicultural content. "We haven't faced up to the challenge," he says. "We're not doing the job we should be doing."

Other unions that set aside space for non-English stories often relegate them to the back of the paper. The Amalgamated Clothing and Textile Workers Union once published separate newspapers in Italian, Yiddish, and Lithuanian. Today, like HERE, the union prints just one page each in Spanish and French.[4] The *UE News*, the United Electrical, Radio and Machine Workers of America (UE) paper, prints one of twelve pages in Spanish. The January 4, 1991, issue features Spanish-language news with a Latino orientation—one story covers UE protests against repression in the Dominican Republic—but the page still comes off as a throwaway.[5]

Offering non-English translations of a few articles is a step in the right direction, but this step doesn't go nearly far enough. African-Americans who were allowed to ride the buses of Montgomery, Alabama, in 1953 found no satisfaction in being confined to the back seats. For analogous reasons, a few literal translations in the back of a union newspaper may strike non-English-speaking readers as a mere sop to their language and culture.[6]

By now you may be wondering whether we have any good news. Fortunately, we do. We think the national publication of the Interna-

---

4. For these pages the ACTWU newspaper, *Labor Unity*, does select stories that appeal to Latino and French-Canadian readers. The French and Spanish versions of the president's message are usually just excerpts from the English, however. In one recent issue the president treated his Canadian readers to a fervent call for reform of the U.S. labor laws.

5. Ironically, the UE is the only union we know whose convention delegates demanded a non-English page in their national newspaper. They adopted a resolution to this effect in 1985.

6. A technical problem in Spanish and other global languages is the idiomatic differences among speakers from different parts of the world. In Puerto Rican Spanish, "to file a grievance" is *radicar una querella*; in Mexico, it is *archivar una queja*. Puerto Rican Spanish also seems to contain more Americanisms than Mexican or Guatemalan Spanish. Puerto Ricans and Guatemalans can understand an article in Mexican Spanish, but they may not view it as their story in the way that Vermonters, Texans, and Californians do when they read English. Some editors and translators believe that Spanish can be written in a common-denominator style capable of making any Latino feel at home. Others disagree.

tional Ladies' Garment Workers' Union (ILGWU) has many strong features. We see some promising bilingual developments in local union papers. And we've found an extraordinary regional newspaper that, though published outside the official union movement, can serve as a model for union journalism in a bicultural setting.

Immigrant Union, Immigrant Press

The ILGWU is America's immigrant union par excellence. Founded in 1900 by workers from Russia and eastern and southern Europe, the union became a dominant force in the garment industry after a spectacular 1909 strike led by young immigrant women. Since that time, the ILGWU has been an industrial union for all kinds of workers in the needle trades. Most of these workers are new immigrants to this day.

In 1909, the ILGWU began publishing its national newspaper, *Justice*, in English and Yiddish. An Italian edition appeared shortly thereafter. These multiple editions lasted long after the great European influx subsided after 1924. But by the mid-1960s, with only a handful of ILGWU members still speaking Yiddish, the Yiddish edition of *Justice* was canceled. The Italian edition survived through the late 1980s.

Meanwhile, a new wave of Asian and Latin American workers has flooded into the garment industry's sewing jobs. Chinese, Mexicans, Salvadorans, Puerto Ricans, Haitians, Cubans, and Dominicans far outnumber the ILGWU's native-born members, while tens of thousands of Koreans, Filipinos, and southeast Asians toil in unorganized sweatshops and kitchens.

The languages of *Justice* have, accordingly, changed. The newspaper now publishes monthly twelve- to sixteen-page English and Spanish editions. The English edition also carries quarterly four-page inserts in Chinese and Italian.

Publishing all these editions is a formidable undertaking to which the ILGWU leadership has committed a substantial budget. Translating and printing the fifty thousand copies of the Spanish edition alone costs nearly $100,000 a year. What the union's Chinese, Latino, Italian, and English-speaking members get for their dues money, however, is one of the liveliest union papers around. *Justice*, like *Solidarity*, is full of their faces, voices, and workplace concerns. By quickly scanning its pages, you can tell who pays the ILGWU's freight.

The English and Spanish editions are identical. We don't think this is a good idea, though identical treatments do have their advantages.

Because photos and stories are the same, Spanish-speaking and English-speaking members can see and read about each other. They can shake hands, so to speak, in a unifying gesture that is obligatory for a multicultural labor press. And *Justice* obviously saves photo, writing, and layout costs by doing things this way.

The disadvantages, however, are severe. There is no recognition in *Justice* that Latinos have *any* concerns or *any* ways of thinking and seeing that differ from those of English-speaking members. Unity is the essential aim of a union newspaper, but absolute conformity should not be.

"When I started here," notes *Justice* editor Dwight Burton, "the Spanish and Italian editions *were* different because they were just quarterly inserts in the English edition. Our Italian editor also had a European sense of design. Most of the stories and photos were the same, but some weren't. But after giving our Spanish-speaking members their own edition, we hired a designer who wanted this edition to be as 'professional' as the English. That's how the two editions came to look the same. Today I don't think there's much advantage in doing separate layouts. Latinos in the U.S. see the same TV, the same billboards, and many of the same magazines and newspapers that other Americans do. They end up with the same sense of design."

Well, maybe in the second or third generation they do. We're not so sure about the first. But Burton does agree that the content of the two editions shouldn't be identical. "Our original idea was to have the Spanish editor write stories for both editions, including some tailored for Latinos," he says. "One of my predecessors hoped the Spanish editor would become a force in the Latino community, but it didn't turn out that way."

Getting *Justice* to the point where the two editions are mostly similar but culturally distinctive will require staffing and budget decisions that have yet to be made.

The Multilingual Challenge

Ideally, you can argue that bilingual labor newspapers should weave both their languages into *one* edition. This would be the clearest possible expression of the diversity within unity that we have been talking about. Unfortunately, we can't generalize about the costs involved.

The English and Spanish versions of *Justice* total thirty-two pages. Would one twenty-eight-page edition cost less than two sixteen-page editions?[7] Probably not. Publishing one edition would eliminate the need to duplicate photos and illustrations and lower pre-press costs somewhat, but every ILGWU member would get a twenty-eight-page newspaper instead of a sixteen-page one. The extra printing and mailing costs might be prohibitive for newspapers like *Justice* and *Solidarity* that have large print runs.

But local unions with fewer readers can always consider this option. Let's revisit HERE Local 11, which represents ten thousand hotel and restaurant workers in Los Angeles. Most of these workers are Latinos, and the proportion of recent immigrants among them is very high. By virtue of its demographics, Local 11 must put out a bilingual newspaper. *Noticias del Local 11 News* is bilingual from cover to cover, but it tries to do more than communicate with members in two languages. As its title suggests, *Noticias del Local 11 News* conveys the idea that, in Local 11, members from different cultures stand side by side.

This integration is accomplished by locating the English and Spanish versions of stories on the same page or two-page spread, with bilingually captioned photos as the unifying design feature. To avoid a boxy, symmetrical look, *Noticias* varies the layout. Sometimes the Spanish story runs at the top outside corner of the page, at other times the English does. English stories are lightly screened to enhance readability.

Another publication using the same integrated format is *El Clarín*, the monthly newsletter of the California Immigrant Workers Association (CIWA). The AFL-CIO's only formal association of immigrants, CIWA was created in 1989 by the Los Angeles County Federation of Labor. It has four thousand members, mostly Spanish-speaking new immigrants from Mexico and Central America. CIWA offers members a modest range of benefits (like most AFL-CIO associate-member programs), but the association's main purpose is to organize immigrant workers culturally, politically, for labor solidarity actions—and eventually into unions.

El Clarín is a trim, well-designed eight-page newsletter. It features "know-your-rights" columns, background pieces on themes that matter to its readers ("New Immigration Law Affects Latinos"), and success

---

7. Why twenty-eight pages? It's a guesstimate. Photos and illustrations would only have to be used once. In a visual newspaper like *Justice* this could easily save four pages.

NOTICIAS DEL Local 11 NEWS

Otoño/Fall 1990
Volúmen/Volume 1
Número/Issue 8

Hotel and Restaurant Employees International Union, AFL-CIO
Sindicato Internacional de Empleados de Hoteles y Restaurantes, AFL-CIO

HYATT ACTION — SEE PAGE 4
ACCION EN EL HYATT, VEASE PAGINA 4

LOCAL 11 FIGHTS BENEFIT CUTS AT CANTER'S DELICATESSEN

The largest and most famous delicatessen in Los Angeles, Canter's, is quickly losing its good reputation.

Long-term employees and customers have joined together to fight a plan by Canter's management to impose severe pension and benefit cuts on its 125 workers.

Local 11 has organized a series of late-night protests at the restaurant which is located in the Fairfax section of Los Angeles. Thousands of customers have been leafleted. Many have expressed their support and their willingness to help employees.

Management has been so shaken by union action, it has leafleted alongside Local 11 to try to convince customers that its anti-worker proposals are necessary.

"It looks totally ridiculous to see management standing outside the restaurant and confronting customers with anti-union statements," says Canter's committee member Alvaro Gonzalez. "Most customers realize that the workers are entitled to decent health insurance and a pension."

Canter's wants to replace the current medical coverage with an inferior plan; they also want to eliminate the pension for all employees who have worked less than ten years. That includes many workers who have paid into the fund for a long time.

The local Jewish community is very upset with Canter's break

Continued on Page 6

EL LOCAL 11 DICE NO A LOS RECORTES DE BENEFICIOS POR CANTER'S DELICATESSEN

Canter's, el restaurante de comidas preparadas más grande y famoso de Los Angeles, está perdiendo rapidamente su buena reputación.

Los empleados que han trabajado allí mucho tiempo y los clientes se han juntado para luchar contra el plan de la gerencia de Canter's de recortar drásticamente los fondos de jubilación y los beneficios de sus 125 trabajadores.

El Local 11 ha realizado una serie de protestas tarde en la noche en el restaurante ubicado en la zona de la Fairfax de Los Angeles. Se les han repartido volantes a miles de clientes. Muchos han expresado su apoyo y su buena voluntad para ayudar a

los empleados.

A la gerencia le ha afectado tanto la acción del sindicato que se ha puesto a pasar volantes junto al Local 11 para tratar de convencer a sus clientes de que sus propuestas anti-trabajadores son necesarias.

"Es una cosa ridícula ver a la patronal parada afuera del restaurante y enfrentandose a sus clientes con declaraciones anti-sindicales," dice el "shop steward" de Canter's Alvaro Gonzalez. La mayoría de los clientes se dan cuenta que los trabajadores tienen derecho a un seguro médico y una pensión decente."

Canter's quiere sustituir el ac-

Continuado en la Página 6

The Hotel and Restaurant Employees Local 11 paper in Los Angeles, Noticias del Local 11 News, *runs each article in English and Spanish on the same page.*

stories showing how CIWA members have organized themselves into unions or helped other workers join.

El Clarín first appeared in September 1989 and initially gave equal weight to Spanish and English articles. But Spanish clearly dominates now, both in page placement and headlines. "The *Anglo* influence is dominant everywhere you look in L.A. union publications," says editor Joel Ochoa. "When they do translate something, it's an 'oh, by the way' afterthought. We're the opposite."

An alternative some unions use is the back-to-back, half-and-half newspaper. This format gives each language its own cover and self-contained section, running upside down from the other's. Unfortunately, this format wastes space by duplicating photos and captions—and it still fails the test of true integration.

We can understand the back-to-back format, however, when readers speak *three* or more languages. That's the case in ILGWU Local 23–25 in New York City. Known as "the Chinatown local," it has organized Latino, African-American, white, and Chinese workers.

How do you work three languages into one publication and still make the layout attractive? The twenty-four-page monthly *Local 23-25 News* runs Spanish and English back-to-back and places the Chinese version in the middle as a removable insert. Each language gets eight magazine-size pages. Each section covers the same stories in similar layouts, with some variation in photos. Given the alternatives—separate editions for each language or a heroic but doomed effort to cram three languages onto each page—we think the *Local 23-25 News* has come up with a reasonable solution.

A five-thousand-member meatpacker local in Fresno, California, faces an even more imposing language problem. The membership of United Food and Commercial Workers Local 126 is about 60 percent Latino, 18 percent white American-born, 10 percent Portuguese, 8 percent Punjabi, and 4 percent Vietnamese. Most unions with these demographics would settle for a bilingual Spanish-English publication. Local 126 is instead developing a newspaper that will accommodate this staggering ethnic diversity.

President Marcello Salcito intends to distribute an English-language publication with inserts in the other four tongues. On the cover will appear notices in all five languages offering the translated inserts. These will be included in subsequent mailings to members who request them. Salcito believes that enough Local 126 members read English to

EL CLARÍN

ORGANO INFORMATIVO DE CALIFORNIA IMMIGRANT WORKERS ASSOCIATION

VOL. 2, NO. 2   JULIO 1990

Victoria De Los Conserjes

Cientos de personas celebran la victoria de los conserjes.
Hundreds of supporters celebrate Justice for Janitors victory.

Joel Ochoa, Organizador de CIWA

El pasado 28 de junio los conserjes de Century City acompañados por cientos de sus simpatizantes pasaron por el mismo lugar donde dos semanas antes, habián sido brutalmente golpeados por la policía cuando pedian justicia.

Esta vez se celebraba una victoria después de una larga lucha que culminó con una huelga de casi un mes, habian logrado doblegar a una poderosa compañia de limpieza que se negaba a darles aumentos salariales, beneficios y demás prestaciones.

Con su lucha y determinación los conserjes, en su mayoría inmigrantes latinos, ganaron un contrato que les garantiza aumento inmediato de 10% a 15% del salario más seguro médico, vacaciones y otras prestaciones que vendrán a principios del año entrante. También ganaron el respeto de toda la sociedad porque demostraron que cuando se esta en lo correcto y se pelea decididamente por la defensa de derechos humanos y laborales, ni el poder de las grandes corporaciones, ni los golpes de la policía pueden evitar una victoria.

En **CIWA** nos sentimos muy orgullosos de esa victoria porque le demostró a todo mundo que los inmigrantes estamos más que listos para empezar a organizarnos y buscar la mejoría en nuestras comunidades y lugares de trabajo.

Que la victoría de los conserjes nos sirva de inspiración para que en forma más decidida participemos en **CIWA**. ¡SI se puede! Cuéntele a un familiar, un amigo o un vecino sobre el triunfo de estos trabajadores e invítelos a participar en **CIWA**. Recuerde — tarde o temprano triunfará toda nuestra comunidad porque ¡la unión SI hace la fuerza!

Miembros de CIWA Presentan "Fronteras/Borders"

Las 420 personas que atendieron la función a beneficio del Proyecto Laboral de Asistencia al Inmigrante (LIAP), gozaron de un excelente programa que tuvo como atracción principal la premier teatral de "Fronteras/Borders," la cual fue elaborada y actuada por miembros de **CIWA**.

La función fue todo un acto de solidaridad en el cual convivieron lideres laborales, religiosos, activistas y muchos miembros de **CIWA**. De acuerdo a la Directora de LIAP, Teresa Sánchez, "Este acto representa el inicio de una tradición que repetirermos año con año para reconocer y saludar a quien luche por los inmigrantes."

Este año, el Padre Luis Olivares fue el recipiente del "Premio Humanitario" por su tremenda dedicación al mejoramiento de la vida entre los inmigrantes.

El platillo fuerte de la función fue la presentación del teatro de **CIWA** con su obra "Fronteras/Borders." Por medio de su trabajo artístico, siete miembros de **CIWA** apoyados por todo un equipo de profesionales pudieron contar sus experien-
(Continuá en la página 8)

Victory for Justice for Janitors
Joel Ochoa, CIWA Organizer

Janitors from Century City, accompanied by hundreds of their supporters, marched through the streets of that business district on June 28th. They had been brutally beaten by the Los Angeles Police Department as they demanded "Justice for Janitors" in a similar march two
(Continued on page 6)

REUNION GENERAL EL 29 DE JULIO / PICNIC EL 19 DE AGOSTO
VEA PAGINA 8

Published in Los Angeles by a membership project of the AFL-CIO, El Clarín *mixes articles in Spanish and English throughout its pages.*

make this flexibly bilingual publication more effective than separate language editions.

Another advantage of this approach, he says, is that it doesn't "rile up the rednecks in the foothills" who might take offense at a multilingual publication.

Beyond Bilingualism

We have taken pains to describe some of the publications that try, with widely varying results, to communicate with non-English-speaking union members. Up to this point we have not challenged the assumptions these newspapers and newsletters make about themselves. Let's examine these assumptions.

The U.S. labor press has an extremely tight focus. It literally *sees* people as workers, not workers as people. Accordingly, it devotes 95 percent of its space to workplace issues, largely ignoring the cultures, histories, and ideologies people bring to work, the problems they face at home, the games they play or watch, and the community dynamics that knit them together or drive them apart. The "vulgar Marxism" of the labor press colors everything it does.[8] When the typical union paper ventures into politics, for instance, it concentrates on "worker" demands—for a fair minimum wage, labor law reform, import controls, and so on.

We agree that a good deal of this content is obligatory for the labor press. But its narrow focus limits the enthusiasm with which both multilingual and English-only newspapers are read. Workers, after all, are people with many interests and problems. The workplace is only one of them. If their union paper insists on treating them as walking grievances, they will look elsewhere for information and entertainment.

Immigrants, in particular, will turn away. As "strangers in a strange land,"[9] they face as many crises off the job as on. It's not just the

---

8. The phrase "vulgar Marxism" may strike most labor editors as off the wall, given their liberal to conservative ideology. But we believe it is apt. Some followers of Marx and legions of anti-Marxists have vulgarized his emphasis on the relations of production, reducing them to the relations of *work*. Out of this confusion has emerged work-driven man and (somewhat later) work-driven woman, not to mention the labor press that tries to communicate with them.

9. This is how an immigrant Italian machinist living in Windsor, Ontario, described himself during a 1979 interview with Stansbury. Sam DiMaio went on to make a key point about immigrants, whatever their crises of the mo-

Publication of the
Hotel and Restaurant Employees
And Bartenders Union, Local 2
209 Golden Gate Avenue
San Francisco, California 94102

February 24, 1988

LOCAL 2

Queremos
Un Nivel
Justo A
Nivel-
Ciudad

We Want One Fair Standard City-Wide

Emily Hartshorn
Dishwasher/Davre's
- 9 years.

The trilingual paper of the Hotel and Restaurant Employees and Bartenders Union Local 2 in San Francisco runs articles in English, Spanish, and Chinese.

100

dunning landlord, or the emergency room in lieu of a doctor, or the battered old car running on hope that worries them—it's the loss of their parents to the old world and their children to the new. Amid all these cross-pressures, their relationship to production is the dominant force, but an effective labor press must meet them where they live as well as work.

Such a labor press does not have to be invented. For over a century new immigrants to this country have created, supported, and read a long line of newspapers printed in their native languages and devoted to the totality of their lives. Many of these newspapers have won a loyal following among working people.

Continuing this tradition today is *Unión Hispana*, a Spanish-language weekly published in Santa Ana, California and circulated gratis throughout the Los Angeles basin. A lively tabloid, *Unión Hispana* first rolled off the presses in July 1988 and has already attracted some thirty-seven thousand readers.

The *Unión Hispana* logo features the words *Vocero del Trabajador Latino* and *Un daño contra uno es un daño contra todos*. The first line means "Voice of the Latino Worker." The second is an old Wobbly slogan: "An injury to one is an injury to all." To understand the working class origins of *Unión Hispana* you need to know a little about La Hermandad Mexicana Nacional (National Mexican Brotherhood/ Sisterhood), the national organization that publishes it.

La Hermandad was founded in 1953 by Felipe Usquiano, a San Diego organizer from the old Spanish-Speaking People's Congress. Fourteen years later the organization opened a Los Angeles office. Its leader here was and is Bert Corona, who organized warehouse workers for ILWU Local 1–26 in the early 1940s before becoming that union's president. Under Corona, La Hermandad vigorously defended undocumented workers against INS raids and abuses while offering them housing, health, and immigration services through its Centros de Acción Social Autónomo (CASAs). Many CASA activists later became union organizers, particularly for the ILGWU.

From the late 1960s into the 1980s, Corona and his intrepid colleague, Soledad Alatorre, organized parts-fabricating, restaurant, and hotel employees into the Hermandad General de Trabajadores. This group fought the stigmatizing of hardworking Mexican immigrants as

---

ment. "The hardships, the bad times," he said, "we can get through them easier than most people who never had to turn their back on home."

"illegals," welfare leeches, and job thieves. It defended their right to earn the legal minimum wage, work under safe conditions, and maintain their original dates of hire after returning from visits to Mexico. Rejecting dual unionism, La Hermandad helped its members join the UAW, ILWU, Teamsters, and other established unions.

Corona is a controversial figure within the labor movement. He is also indefatigable, honest, and effective. Long before most Los Angeles unions organized undocumented workers, Corona and Alatorre were out there signing them up. While the AFL-CIO lobbied to criminalize millions of immigrants at the point of hire, La Hermandad was defending their right to work and unionize, to learn English and get an education, to live in decent, affordable housing, and to become citizens. Because La Hermandad deals with so many aspects of immigrants' lives, it is no surprise that *Unión Hispana* does, too.

The newspaper's pro-union, pro-immigrant stand is clear. In the April 12, 1991, issue, an article describes how Latino immigrants have spearheaded many recent organizing drives and suggests that they may be "the seed that will reactivate the weakened U.S. labor movement." Each thirty-two-page issue has a section on unions, some of which seek organizing leads through ads in the newspaper. Elsewhere in *Unión Hispana* you'll find news stories and editorials on strikes, boycotts, *la migra* (the U.S. Immigration and Naturalization Service), the proposed Mexico-U.S. free trade agreement, and other issues familiar to readers of most union newspapers.[10]

Unlike most union newspapers, however, *Unión Hispana* doesn't stop there. The March 29, 1991, issue leads off with a report on the widespread demands for L.A. Police Chief Daryl Gates's resignation in the wake of the savage police beating of an African-American, Rodney King. The front page also features an article on the Santa Ana city council's decision to shut down a swap meet where thousands of immigrants often found low-cost food, clothing, and household articles. On page 5, an editorial protests the market's closing.

---

10. The April 5, 1991, issue of *Unión Hispana* dealt with the subject of this essay—the emerging multilingual labor press. It carried a story on a new United Brotherhood of Carpenters newsletter, the *Hammer*, which is handed out at nonunion construction sites in southern California. In straightforward didactic prose with a few illustrations, the *Hammer (El Martillo)* tells immigrant workers about job safety and other workplace rights. Readers can get a free subscription by filling out and returning a mini-survey in the newsletter. Future organizing contacts are obtained in this way.

The Gates story dominates the next three or four issues, but not to the exclusion of news reports or features on year-round school classes in Los Angeles, the effect of diet on cancer, American and Mexican sports events, the life of Martin Luther King, bilingual education, the influence of Mexican art on American artists, a proposition limiting the terms of California lawmakers, economic and political developments in Latin America, progress against alcoholism and diabetes, whether Fernando Valenzuela has a future in baseball, the 1991 Oscar won by *Dances with Wolves*, a campaign against ethnic stereotyping in Hollywood, an exhibit of Mexican popular religious art, the health effects of smog, a literacy campaign, nutrition, a *salsa* concert at the Hollywood Palladium, how Texas was stolen from Mexico, racial violence in Compton (just south of Los Angeles), the death of the Cuban artist Juan Boza, postpartum blues, and the life of Martha Graham.

Compared to most labor papers, the design of *Unión Hispana* is a little raggedy and rambunctious. Some pages look professional, others look thrown together in no particular alignment. The newspaper is chockfull of ads that have phone numbers; they add energy, not class, to the layout.

Class, however, is not what *Unión Hispana* is striving for—unless it's working class. This newspaper is alive. It's readable. And it's right on target for its immigrant readership. As that readership enters its second and third generations, *Unión Hispana* will gradually begin translating its stories into English.

"We cover people's social and community lives because that's La Hermandad," says the paper's editor, Juan Garcia. "We *are* the community. We mix popular culture with a political point of view that benefits working people. Believe me, if union newspapers did this, there'd be no need for *Unión Hispana*."

Well, union newspapers *should* be doing what *Unión Hispana* does. If we have described this lively rag in more detail than any other publication, it's because we consider it a model for the labor press. Not in every respect, of course. Multicultural labor papers should generally be multilingual. Few will have the resources to publish 128 pages a month. But all can learn from *Unión Hispana*'s broad focus on, and involvement with, its readers' lives. Why should we let the downtown dailies do all the talking to union members about Daryl Gates, *salsa*, and Fernando Valenzuela?

There are other things *Unión Hispana* can teach us. For one thing, its staff reflects its readership. They speak the same language, breathe the same culture, and live in the same neighborhood. "Every once in a while we bring rank and filers in and train them to write," says Garcia. "We get them into print and help them along. In time, some of them come on staff. It's something we don't do enough of. We should do it more."

So should union newspapers. Very few have regular programs for recruiting, training, and placing union members on editorial staffs. Multicultural papers should lead the way in making this happen.

Finally, *Unión Hispana* doesn't just talk to Latinos, it helps *organize* them. La Hermandad often sends its activists into the field. When they go door-to-door, recruiting people for English and citizenship classes or for political action, the newspaper is their calling card. They say, "Here's a copy of *Unión Hispana*, it's free," and people let them in.[11] Usually, the issue they're handing out has a story or editorial about the subject of the organizing drive. This helps people see a direct connection between *Unión Hispana* and the steps they are being asked to take to improve their lives.

The Multicultural Labor Press in the 1990s

By the end of this decade Spanish editions, sections, and pages will be a routine feature of the labor press. You'll see many more stories in Asian-Pacific languages, too. Spurring on these developments will be organized labor's realization that its future is intimately bound up with new immigrants.

How can the labor press meet the challenge of unity within diversity in the 1990s? It's already beginning to, but we have a few suggestions.

First, don't relegate your immigrant readers to the back of the bus. Give them their due on page 1. If they are a majority or substantial minority of your union, give them equal space.

Second, feature their bylines, not just their faces. No newspaper can be multicultural in print if it's not multicultural in staffing. You need to recruit, train, hire, and encourage writers, photographers, and graphic artists who come from your rank and file. Resisting this challenge on the grounds of professionalism is a copout.

Third, don't farm out your local union newspaper to a professional media consultant. No matter how sensitive your consultant is, that consultant will drive a wedge between the publication and its readers. A

---

11. The Carpenters and other union canvassers use *Unión Hispana* as an icebreaker, too.

consultant may be useful, however, if you want to train workers to write, lay out, and take pictures for your paper. Consultants can set up on-the-job training programs and make sure a paper maintains an acceptable quality while the new recruits are learning. With a cadre of contributors out in the field, your paper can be a powerful organizing tool.

Fourth, do what *Unión Hispana* does: respect the fullness of your readers' lives. Immigrants and other workers spend sixteen hours off the job, eight hours on. The workplace is their crucible, but other things matter to them just as much. Your pages should reflect this reality.

Finally, we call on the International Labor Communications Association to recognize the immigrant challenge. It's time for ILCA to provide a multilingual news and feature service for union newspapers. The stories and art it sends them should be camera-ready, in a format that satisfies their most common typeface, column width, and screening needs.[12]

The U.S. working class is growing more polyglot by the day. Unifying it and mobilizing it for action will require an *enthusiastic* recognition of its diversity. If the labor press fails to meet this challenge, it will lapse into irrelevance.

---

12. The UAW has offered such a service to its more than four hundred local union newspapers since the early 1980s, tailoring it for mimeo sheets as well as printed (offset) papers. At no great cost, this service should now become multilingual—and multicultural.

Women and the Labor Press: Emerging from the Shadows

Carolyn J. Jacobson and Susan L. Phillips

Once upon a time, not too many years ago, the International Association of Machinists newspaper, the *Machinist*, published a regular photo feature entitled "Miss Union Maid." Despite the label, there was nothing union-related about "Miss Union Maid," just a wire-service photo of a woman in a brief bathing suit intended to capture members' attention. And "Miss Union Maid" did just that for about twenty-five years—until the photos generated so much negative attention that the editor dropped them in 1976.

By the mid-1970s, not too many union publications were carrying outright cheesecake features like "Miss Union Maid." For the most part, union papers ignored women workers and the issues that mattered to them. Union papers highlighted older white men almost exclusively in photos and as spokespersons. Workers universally were referred to by the generic pronoun "he." What were perceived as women's concerns were addressed primarily through "women's pages" and special columns devoted to ladies auxiliary news, recipes, and homemaking tips.

Today, fifteen years later, union publications have a distinctly dif-

Carolyn J. Jacobson, the director of public relations for the Bakery, Confectionery and Tobacco Workers International Union, serves as managing editor of the BC&T News, *the union's membership publication. A member of the Executive Council of the International Labor Communications Association since 1980, Jacobson served as its president from 1986 to 1989. She is a charter member of the Coalition of Labor Union Women. Susan L. Phillips is publications director for the 1.3-million-member United Food and Commercial Workers International Union. She serves as managing editor of* UFCW Action, *the union's bimonthly membership magazine. Currently secretary-treasurer of the International Labor Communications Association, Phillips tabulated and analyzed the ILCA's 1987 survey of union editors.*

ferent look. Photos of women—and minorities—appear regularly in most union publications. Gone almost totally are the ladies auxiliary news and homemaking tips. A few papers do still run recipes, but the recipes aren't intended just for women. Contemporary labor editors carefully refer to workers using both male and female pronouns and work consciously to eliminate sexist language from their writing. In today's labor papers, it's not unusual to see news on child care, sexual harassment, and pay equity lawsuits—even in the papers published by unions that have only small percentages of women members.

What explains these changes? How widespread are they? What can union publications do to improve their coverage of women in the work force and in the labor movement? We recently put these questions to labor editors around the country in a survey on women and the labor press. Their answers can help point the way to a stronger labor press— and a stronger labor movement.

Changing Demographics, Changing Attitudes

The labor press, like the labor movement as a whole, has felt the impact of the demographic trends that have shaken America over recent years. In the 1980s, women flooded into the work force in record numbers. In the 1990s, two of every three new workers will be women. By 1995, women are likely to become the majority of all workers in the United States.

Unions have noticed. They're increasingly targeting organizing efforts toward predominantly female occupations in sectors as varied as health care and data processing. With the number of unionized, male-dominated manufacturing jobs still shrinking, unions have recognized that women are absolutely essential to labor's future.

Union editors cite two landmark events in the 1970s—the 1973 AFL-CIO endorsement of the Equal Rights Amendment (ERA) and the founding of the Coalition of Labor Union Women (CLUW) in 1974— as critical steps toward that recognition.

Until 1973, the AFL-CIO opposed the ERA on the grounds that women needed "protective" labor laws to shield them from the vagaries of the workplace. But that position became increasingly untenable as courts threw out one outmoded "protective" measure after another and job discrimination against women remained widespread.

The next year, in Chicago, some thirty-two hundred union women from fifty-eight unions gathered to form the Coalition of Labor Union Women. CLUW aimed to unify union women into a viable organization that could help define common concerns and develop action programs within the framework of the labor movement. The AFL-CIO formally endorsed CLUW in 1977.

John Barry, managing editor of the AFL-CIO's weekly newspaper, the *AFL-CIO News*, until he retired in 1988, credits CLUW for "stirring up our consciousness on women's issues." CLUW both made news, Barry explains, and influenced AFL-CIO policy on a variety of women's issues.

In the mid-1970s, when CLUW was founded, the *AFL-CIO News* and other labor papers were running precious little coverage on women, who even then made up 40 percent of the civilian work force and 25 percent of all unionized workers. But there were exceptions to this silence on women's issues, especially among unions with substantial numbers of women members. In 1975, for example, the Association of Flight Attendants was actively addressing discrimination and women's rights issues in its publications. In that same year, the *Retail Clerks Advocate*, the Retail Clerks International Association's national magazine, devoted sixteen pages to a special feature on working women. The special section profiled women who had helped build the union as well as contemporary women local union officers and influential international union staff members. The Retail Clerks membership was then approximately 50 percent women, though all of its officers and editorial staff were men. In 1979, the Retail Clerks merged with the Amalgamated Meat Cutters and Butcher Workmen to create the United Food and Commercial Workers union.

As the 1970s progressed, union papers started catching up with the exceptions. The *AFL-CIO News* began regularly running photos that featured women and eliminated the generic pronoun "he" when referring to workers. The paper's managing editor since 1989, Michael Byrne, says that the *AFL-CIO News* staff, which now includes women, has become particularly conscious of the labor movement's women members, as well as the large potential for membership growth among women. The AFL-CIO, adds Byrne, is redefining "women's issues" as "working issues."

Individual AFL-CIO affiliates, meanwhile, are making deliberate efforts in their publications to focus on issues that appeal to working women, especially during organizing campaigns. The American Federation of State, County and Municipal Employees began championing pay equity on behalf of its women members—half the union—in the late 1970s. AFSCME's role in the passage of a precedent-setting pay equity law in Minnesota made big news not only in AFSCME's magazine, the *Public Employee*, but also throughout the labor movement.

AFSCME became one of the first unions to publish a newsletter for women members. In 1990, however, the union decided that the issues the newsletter spotlighted were relevant to all members and discontinued that publication. The *Public Employee*, notes editor Marshall Donley, now devotes one page in each issue to a feature entitled "Not for Women Only."

The Service Employees International Union, whose membership is also half women, has increased coverage of women in its membership magazine, *Union*, says SEIU's former field communications director, Bill Pritchett. *Union* features more pictures and quotes from women spokespersons, more stories on women's issues and female-dominated professions, more profiles on women who have made contributions to the labor movement, and more organizing stories about clerical workers.

The United Food and Commercial Workers places its highest institutional priority on organizing, a priority directly reflected in *UFCW Action*, the union's membership magazine. *UFCW Action* regularly and deliberately includes stories about women and women's issues, including cover stories aimed to appeal to potential as well as current members. Cover story topics over recent years have highlighted sexual harassment, child care, women's health issues, and two-earner families.

The Amalgamated Clothing and Textile Workers Union, with a membership that is 80 percent women, has increased coverage of women workers largely because "of a society that is more aware of these issues generally and a staff that is sensitive," says *Labor Unity* editor Anne Rivera. The paper has run profiles on women local union leaders and articles on the double role that working women play.

Women make up about one-third of the Bakery, Confectionery and Tobacco Workers Union membership, and coverage of women workers and issues of particular concern to them has increased in the *BC&T News*. Increased coverage of these issues by the AFL-CIO has helped this process along.

The National Association of Letter Carriers has increased coverage of women workers substantially in its membership publication, the *Postal Record*. "Fifteen years ago, the NALC had very few female members," says editor Lorraine Swerdloff. "Today, about 19 percent of the membership is female. I make it a point to have articles that concern women and photos of women." Recent *Postal Record* issues have featured a history of women in the profession, profiles of women who perform exceptional community service, a cover story on how women contribute to the union, and a back cover explaining why unionization is the best way to achieve pay equity.

The Allied Industrial Workers, with a membership between 35 and 40 percent women, has taken progressive stances on issues of concern to women, such as child care and the ERA. The *Allied Industrial Worker*'s editor, Ken Germanson, credits improved coverage on women's issues to the emergence of organizations such as CLUW, which provide stories on sexual harassment, the ERA, and women workers in general.

The percentage of women in Communications Workers of America (CWA) has declined slightly in the past fifteen years from over 50 percent to about 40 to 45 percent, largely because of changing technology. The CWA addresses women's concerns institutionally through a women's activities office, regular conferences that focus on women's issues as well as job-related concerns, and convention resolutions addressing child care, flexible hours, wage discrimination, and more—all of which are covered in the *CWA News*, says editor Jeffery Miller.

Coverage of women's issues has increased even in unions that traditionally have had predominantly male memberships. The Machinists union's coverage of women has increased slightly, reports the *Machinist*'s Pat Ziska, as has the union's overall female membership, which now stands at about 20 percent.

The Carpenters Union's recently retired editor, Roger Sheldon, notes that the percentage of women members in that union has increased only slightly, to about 15 to 20 percent. But features on women and stories about women apprentices have appeared routinely in the *Carpenter*, after a deliberate decision on his part to include them.

With women making up about 30 percent of its membership, the International Brotherhood of Electrical Workers emphasizes women working in nontraditional jobs in the *IBEW Journal*, along with a variety of other women's issues, reports Mary Ann VanMeter. *Journal* articles often aim to enlighten IBEW members about the changing relationship of women and men and society, adds VanMeter. One recent *Journal* article, headlined "It's Time to Stop the Role Playing: 'Women's Work,' 'Men's Work' Not Valid in a Modern Society," explored both what employers should be doing for working women and the need for society as a whole to change its attitude about women's roles. The article's intent, VanMeter explains, "was to get those who read it thinking, 'Am I doing my share to bring real equality for women? Can I in some way help relieve the stress the women around me experience because of a lack of understanding on my part?'"

Coverage of women workers and the issues that affect them is also improving at the local union level, although progress has been mixed.

In the Bakery, Confectionery and Tobacco Workers Union, a local or regional editor will occasionally refer to a member "and his lovely wife," but, for the most part, local coverage of women and women's issues has improved. Much of the credit needs to go to materials provided by CLUW on Working Women's Awareness Week, observed annually in May, and other topics. The International Labor Communications Association's monthly publication, *ILCA Reporter*, also widely distributes articles and graphics on Women's History Month and other issues relating to women union members. About 750 local union publications belong to the International Labor Communications Association, and these locals frequently make use of the camera-ready materials provided.

Still, apart from avoiding overt sexism, local union publications in the Bakery, Confectionery and Tobacco Workers Union—like locals in other unions—seldom use their pages to showcase women or educate members on the issues that affect them.

In some unions, progress at the local level has been more noticeable. Nancy Brigham, the coordinator of the United Auto Workers Local Union Press Association, feels that UAW local union publications have taken important steps forward over the past fifteen years. LUPA distributes articles on a variety of issues, including women's concerns, to some 450 UAW local union publications.

The proportion of UAW local union editors who are women could be as high as 40 percent, says Brigham, who notes that just 13.5 percent of the union's members are women. All the editors, men and women, receive support from the UAW Women's Department, which has raised the consciousness of members and leaders on women's and family issues. Department staff conduct programs in local unions on sexual harassment and other issues, and the local unions often report on these programs in their publications. The UAW Public Relations and Publications Department also generates material on women's issues used for both the UAW national magazine and local union publications.

The UAW isn't the only union with disproportionately high numbers of women serving as local editors. Louise Walsh, a senior staff associate at the George Meany Center for Labor Studies, has noticed an increase in the number of women, especially minority women, who attend the newswriting and editing class she teaches.

In the early 1970s, few women served as editors or managing editors of union publications. In 1974, the International Labor Press Association—known today as the International Labor Communications Association—surveyed the labor press and found that only 22 percent of the editors and managing editors of union publications were women. Another survey in 1987 showed definite improvement. The number of women editors and managing editors had increased to 32 percent.

The increasing number of women in labor journalism, some labor editors suggest, reflects a higher consciousness among union leaders on the need to promote affirmative action—not just in union contracts but also within their own ranks.

As more women join unions, unions are clearly seeking more women for professional and technical positions. But few of these women appear to end up in top-level positions of responsibility—either appointed or elected. By and large, women have been recruited to fill writing and "special projects" positions rather than top-level "mainstream" union jobs that involve organizing and collective bargaining. Some editors postulate that this pattern mirrors the popular perception that women possess special communications skills. One editor we surveyed points out that one union increased its number of women publications specialists because the union could pay women less than men and get "more bang for the buck."

Whatever the reason, the greater numbers of women in labor journalism have directly affected both the amount and content of labor press coverage of women workers. A few unions have offices or departments responsible for "women's issues"—which theoretically could take the lead on pushing for inclusion of such information. Yet having a special department or person to promote these issues does not appear to be the catalyst for ensuring that these issues receive attention. Coverage of women's issues in union publications has almost uniformly increased and improved because of the initiative of individual editors, many of them women.

Several older male editors will admit candidly that they do not often think consciously about including photos and features about women. In contrast, male editors a generation younger point out that coming of age during the women's and civil rights movements attuned them to be sensitive about cultural and gender diversity.

Choice: A Difficult Test for Labor Journalism

No single social issue has generated more controversy within the labor movement in recent years than reproductive choice. Unions traditionally avoid controversy in their publications—one reason why few national union publications publish letters to the editor. On the issue of choice, this traditional tendency to shun controversy has collided head-on with a concern of high and direct importance to women, a concern that ought to be discussed and debated.

The choice controversy first boiled onto the national labor scene in 1989 when several pro-choice resolutions were submitted to the AFL-CIO convention. The convention debate on whether the federation should adopt a pro-choice stance quickly surfaced strong differences of opinion about whether choice was indeed an issue that should be considered within labor's purview.

Opponents argued that reproductive issues are moral and religious concerns and strenuously objected to the prospect of unions endorsing and supporting political candidates on the basis of their positions on choice. An AFL-CIO position, opponents argued, would only be divisive and lead many members to resign.

Pro-choice proponents contended that the labor movement was already working to guarantee workers the right to privacy on random drug and polygraph testing. That right to privacy should also encompass reproductive choice. Moreover, proponents pointed out, choice is most definitely a labor issue, in the most basic of labor terms, because many collectively bargained health plans address it.

The reproductive choice issue made its first *AFL-CIO News* appearance in the edition published immediately after the federation's 1989 convention in Washington, D.C. The coverage revealed considerable ambivalence, to say the least, about how to deal with the choice issue within the house of labor. The article that mentioned choice appeared on page 13 of a sixteen-page edition, with the nondescript headline, "Delegates refer 17 resolutions to council." The article's first paragraph mentioned the seventeen resolutions in general. The second paragraph noted that choice had been discussed, pointing out that "six of those resolutions examined women's rights to reproductive choice." The article went on for 11 more paragraphs with details of the floor discussion, including quotes from pro-choice delegates.

The choice resolutions introduced at the 1989 AFL-CIO convention were ultimately referred to the AFL-CIO Executive Council for further consideration. At the February 1990 council meeting, an ad hoc Committee on Reproductive Issues was named to study the appropriateness of an AFL-CIO position on choice. The council accepted the committee's recommendation against taking a choice position six months later. The lead article of the next *AFL-CIO News* reported, in the second lead headline, the federation's decision. The headline read, "Council defers to membership on fetal issues."

The article noted that the AFL-CIO had decided "to yield to the good and sound judgment of union members on abortion, leaving the emotionally charged issue to the consciences of individual members." The article also referenced the "several unions" that "have adopted pro-choice resolutions" and explained that "some Executive Council members argued for abortion rights even as they agreed to support the federation's impartiality on the issue."

At the time of the AFL-CIO decision, thirteen national and international unions had taken pro-choice positions, which were covered in different degrees of prominence in the respective union publications.

The Association of Flight Attendants has been one of the few unions that actively involved its members in the reproductive rights debate. The magazine ran side-by-side viewpoints by two national union presidents stating opposing positions on choice. The union later mailed members a postcard on which they could express their views about choice directly to the national office.

In local labor publications, coverage of the choice issue has been nearly nonexistent. One notable exception has been *Trade Winds*, the 7,500-circulation newsletter of Machinists Local Lodge 1781 in Burlingame, California. Fewer than 17 percent of the local's members are women, but that didn't stop *Trade Winds* editor Dennis Hitchcock from publishing an article on why women's reproductive freedom is a labor issue, written by a member who attended a pro-choice rally in Washington, D.C. The union had no position on the choice issue at the time, and Hitchcock knew that publishing the article would cause controversy. But he ran the article anyway, with the member's byline and an editor's note explaining that the article did not reflect union policy and inviting other opinions. Hitchcock expected letters—and got them. He published these letters in subsequent issues to provide "a forum for free and open discussion." Members, he reports, were "extremely pleased at the local's openness in discussing the issue."

A Status Report

The labor press coverage of the choice debate raises important questions about the overall labor press coverage of issues that affect women.

"Coverage is getting better," says Bill Pritchett of SEIU, "but the attention to and coverage of women is still not commensurate with the need or the percentage of women in the work force. We still have a very, very long way to go."

"Many national unions do an excellent job, but *real* improvement will come about only when more women become union leaders," asserts Lorraine Swerdloff of the Letter Carriers.

In the meantime, labor editors, men and women alike, are emphasizing, as IBEW's Mary Ann VanMeter puts it, that issues once limited to women now affect men as well. In a society in which two wage earners in a family are the norm, not the exception, adds Ken Germanson of the Allied Industrial Workers, "many workers' issues are also 'women's' issues."

The labor press, on the whole, still needs to treat women as part of the mainstream of the labor movement and not as peripheral. All workers share common concerns: economic and job security, dignity on the job, a fair share of the wealth workers help create, a better life for our children. Labor publications need to deliver this message, and, fortunately, more and more are doing so.

This trend is not driven by the growing numbers of women represented in top union leadership positions. In fact, the number of women in top leadership is not growing nearly as fast as the number of women entering the work force. What is driving the labor press to better coverage of women's issues is, in part, a growing consciousness about women in labor among union leaders.

Labor leaders today understand the demographic trends. In the huge influx of women into the work force, they see a vast potential for organizing, particularly because polls show that women as a group generally support unions more than men. Any labor leader concerned about labor's survival and growth will naturally be open to steps that make union publications more appealing to the rapidly expanding number of women members and potential members.

The increased overall national attention to sexual harassment and other women's workplace issues is also helping to broaden the content of labor publications. National headlines frequently offer editors salient angles for addressing important women's issues. The International Labor Communications Association is helping this process along by providing editors both a forum for discussing these current events and ideas on how to present them effectively from a labor perspective.

Union publications are often the only direct link unions have with their members. In recent years, more union presidents have come to understand the importance of these links. Top union leaders are permitting their editors a degree of freedom many weren't allowed in the past—the freedom needed to serve as sensors of currents within the labor movement and society at large. Today, more and more labor editors are sensing these currents. They are increasingly defining the concerns characterized in the past as exclusively women's issues as work and family issues of interest to all workers. This trend isn't uniform, but it's real—and it's growing. The coverage of women and issues of concern to them has become far more prominent in union publications.

The Labor Press: Solidarity and the Fight against Racism

J. J. Johnson

The best labor publications in America today consistently make notable contributions to the fight for racial and economic justice. This should be no surprise. Unions unite individuals with common problems across broad racial and ethnic lines. Their press is well positioned to record the activities of these diverse groups, working and struggling together.

Unfortunately, on an overall basis, the labor press effort to cover racial and ethnic groups as they work and struggle together falls far short. Union newspapers too often consider coverage of the concerns of any particular group as either divisive or outside their purview. This stance springs from a narrow view of the labor press role, a view that treats labor publications as house organs for self-promotion that report leadership accomplishments and a limited range of union activities.

The failure to take a broader view consigns the labor press to a role of chronicler, not shaper, of events. The labor movement today needs more than chronicling. The fight for racial equality requires an activist press nurtured in the soil of democracy, inclusion, and empowerment, not choked by the weeds of strict censorship and control.

An activist publication is an organizer and an educator. It encourages debates and provides a forum for the frank discussion of controversial issues.

After the victory of the United Mine Workers against the Pittston coal company in 1989, UMW President Richard Trumka announced that "the 1980s belonged to them, but the '90s are ours." Some strug-

J. J. Johnson edits the publication of District Council 1707 of the American Federation of State, County and Municipal Employees. AFSCME Council 1707 represents workers employed by New York City–area nonprofit agencies.

gles since then, at Eastern Airlines and the *New York Daily News*, have indeed forced management retreats. Yet, overall, labor at the outset of the 1990s remains on the defensive, with bargaining limping along and membership eroding. Today, less than 17 percent of the work force is unionized. The labor movement needs a net annual increase of 1 million members just to increase its membership by 1 percent per year.

Labor's declining fortunes in the 1980s mirrored, not coincidentally, the declining fortunes of African-Americans in the very same years. The advances of the 1960s and 1970s have largely been undone. In 1970, for instance, the median income of African-American families was 61.3 percent that of white families. By 1989, the percentage had fallen to 56.2. In 1980, the African-American poverty rate was 2.8 times the poverty rate for whites. By 1989, African-Americans were more than three times as likely to be poor.

Perhaps the most alarming statistic of all is that, according to the Sentencing Project, a nonprofit organization that promotes alternative punishment and sentencing reform, nearly one of every four young Black men in the United States today is behind bars, on probation, or on parole. In 1989, 609,690 African-Americans age twenty through twenty-nine were under the control of the criminal justice system. That total represented 23 percent of the Black male population in that age group. For white men in the same age category, the figure was 6.2 percent. In the late 1980s, the Sentencing Project adds, the number of Black men of all ages enrolled in college stood at 436,000. In a very real sense, the social safety net has been replaced by the dragnet.

The 1991 recession has made matters worse. Past recessions have had a disproportionate impact on the Black community, which traditionally fails to regain the lost ground in previous recoveries. How families fare in recessions is a function of several factors, including the amount of reserve financial assets a family has at its disposal. Based on data from the Bureau of Labor Statistics, the National Urban League concludes that "lower income whites, on average, could be expected to survive the recession more than 3.7 times longer than similarly situated African Americans."

The interconnection between the crisis in the labor movement and the crisis in the Black community suggests a unity of interest that should inform the strategy of the labor movement and the labor press. The struggle for racial equality needs to be placed within the context of the campaign to revitalize the labor movement as a whole, with the labor press enlisted as a critical weapon in such a campaign.

How? One example: During preparations for the AFL-CIO Solidarity Day 1991 demonstration and rally in Washington, most union publications highlighted the three major goals of the action: legislation banning the permanent replacement of strikers, national health care reform, and full freedom of association abroad and at home. Some union publications, including most AFSCME newspapers and newsletters, featured two other Solidarity Day demands: aid to states and cities and passage of the Civil Rights Act. The added AFSCME demands recognized that communities the nation over face inhumane budget cuts and a rising tide of racism and sexism. The inclusion of these two demands helped broaden minority participation and cement labor's ties to minority communities.

Demographic changes also necessitate a reassessment of labor's approach. The 1990 census revealed, to give one example, that minorities now constitute more than half the resident New York City work force. Based on the census figures, the U.S. Bureau of Labor Statistics predicts that by the year 2000, one-third of the new entries to the U.S. labor market will be people of color.

If the labor movement is to reverse its decline, it must develop methods to reach and influence these new entrants into the labor market. To do so, labor cannot restrict itself to workplace issues. Unions need to reach beyond the workplace and build bridges with labor's natural allies—and labor has no more important ally than the African-American community.

Unions can be more than mechanisms for winning pay raises or protecting pension benefits. Unions can and must become leaders in a movement that advances social justice and universal human values, a movement that helps our society find a way to provide every man, woman, and child with the opportunities that the wealthiest society on earth should be able to offer all its people: decent health care, world-class education, affordable housing, safe streets and drug-free communities, and protection against all forms of discrimination.

The labor press, for its part, needs to follow members beyond the workplace, into their communities and homes. The labor press ought to be exposing the failure of banks to provide mortgages for minority families, spotlighting the overcrowding of America's urban schools, telling the stories of members denied quality health care.

The press does not have to venture beyond the labor movement itself to highlight concerns in the African-American community. For twenty years, the Coalition of Black Trade Unionists (CBTU) has toiled to make the issues of concern to Black trade unionists the concerns of the labor movement as a whole. But few trade union publications cover the CBTU and even fewer seek the opinions of CBTU leaders on relevant issues.

Jobs and freedom, economic justice and civil rights, are indivisible. Economic justice is a precondition for social progress and political democracy. As long as barriers to equal access to jobs, promotions, and union cards remain in place, the labor movement will fail to broaden its appeal.

Workers who have lost their jobs and those who have never held jobs can either be a force to strengthen the labor movement or a force to be used against it. What approach the labor movement and its press takes to the often minority unemployed will in large measure determine their allegiance.

One case in point is the 1990 *Daily News* strike in New York. During this strike, the *Chicago Tribune* parent company of the *News* charged that some of the striking unions were racially exclusive. Sadly, the printing trades unions had not vigorously opposed the exclusionary policies of *News* management during the 1960s and 1970s, and that inaction left them in a weak position to rebut management claims.

Right from the start of the *News* strike, the *Tribune* took pains to hire Black scabs and provide papers at no charge to the homeless, also predominantly minorities, to hawk on the streets and subways. But the unions and the strike support committee worked hard to counter management's gambit. The strikers and their supporters helped organize the homeless to fight for essential services and employment opportunities. Some union publications carried pieces that acknowledged the homeless and unemployed as the strikers' fellow victims.

These efforts at outreach to the broader community kept the boycott against the *News* an effective strike tactic. But the questions raised by the strike continue to bedevil the labor movement as a whole. Too many unions continue to exclude minorities and women as active participants, and management continues to exploit this cleavage.

The outreach effort by striking *Daily News* unions recalled campaigns won by unions and other progressive forces in the 1930s. As part of President Franklin D. Roosevelt's New Deal, several million workers were employed by the government on public works projects that constructed thousands of schools and other public facilities. The Civilian Conservation Corps and the Work Progress Administration's Federal Theater Project put hundreds of thousands of people to work. Unions were at the forefront of these developments. The labor press championed these causes. And many of those who were aided by the programs subsequently joined unions and became militant activists.

By identifying unions with the problems of all working people and their communities, labor in the 1930s won the allegiance of those beyond union ranks. Such an approach can be equally useful today, throughout the nation but particularly in the South, where the nation's lowest unionization rate and wages are found.

The late Dr. Martin Luther King once remarked that southern and northern reaction was the major roadblock to social advancement in the United States. It was in the southern city of Memphis, Tennessee, that Dr. King was assassinated. He was in Memphis to aid a strike of AFSCME sanitation workers. William Lucy, AFSCME secretary-treasurer and president of the Coalition of Black Trade Unionists, later remarked that the strikers' subsequent victory "demonstrated that the struggles for human dignity, civil rights and workers' rights are linked by a common thread of solidarity."

Mindful of this reality, in the spring of 1990, the Reverend Jesse Jackson and Jack Sheinkman, the president of the Amalgamated Clothing and Textile Workers Union, embarked on a four-day organizing tour of the Deep South. The presence of Jackson and Sheinkman together had significance far beyond the tangible results of the tour. Their unity embodied the conjunction of labor, civil rights, and political empowerment. The two told a Rainbow Coalition conference that their task in the South was to organize the unorganized *and* register the unregistered.

Unfortunately, such cooperation is more the exception than the rule—and the exceptions are not generally accorded the importance they deserve even in the labor press. The mainstream media alerted the entire nation to the United Auto Workers 1989 election defeat at the Nissan factory in Smyrna, Tennessee. Yet few Americans or trade unionists know of the UAW victories at Mack Truck in South Carolina, Freightliner in North Carolina, or Coats, an equipment manufacturer not far from Nissan's Smyrna plant.

In its victory over the S. Lichtenberg drapery manufacturing plants in Georgia, ACTWU formed a Citizens Commission on Justice that included civil and women's rights leaders. Of the five hundred workers who won reinstatement and back pay at Lichtenberg, more than 90 percent were African-American women. So, too, were the twenty-five workers whose lives were snuffed out at the Imperial Foods processing plant in Hamlet, North Carolina, when they were trapped behind locked doors during a fire in an uninspected building. Only occasionally do we catch a glimpse of these women in the pages of labor publications.

Other southern organizing victories have been won in recent years by the United Food and Commercial Workers, the United Rubber Workers, and the National Union of Hospital and Health Care Employees. These victories have received precious little attention.

To multiply these gains would require a multi-union campaign and a commitment on the part of unions to battle racism and reaction. The labor press would have to be in the front ranks of such a battle. A coordinated organizing drive in the South would probably take tens of millions of dollars—a princely sum, but no more than the United Auto Workers, the American Federation of Teachers, and the American Federation of State, County and Municipal Employees spent during the 1990 campaign to win the right to represent Indiana state workers. However large the cost to launch an effective campaign across the South, the cost of the failure to do so already has been much greater.

Cost is just one reason for labor's reluctance to organize in the South. Chief among the others is labor's unwillingness to tackle the racist divisions that plague the region. Unions, for example, were correctly concerned with former Klan leader David Duke's 1990 senatorial and 1991 gubernatorial campaigns in Louisiana. Some dispatched organizers to the state to work for Duke's defeat. These organizers talked largely to Black voters about the need to defeat Duke. Few made concerted attempts to reach white workers with their message.

One organizer noted that one of his most militant trade unionists was a Klan member and that he didn't know how to raise the issue. UAW's *Solidarity* magazine provided the answer several years ago when it ran a story about a member who had forsaken the Klan after becoming involved in the union. Such a personal story is a far more effective antidote to racism than a pronouncement from on high.

In 1991, during Duke's gubernatorial campaign, few unions followed up creatively on *Solidarity*'s approach. The labor press missed an opportunity to run stories that explain exactly what the policies of the Dukes of this world mean for working people.

These stories do not come easily; they require research and digging that sometimes are beyond the reach of publications strapped for resources. But labor editors too often don't tap the resources that *are* readily available. They overlook their own members who are activists in organizations such as the CBTU, the A. Philip Randolph Institute, the Labor Committee for Latin American Advancement, and the Coalition of Labor Union Women. A telephone call to a member of one of these organizations can create a "hook" for a dramatic and personalized story. Jobs with Justice, the labor-community coalition initiated in the mid-1980s, offers editors another important vehicle for merging union issues with community struggles. But union publications, by and large, have not taken full advantage of these opportunities.

New York City, for example, has recently been torn by racial strife, with the commercial media often fanning the flames. The labor press has tended to remain aloof, as if New York's racial strife were happening to "them" and not "us." Such provincialism only plays into the hands of labor's enemies.

Union publications like the *Public Employee Press* of AFSCME's District Council 37, *The Voice of 1707* of AFSCME's District Council 1707, and the *1199 News* of Local 1199 of the Hospital and Health Care Workers Union are notable exceptions. These labor journals have carried effective stories and editorials. The memberships and leaders of these unions are predominantly Black and Latino. We need to see similar effective coverage in unions led by white labor officials.

Organizing campaigns and political and electoral struggles require vast resources, human and financial. They also necessitate a long view, or strategic approach, as opposed to a quick fix. It is the task of the labor press to agitate and educate in this arena. Labor papers must find the unifying issues that build the bridges between unions and those movements outside labor so important to the labor movement's revitalization and growth. Labor must take the lead in the unionization of low-pay sectors in which minorities and women are disproportionately represented—and fight to ensure that all Americans have access to the material resources necessary to exercise their rights and liberties. Labor must place the fight against race and gender discrimination on the top of its agenda. And to do so, unions must fight for the application and extension of affirmative action laws.

No issue may be more critical to the trade union movement than affirmative action. Wthout the strict application of affirmative action, America will never balance the ledger of racial justice. Affirmative action represents more than just doing the right thing; it is intimately interconnected with labor's ability to democratize and revitalize itself.

Unfortunately, in some instances, individual unions have not just failed to make peace with Black, Latino, Asian, and other minority communities. They have gone to lengths to widen the rift. No organization in the United States, for instance, has activated more reverse discrimination suits than the International Association of Fire Fighters. The IAFF helped finance the litigation for white firefighters in Birmingham, Alabama, an action that led to the 1989 Supreme Court ruling, in *Martin* v. *Wilks*, that opened court-approved consent decrees to challenge. The IAFF has entered suits on behalf of applicants who were not even members of the union, while permitting the harassment, firing, and expulsion of dues-paying Black members who sought to integrate fire departments. The situation has improved somewhat since the last convention when members of the International Association of Black Fire Fighters and other progressive firefighters passed a resolution preventing the international from continuing to fund local anti-affirmative-action suits.

Today, affirmative action is the primary tool used to splinter the labor movement. Racial quotas have replaced Willie Horton as the buzzword for the 1990s. Talk of quotas serves to obscure the meaning of affirmative action by introducing the notion of the unqualified absconding with the jobs of the worthy. Affirmative action is truly a complex and emotionally charged issue. Answers do not come easily. What is clear is that attacks on it are being used to perpetuate the consignment of minorities and women to subordinate status.

A publication that engages the affirmative action debate would be making a most important contribution to the entire nation. A dialogue here is sorely needed within the house of labor.

Solidarity, the UAW journal, recently made an important contribution to this dialogue by featuring commentary by Paul Rockwell, a member of SEIU, in its June–July 1991 issue. "Opponents of affirmative action for minorities have overlooked the key American reality— the role of affirmative action in the lives of white men," Rockwell wrote. "Minority programs are in fact only a small part of the spectrum of preferential policies. Tax breaks for corporations, subsidies for homebuyers, mass transit subsidies for white suburbs, bank bailouts for bank executives, selective allotments for immigrants and refugees, price supports for corporate farmers are all shot through with considerations of need and preference."

Concluded the *Solidarity* piece: "Special considerations may be valid or invalid, but preference for those perceived to be in need is a basic concept of American society."

Progressives, in and out of the labor movement, seek a color-blind society. But the tomorrow we seek when race is no longer an issue will never be a reality unless race is recognized as a decisive issue today.

Any organization that seeks to defend the interests of its members by *uniting* them in struggle must address all the stratagems of *division*. By so doing, an organization provides hope, direction, and vision.

Labor has failed to keep pace with the profound demographic and structural changes taking place within the United States. This failure has deepened divisions among workers and sharpened the political crisis spawned by these divisions.

Sadly, the demands of African-Americans and other marginalized victims are viewed as the cause of the crisis, even though the erosion of working class support for the Democratic party has been long in the making. As early as 1984, for example, after President Reagan had busted PATCO, more than half of all white families voted for the Reagan-Bush ticket.

The labor press can play its needed role by helping members make informed decisions. Union papers must see themselves as the alternative, the counterbalance to the divisive themes that echo through the mainstream press. Convincing white workers of the need for affirmative action, cultural diversity, and inclusion is, of course, no easy task. But whatever price labor will pay in this battle is not nearly as great as the cost labor would incur if it turns its back.

Labor Cartoons: Drawing on Worker Culture

Mike Konopacki and Gary Huck

"WORKER NEEDS CARTOONS," announced the *Industrial Worker*, the newspaper of the Industrial Workers of the World union, in 1918. The Wobbly paper wanted "cartoons on industrial union or revolutionary subjects."

That a workers' paper would call for cartoons on union issues is no surprise. That a workers' paper would seek cartoons on "revolutionary subjects" should be no surprise either. Cartoons on revolutionary topics ought to be running in every labor publication.

Revolutionary subjects, after all, have been the stuff of American political cartooning ever since Benjamin Franklin drew his famous severed snake representing eight disjointed colonies above the caption, "JOIN or DIE" (still wise advice for today's workers). A century later, Thomas Nast's indignant and persistent political cartoons helped topple one of America's most powerful politicians, New York City's Boss William M. Tweed, and Frederick Burr Opper's hilarious antitrust satires burst inflated robber baron egos.

America's labor press was, at the start, slow to feature cartooning on such revolutionary subjects. The printing technology of the 1800s required painstakingly difficult wood engravings and expensive machin-

Mike Konopacki began drawing labor cartoons in 1978, between shifts as a Teamster school bus driver, for the Madison Press Connection, *a daily newspaper formed by striking newspaper unions. Konopacki currently works as a labor consultant for Labor Strategies, Inc., in Madison, Wisconsin. Gary Huck draws cartoons full time for the United Electrical, Radio and Machine Workers of America. In 1983, Konopacki and Huck began syndicating their cartoons to the labor press through Huck/Konopacki Labor Cartoons. Konopacki and Huck have coauthored two labor cartoon collections,* Bye! American *and* THEM—More Labor Cartoons by Gary Huck and Mike Konopacki.

ery to print them, machinery too expensive for common workers. As a result, the elaborate woodcuts of the most popular cartoonists of the 1870s and 1880s—Nast, Opper, Frank Bellew, and Joseph Keppler— were found in the establishment publications of the day and not in labor papers.

"Illustrations of any kind were rare in the early American labor press," notes labor humor historian Franklin Rosemont. Other than "the famous arm-and-hammer emblem, first used by the New York General Society of Mechanics and Tradesmen, organized in 1786," early labor papers published little original art. Organized labor didn't develop its own graphic artists "until long after the Civil War," and it wasn't "until the second decade of our own century that labor cartooning really came into its own."

Labor cartooning blossomed, ironically, at the very time new printing processes were undermining the importance of art in the commercial press. In the early 1890s, nearly every large newspaper had a stable of artists to illustrate everything from advertisements to news stories. But with the advent of the photomechanical process and the more widespread use of the halftone, newspaper illustrators and artist-reporters were soon replaced by photographers.

"The political cartoon was driven off the feature pages," Richard Fitzgerald notes in *Art and Politics*, "because photographs were easier and cheaper to produce, and could be supplied in great quantity." This switch from cartoons to photographs carried important consequences. Political cartoons, Fitzgerald points out, are by their very nature "subversive." Photographs mirror life's daily structure. Political cartoons disrupt it, making "jokes and stage whispers and asides at the process of everyday life."

The new printing technologies created more unemployed daily newspaper cartoonists. But they also enabled any worker with a pen and a bottle of ink, or a graphite pencil and sheet of coarse paper, to draw cartoons that were reproducible. As a result, political magazines like the *Masses* (1911–17) attracted numerous cartoonists eager to denounce their plight and the system that created it.

The *Masses*, one of the leading left magazines of the time, had a great impact on cartooning. Cartoonist John Sloan, famous for his *Masses* cover that depicted the Ludlow Massacre, came up with the idea of featuring full-page cartoons with one-line captions. He also chose to reproduce cartoons using linecut instead of halftone. The result was a sharper and more graphic reproduction, simply created by using

John Sloan.
Ludlow, Colorado.
The Masses 5
(June 1914)
Cover.

graphite on pebbled paper. This style, perfected by Sloan and fellow *Masses* cartoonists Art Young, Maurice Becker, and Robert Minor, influenced both labor and establishment cartoonists for decades.

The door was now open. The new technology made newspapers and magazines cheaper to produce, and labor cartoons flourished. Cartoonists such as Ryan Walker, William Gropper, K. R. Chamberlain, and Boardman Robinson appeared regularly in labor and socialist publications. The Industrial Workers of the World (IWW), for its part, developed a cartoon culture that was uniquely its own. The famous Ralph Chaplin, author of our labor anthem "Solidarity Forever," was also an accomplished cartoonist who, along with "Dust" Wallin, C. E. Setzer, and Ernest Riebe, created some of the best work of the 1910s and 1920s. Riebe created what is probably the earliest known labor comic strip, Mr. Block, which first appeared in the *Industrial Worker* on November 7, 1912.

"Mr. Block is legion," IWW editor Walker C. Smith wrote in 1913.

Robert Minor. Pittsburgh. The Masses *8 (August 1916).*

"He is the representative of that host of slaves who think in terms of their masters. Mr. Block owns nothing, yet he speaks from the standpoint of the millionaire; he is patriotic without patrimony; he is a law-abiding outlaw; he boasts of 'our tremendous wheat exports,' yet has no bread on his table; he licks the hand that smites him and kisses the boot that kicks him; he is the personification of all that a worker should not be."

What a worker *should* be is a creator of political art. What the labor press should be is the garden that nurtures the budding worker-artist.

Labor art in today's labor press falls into two categories, the story illustration (often appearing on the cover or within the body of a story) and the cartoon, be it the angry or satirical political cartoon or the occasional comic strip. Given the gradual decline of the labor movement—unions now represent only a small percentage of American workers—and the resulting shrinkage of the labor press, labor art is finding fewer and fewer gardens in which to grow, which means that America's existing labor media have a greater responsibility than ever to cultivate and protect this fragile crop.

Let us fantasize a bit. Let us envision a labor movement rebuilding itself, its media encouraging the best in political cartooning, satire, and

UE News Service

Fred Wright. Copyright UE News.

131

...AND NOW FOR OPINIONS ON LABOR

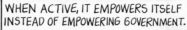

IT'S THE ONE THING POLITICIANS FEAR THE MOST.

WHEN ACTIVE, IT EMPOWERS ITSELF INSTEAD OF EMPOWERING GOVERNMENT.

WHEN ACTIVE, IT PREVENTS LAW-MAKERS FROM PANDERING TO A FEW WEALTHY SPECIAL INTERESTS.

WHEN ACTIVE, IT CAN DEFEAT THE SELF-AGRANDIZING POLITICIAN.

WHAT, IN HEAVEN'S NAME **IS** THIS **HORRIBLE** THING?

A SWARM OF INFORMED UNION **VOTERS!**

KONOPACKI
H/K LABOR CARTOONS

art. The pages of the labor press now run political cartoons that are unafraid to skewer and lampoon both our oppressors and ourselves. We see comic strips that challenge the best in the daily papers. Labor video productions feature the finest animated political cartoons around (at this point, they would be the *only* animated political cartoons around). Labor humor and satire magazines that rival pop culture journals like *MAD*, the *National Lampoon*, and *Spy* appear everywhere.

This is the future we need to create. Labor's media must become outlets for the creative genius of American workers, breeding grounds for the satirists and artists who now toil unknown within the ranks. The voice of labor must be heard in *all* its incarnations, including the snicker, the laugh, and the guffaw.

Cartoon Power

Besides supplying ample doses of snickers, laughs, and guffaws, of course, cartoons play a vital role in the communication of political ideas. People don't just look at cartoons, they interact with them. They cut them out and stick them on refrigerators, bulletin boards, office doors, machines at work. They wear them on T-shirts and carry them on picket signs.

Cartoons communicate with people the way people communicate with each other. They draw upon a full range of emotion, much like an impassioned political discussion. When the cartoon hits upon the right combination of intellect and humor, fact and fantasy, irony and anger, it is recognized in an instant with a "That's it! That's exactly the point!" Of course, the reverse is also true; anger over cartoons generates some of the best reading on the letters-to-the-editor page. But this range of emotion only underscores the effectiveness of cartoons.

Political cartoons rage and engage, criticize and idealize, employ and destroy. They are a language spoken at a shout. Political cartoons are a subjective means of *expression*, not an objective means of *information*. Political cartoons reside in the sovereign state of mind of the cartoonist known as the imagine nation. In the imagine nation politicians are drawn, then quartered. In the imagine nation, like Pinocchio, lying politicians are apt to find their noses growing. Often accused of cynicism, political cartoonists are in truth rabid idealists who speak in negatives but think in positives, criticizing inept leadership because they believe that the ept are out there . . . somewhere.

If there is a science to political cartooning, it is that for every reaction there is an action. The cartoonist would rather reform than inform: "Did you know this? Can you believe this? What are you going to do?!"

As readers, we often have opinions on issues, but we may not know how we *feel* about an issue until we see a political cartoon on it. There is an emotional truth to cartoons that touches people in a way no other form of journalism does.

No one touched the labor press the way labor cartoonist Fred Wright did. For five decades, until his death in 1984, Fred Wright worked in his small office at the headquarters of the United Electrical, Radio and Machine Workers of America. There he almost single-handedly supplied the labor press with the best political cartoons of his era. The thousands of cartoons he drew on contract negotiations, health and safety issues, organizing the unorganized, civil rights, women's rights, shop floor humor, and other aspects of union life were published in the labor press around the world. One could easily compile a history of the labor movement from the 1930s to the 1980s from Fred Wright cartoons. The ultimate tribute to the significance of Fred Wright's work is that his cartoons are as much in demand today as ever.

Fred Wright could not have produced the body of work he did from outside the labor movement. He was a worker-artist, drawing on worker culture to draw worker culture.

Fred Wright drew more than a living history of the struggles of and in the labor movement. He also drew a road map for other cartoonists to follow. But of the cartoonists who attempt to follow Fred's map, almost all have to pull off the road to work for gas money. Of all the affiliated unions of the AFL-CIO, not one has a full-time political cartoonist.

Want to revitalize the labor press, want to move the labor movement? Educate, Agitate, Animate!!

Worth a Thousand Words: Photographing Labor

Earl Dotter and Deborah Stern

Unlike the written word, photographs make an instant impression. In the labor press, a photograph declares, in a glance, an issue's importance to a union. Whether the subject is bargaining, a strike, health care, or job safety, a photograph immediately lets readers know how committed the union may be to the matter at hand. Even more important, photographs can reveal how personally involved union members are in their union. You can thumb through any union journal or magazine and know, by reviewing the photographs, whether that union has the vitality that comes from an active, respected rank and file.

Good photographs will lead readers past headlines and captions into the article itself, just as dull, uninspiring photographs may signal that the articles they illustrate aren't worth reading. Unfortunately, the labor press abounds with uninspired, ineffective photos. The same tired photos appear again and again in union publications: the talking heads with dark shadows rearing up behind them, the grinning back-pay award winner accepting a back-pay check from a grinning union leader, the union official speaking from behind a lectern, union mem-

Earl Dotter began his photojournalism career while attending the School of Visual Arts in New York City in the late 1960s. A VISTA volunteer in the early 1970s, Dotter met coal miners working to reform the United Mine Workers union and later became the photographer for the revitalized United Mine Workers Journal *from 1973 to 1977. Since that time, Dotter has worked for many labor unions, emphasizing workplace and occupational health and safety subjects. Deborah Stern, a graduate of the George Washington University National Law Center, has served for the past nine years as in-house counsel to the United Mine Workers in Washington, D.C., and has recently taken a leave of absence to work with her husband, Earl Dotter.*

Working together, photographer and subject can create photographs that communicate with sensitivity and impact. Earl Dotter shot this photograph in 1976 on assignment with the United Mine Workers Journal *in Clearfield, Pennsylvania.*

bers standing around at a rally, holding ready-made, preprinted plac-ards.

These sins of poor labor photography are readily correctable. But using photos right, using photos to drive home a union's determination to serve members and pursue the issues that concern them, takes real understanding—on the part of the photographer, the labor editor, and, of course, the union leadership. Each has an important role to play. Photographers must be able to seek out opportunities for photo-graphs that draw attention to the issues. Editors must understand how such photographs give the union publication added impact. Union officers must support the use of photographs that do more than just campaign for incumbents.

A good editor understands that photographs serve the labor press best when they don't just embellish a story, but tell it. Unions offer photographers a high drama environment, particularly at the local level, where stories of security versus poverty, safety versus disability, health versus disease unfold on a regular basis. Good photographs can capture that drama.

For bad photographs, there is simply no excuse. There are always alternatives. Instead of publishing photos of talking heads, for instance, why not illustrate the subject the heads are talking about? Instead of running a mug shot of a member quoted in support of union-backed health and safety legislation, why not picture that member in the work environment, either exposed to the hazard at issue or protected from that hazard by the union contract?

Instead of always publishing photographs of grinning grievance winners accepting back-pay awards, why not run photos that dramatize the impact of management's improper behavior? If an illegal firing cost a grievant considerable income, why not show the grievant riding the bus to run errands because her car had been repossessed? Instead of boring photos of leaders speaking at union meetings, why not focus the camera on the response of union members to the speaker? If members are debating a topic, why not shoot photos that show debate taking place?

As these questions make clear, a little effort and imagination can create photographs that engage readers and speak to the hearts and minds of the union rank and file. But in today's labor press union members too often take a back seat to union leaders. The boring publications that result do little to invigorate the rank and file.

The most overlooked area of rank-and-file life, in union publications, is the home. Labor publications are edited as if there were an invisible barrier between the job site and the home. But nothing can dramatize the positive effects of union representation better than the photographs shot when a photographer enters the worker's home. In a country where so many workers have no health insurance, for instance, a photograph of a worker's child home from a life-saving, fully paid hospital visit can speak volumes about the impact of the union on daily life.

Company abuses can also be graphically illustrated by photographing off the work site. The camera is uniquely positioned to document, with unparalleled intensity, the impact of corporate "profits first" policies on union families: the laid-off worker holding a stack of unpaid bills, the children who can't concentrate on schoolwork because they're hungry, the visits to crowded emergency rooms that become absolutely necessary when private health insurance terminates. The camera can

MARCH-APRIL 1991

PROUD TO BE UNION

WE DARE DEFEND OUR RIGHTS

These striking photos by Jackson Hill originally appeared in color in the United Auto Workers Solidarity *magazine.*

document both the dignity of workers who cope with these difficulties and the support they receive from their union. Photos in these situations can both highlight the union in action, helping members overcome hard times, and help expose company practices that are callous to employees.

Labor publications can be powerful public relations tools when they use photography skillfully to cover rank-and-file life because publica-

144

tions oriented to the rank and file don't just have a positive impact on union members. They also have an impact on employers and larger public audiences.

In the early 1970s, for instance, a rank-and-file rebellion in the coalfields overthrew the entrenched leadership of W. A. "Tony" Boyle at the United Mine Workers of America. The Miners for Democracy movement eventually installed a new president and instituted democratic reforms that included a new approach to the union publication, the *UMW Journal*. Gone were the photographs of union officers on each page, framed by obeisant captions. Instead, the new editor and *Journal* staff were given unprecedented editorial independence, and the publication began to focus on exemplary rank and filers and featured photographs and articles that inspired pride and action among UMW members.

As the photographer for the *UMW Journal* at that time, coauthor Dotter traveled extensively with other *Journal* staffers through the coalfields, visiting miners at the mines and coal preparation plants where they worked, and their families at home. He had the time to get acquainted with members and encourage them to collaborate on his photographs. The miners and Dotter would often talk about the articles that his photographs would illustrate and toss around suggestions for settings that would send the best pictorial message to the readers. Many times he would photograph miners at home and then meet with them again, the following day, at the mine. At the home, they would discuss ideas for pictures underground, and the miners would prepare

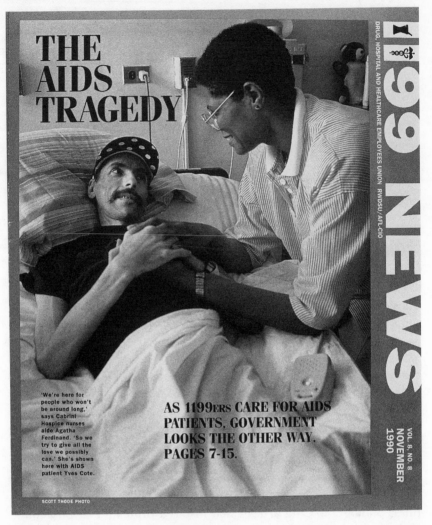

THE AIDS TRAGEDY

DRUG, HOSPITAL AND HEALTHCARE EMPLOYEES UNION, RWDSU/AFL-CIO

1199 NEWS

VOL. 8, NO. 8
NOVEMBER
1990

'We're here for
people who won't
be around long,'
says Cabrini
Hospice nurses
aide Agatha
Ferdinand. 'So we
try to give all the
love we possibly
can.' She's shown
here with AIDS
patient Yves Cote.

AS 1199ERS CARE FOR AIDS
PATIENTS, GOVERNMENT
LOOKS THE OTHER WAY.
PAGES 7-15.

SCOTT THODE PHOTO

This photo essay by Scott Thode, published in the 1199 News, *warmly evokes the bond between patients and the caregiver members of District 1199, Drug, Hospital and Healthcare Employees Union.*

him for potential management restrictions on access and the mine's alien environment.

This collaborative work between photographer and subject brought forth the intimate images of coal miners and coalfield culture that Dotter was able to capture during those years. The photographs didn't just illustrate. They communicated a point of view. The subjects spoke to *Journal* readers. Their involvement in the photographic process could be felt.

146

A Contemporary Survey

Almost twenty years have passed since the Miners for Democracy movement brought profound changes to the UMW, but the *United Mine Workers Journal*, under the administration of Richard Trumka, is continuing along a similar path. The August–September 1991 *Journal*, for instance, was an anniversary issue entitled "The UMWA at 100: Looking Back, Looking Ahead." The issue makes excellent use of historic and contemporary pictures and text to illustrate lessons from the past relevant to the union's future.

Elsewhere in today's labor press, the United Auto Workers publication *Solidarity* offers one of the best examples of consistent use of eye-catching photography. The March–April 1991 *Solidarity* cover features a Jackson Hill photograph of a member whose cap declares "Proud to be Union." The member's proud expression is caught in a full-face portrait and given extra punch by warm colors and tones and a soft-focus background. The issue itself offers three photo essays, all of which present photographs prominently, encapsulated attractively by the text. The inside cover story, also photographed by Jackson Hill, "Storm Beneath the Calm," relates how the Teledyne Corporation permanently replaced strikers. The piece begins with a two-page color spread of a bucolic Alabama scene, over which the article's title is superimposed, with a smaller inset photograph of a determined-looking striker holding a placard reading, "Be Proud, Not Scab." The photo spread and the inset picture counterpoint each other, the hard reality of striker replacement policies leaping out from an illusory peaceful setting.

Every *Solidarity* issue features a two-page color spread called "This Working Life" that always makes exciting use of color or black-and-white workplace portraits of individual union members from a wide variety of unions. The spreads often have a poster-like quality. Their impact is enhanced by a short corner text block that offers a brief biography of the workers highlighted and points of interest about their jobs.

The *1199 News*, published by the Drug, Hospital and Healthcare Employees Union, AFL-CIO, has recently been redesigned under the administration of its new president, Dennis Rivera. The new format emphasizes both black-and-white and color photographs. The format, a little busy, packs each page with information and photographs. Still, the photos effectively highlight members as workplace activists. In the November 1990 issue, a real standout, photographs by Scott Thode show the loving care that 1199 members bring to their work with AIDS patients. The photographs dignify both the union caregivers and their patients. It is apparent from that issue that the union is proud of its members and that its members are proud of the work they do and of their union.

One of the most professional looking labor publications is the *Union*, published by the Service Employees International Union. What distinguishes *Union* from most labor publications in its general interest approach. The magazine covers topics that would engage anyone interested in labor issues. *Union* is printed on heavy-weight, high-quality, dull-coated stock paper that allows excellent photo reproduction. The layout is uncluttered and easy on the eye. The photographs are generally well-conceived workplace portraits that emphasize individual work and character. The portrait subjects often make strong eye contact with the camera, creating rapport with the reader. The color saturation of the photos is excellent, translating the most subtle hues faithfully. The magazine is a quarterly, and this low frequency presumably permits the single-issue budget necessary to support the expense of producing a union journal of this caliber.

The winter 1991 *Union* features UAW-represented GM-Saturn workers. The cover by *Time* magazine's Ted Thai, entitled "Comeback Time for Union-Built American Cars," shows roughly thirty United Auto Workers members standing proudly around a Saturn automobile. The inside story, "Looking for a New Car," is interspersed with photographs of cars produced by new partnerships between Japanese and UAW-represented American car manufacturers. The photos of the

This Service Employees Union *magazine cover by Ted Thai nicely couples UAW members with the auto they produced.*

cars, standard ad-agency shots, communicate to readers the options for purchasing union-made vehicles. Typical of the magazine's style, the article and photos are upscale and cover a topic of general interest from a union perspective.

Finally, *Labor Unity*, the publication of the Amalgamated Clothing and Textile Workers Union, demonstrates that a labor magazine can

Ernesto Mora both writes and photographs for the Amagamated Clothing and Textile Workers Union's Labor Unity. *This photo illustrated an article on a successful internal organizing campaign in a Texas boot factory. The camaraderie so evident in the photo helps explain why the campaign succeeded.*

make effective use of photographs and high-quality design without paying for glossy paper or using other high-cost production techniques. *Labor Unity*, a tabloid, is printed on good-quality newsprint, with black-and-white reproduction and spot color. *Labor Unity* has always made the effort to photograph union members in the workplace or actively involved in the union's programs. Many successful photos are shot by staff reporters, such as Ernesto Mora, whose portraits on the job convey the strength and dignity of his subjects. Gary Schoichet, a regular free-lance contributor to *Labor Unity* and the UAW's *Solidarity*, excels at taking pictures that exude camaraderie among workers. His cover shot on the March–April 1991 issue, on the subject of International Women's Day, is a fine example.

Working with Photographers

Most labor unions operate under budget constraints. Not surprisingly, photography often ranks low on the list of spending priorities.

150

Labor Unity

Volume 77, Number 2
March - April 1991

THE OFFICIAL PUBLICATION OF THE AMALGAMATED CLOTHING AND TEXTILE WORKERS UNION, AFL-CIO, CLC

ACTWU Celebrates International Women's Day
Organizing ✷ Bargaining
Fighting for Workers' Rights

Gary Schoichet manages to establish an easy informal rapport with his subjects, and the collaborative result is apparent.

Good free-lance photographers can be expensive, and many labor publication editors assume that their services cannot be afforded. But with a little understanding of each other's needs, good free-lance photography should be within the reach of the labor press. By offering a photographer a sufficient number of days of shooting at one time and location to make a job worthwhile, a union might be able to obtain a day rate within its means. By hiring a photographer to shoot a variety of

A conference on meeting the needs of Deaf union members gave photographer Gary Schoichet a fine opportunity to capture Deaf co-workers communicating for ACTWU's Labor Unity.

events, work sites, and members consecutively, an editor can get a variety of photographs that can be used in the union's publications over time, and the photographer gets an overall fee that adds up to a sum that's attractive.

Editors need to understand that free-lancers seek challenging photo opportunities that benefit their stock picture collection over the long run. Stock photo sales to textbook companies or general interest magazines are vital to a free-lancer's income. It is also in organized labor's best interests, of course, for this work to reappear, published by the mass circulation media. Professional free-lancers also look for exhibit opportunities, and the chance to photograph interesting material can encourage a photographer to show flexibility on the question of budget.

Quality photographers look for both quality publications to showcase their work and editors who respect the photographer's product. A labor publication that uses photographs well and returns negatives and slides promptly is likely to find free-lance photographers eager to work hard for that publication.

Labor unions often lose money, and photographers lose valuable photography time and opportunities, because of sloppy planning before a shoot. It is critical that local unions and company management know beforehand why and when a photographer will be on site. Without this advance notice, photographers often must suffer through frustrating down time while staff and management negotiate access and the like. The better the advance work, the faster and more effectively the photographer can work. Whenever possible, the photographer should be accompanied by a union representative who knows the members to be photographed and can handle any misunderstandings or problems that might arise. The photographer would also do well to ascertain, in as much detail as possible, how the union wants to use the photographs it is commissioning. Usually, when an editor and a free-lancer develop a long-term relationship, they can rely on each other to fulfill their respective tasks.

Good labor photographers feel deeply for the subject they're photographing. A photographer who respects and cares for the subject will approach the subject with that attitude. By taking the time to explain to the subject why a photograph is being taken, the photographer can overcome that person's reflex simply to smile for the camera. Subjects who understand the reason the photographs are being made are more likely to act natural and project an attitude appropriate for the circumstances. The photographer's goal should be to produce a photograph that has the same impact on the viewer that the actual moment had on the photographer at the time the picture was taken. This is especially true when photographing a subject who has been victimized. Victims who do not project a sense of their individual uniqueness in photographs can easily become dehumanized freaks for whom the viewer feels little compassion.

The Challenge of Labor Photography

Labor press efforts to document the lives of union members and the social and economic issues that concern them can create a legacy for all time, as the photographs of Lewis Hine vividly demonstrate. Hine photographed working men, women, and children in the first third of this century. His portraits emphasized human traits of dignity and self-respect common to the human family. By stressing the common ground between the viewer and the subject, Hine established a reference point that enables the viewer to identify with the subject's situation. His photographs even today move viewers to understand and empathize with the human plight that he documented.

"There are two things I wanted to do," Lewis Hine once said. "I wanted to show things that had to be corrected. I wanted to show things that had to be appreciated."

Today's labor photographs have the capacity to inform future generations of what had to be corrected in our time and to appreciate and learn from those who worked so hard to correct them.

The Promise of Technology: A Case Study

Mary Ann Forbes

There is no doubt about it: desktop publishing is revolutionizing union journalism. The experience of my union, the Association of Flight Attendants (AFA), offers an interesting case study of how desktop publishing has helped one small union make a qualitative leap forward in membership education and communication, both at the local and the national levels. Our AFA decision to purchase desktop publishing hardware and software in 1986 revitalized our entire communication structure, staff to field, and more than quadrupled membership service the first year of operation.

About the Flight Attendants

The Association of Flight Attendants currently represents thirty thousand flight attendants on eighteen U.S. airlines. AFA is the largest national flight attendant union, but, in size, it's comparable to a large local in one of America's bigger international unions. AFA's small membership dues base means that budgets are always tight. Yet AFA flight attendants, middle-class, college-educated, and employed by some of the wealthiest, most sophisticated airline corporations in the world, expect professional-looking and timely publications from their association.

When I first joined the AFA staff, as managing editor, I entered a newly deregulated industry fraught with labor-management strife. AFA members needed to be kept updated about the latest layoffs,

Mary Ann Forbes is the former director of publications for the Association of Flight Attendants, AFL-CIO. A labor journalist for the past eleven years, Forbes is currently the director of publications and information for the African-American Labor Center in Washington, D.C. She holds an M.A.L.S., specializing in women and workplace ethics, from Georgetown University.

mergers, bankruptcies, and negotiations. Meanwhile, the media needed to be educated about the issues flight attendants face. With outdated technology and limited budget and staff, the AFA Communications Department found these impossible objectives to meet—until desktop publishing.

There was a time in the labor movement, back in the late 1970s, when the mere suggestion of using computers to bring typesetting in-house—to cut costs—would bring accusations of subconscious anti-union tendencies and even threats of picket lines. Those were difficult years for traditional typesetters. All across the United States, new computer technologies were eliminating union typesetting positions. For labor leaders, using traditional typesetting arrangements became an act of solidarity with struggling workers, and they continued to have their publications typeset traditionally, even if that meant paying higher costs and maintaining outdated and inefficient production techniques.

When I joined the AFA staff in 1984, attitudes about in-house typesetting were changing. AFA had rented a computer typesetter that took up two-thirds of our designer's office space. Surrounded by bulky, filthy machinery, our designer, Sarah Shaw, would have to squeeze between the typesetter and her desk to climb to her light table to work. Wet, typeset slicks hung to dry on every available door, bookcase, and wall. I don't remember which was worse to face each morning, drinking Sarah's hot "toxic" tea that smelled like herbal toner solution, or trying to interpret Sarah's esoteric commands as she tried to coach me how to typeset last-minute copy changes—so she could kneel on the floor and paste down page mechanicals due to the printer any minute.

The most frustrating part of all was that we could typeset only one project at a time. If a large AFA council demanded service, every other project came to a halt, including the national magazine. In a crunch we might be able to send a newsletter to an outside vendor to be typeset, at considerable cost, but AFA's limited funds did not allow for much of that. Our staff was frustrated and overworked, not by demands from the field but by technological inefficiency.

Finally, our production assistant quit. The day her replacement started, our department head announced her own departure. Sarah and I were shocked. Our industry was in chaos. Our members were desperate to hear from their union. Our union couldn't afford expensive outside services. Something needed to be done.

AFA Invests in Desktop Publishing

Aware that her Communications Department was in trouble, then AFA president Linda Puchala stopped in to chat with the staff one day. She listened to our problems, and then, like the experienced politician she was, Puchala turned back and challenged us to create a proposal that would turn the department around.

Sarah was well-informed about the new desktop publishing systems, at that point mostly Macintosh, that were just coming on the market. I was skeptical. I felt it was one thing to be able to set type, but I wasn't confident that a writer could learn to design and produce newsletters well. Soon Sarah had me convinced. Together Sarah and I confidently proposed to President Puchala that the Communications Department be split into a Publications Department and a Public Relations Department. That way, we could focus our energies on internal membership education, and a separate PR department could focus on educating the public. For too long we had been stretched and torn between trying to service the locals while attempting to put AFA's name in the news. Sarah and I wanted to meet the communication demands of our local leaders by specializing in desktop publishing.

We proposed spending $22,000 to purchase new Macintosh desktop hardware and software that would allow four employees to work on four separate projects simultaneously, cleanly, and efficiently.

President Puchala was immediately interested. She remembered joining us late one evening, with the union's collective bargaining director, on a paper-strewn floor, working feverishly to paste together the dried slicks of a critical tentative agreement for United flight attendants. She understood our situation. Several weeks later, we had the go-ahead we were after. Before long, our new Publications Department had new space and new staff.

The new desktop hardware and software did just what we had hoped. After a simple installation and a few days training, we were producing a twenty-four-page council newsletter and our national magazine simultaneously.

We divided staff responsibilities in half. The art director and the managing editor focused their time and effort on producing the national magazine, while I, as director of publications, and a production assistant served locals by producing their newsletters. In one year we had tripled the number of projects we sent to the printer—and saved the union expensive typesetting costs as well.

Expanding Service to the Field

The more our staff became proficient with our desktop publishing resources, the more creative ideas we had for improving service to the field. We soon turned our quarterly leadership newsletter into a monthly bulletin board update of industry and union activities, written, edited, and laid out by our Publications Department staff. We saved $920 an issue for printing and postage, as well as long hours of manual paste-up. On top of that, we began

■ developing original mastheads for local union publications;

■ producing departmental updates on safety, research, government affairs, and the airline industry;

■ publishing bulletin board pieces and flyers announcing union meetings in-house for overnight delivery to the field for next-day distribution;

■ helping AFA local councils produce letters to members on their own personalized stationary; and

■ helping negotiating and organizing committees put out their own quick and inexpensive newsletters and bulletin board pieces.

No longer did staff members wait for slicks to dry or for another staffer to complete typesetting a project so someone else could use the typesetter. AFA staff were using their time and talents completely and efficiently throughout the day.

Computerizing the Councils

The situation out in the field was a different story. No one in the field yet had access to desktop publishing, and each AFA local was still submitting its local newsletter in handwritten and typed copy. The largest of these newsletters, a sixteen-to-twenty-four pager for United flight attendants, took AFA staff nearly three days to typeset and ready for layout. The editor of this newsletter, a volunteer flight attendant with no professional journalism experience, was paid for time away from flying to collect the articles and type them on a typewriter for AFA staff to retype into the computer. The system was inefficient, frustrating, and expensive.

About one year after the AFA national office put its desktop publishing system in place, the United Council bought its editor a desktop publishing system. By the next issue, AFA was receiving all copy for the newsletter on a diskette, proofed and ready to be designed and pasted up. Just by providing the department with clean, workable copy already set on the computer, the council had saved at least three days in production time, as well as money for the editor's time off the job.

The next United volunteer editor, flight attendant Bill Gentes, quickly became fascinated with the new desktop system. By working closely with AFA staff, Bill was able to design an efficiently produced, award-winning publication with a predetermined computerized format. Today, Bill and AFA production coordinator Darlene Dobbs are able to move the entire newsletter in and out of production in about one week, not the three weeks production used to take.

As word about desktop publishing spread throughout the union, other local councils followed United's example. With some training and a relatively small investment, the editors of these locals have found that desktop publishing saves them both time and money.

USAir flight attendant leaders recently purchased a computer and laser printer for their editor and completely computerized their publishing operation. Thanks to desktop publishing, an Alaska Airlines AFA local editor can now do editing all across the continent, working either on the equipment he has at home or using the hotel systems available for rent during his trip layovers. This editor even drops by the national office in Washington, D.C., for final editing.

With desktop publishing at hand, local editors are less intimidated by the task of communicating with their members. Local editors enjoy the challenge of learning to operate their desktop publishing systems and come to understand quickly that, in developing their own talents and skills, they are providing a valuable service to their members.

Continuously Improving Service

Over recent years, the AFA Publications Department has gradually upgraded the system we bought in 1986. We now have

- TOPS network software that allows us to transfer documents to other stations through the computer network instead of having to hand-carry disks back and forth.

- Two full-page monitors for the designer and publications coordinator. The large screens save time by allowing the staff to work with two full pages on display at once instead of wasting time scrolling through a partial page every time they want to make a change.

■ Increased storage space and memory that allows us to work faster and store more information.

■ A new, faster Laserwriter NTX printer that allows us to use more fonts.

■ Upgraded PageMaker and Microsoft Word software that give us the state-of-the-art design and word-processing capabilities we need.

■ Antivirus software that protects the system from viruses.

■ A flatbed scanner that permits us to pick up documents and graphics to save copy inputting time and enhance our publications.

We've also added the AFA Public Relations Department to our Macintosh network. AFA PR will now be able to send a fax to an entire media distribution list with only one command, and that should help the department continue its successful media outreach efforts. In 1987, AFA PR received only one unsolicited media call a day. By 1990, coverage of flight attendants' issues was appearing in approximately one hundred newspapers and magazines each month.

The Unexpected Challenges of Desktop Publishing

Desktop publishing has changed forever the way we communicate to our members. It has been a tremendous asset to our union. But the transition to new desktop technologies has also confronted us with many challenges.

Just Saying No

Soon after we installed our desktop system, we realized what our toughest challenge was going to be. Everyone wanted to use the new equipment. We were asked to do everything from word-processing projects to name tags.

At first, Publications staff were willing to try everything we could on the new machines. But then reality hit home. We began to see an increase in the number of less critical projects and more and more evening or weekend hours needed to fulfill them. Eventually, we had to sit down with former AFA national vice-president Juliette D. Lenoir, to whom we reported, and clarify exactly what the department's services should be. We all agreed that prompt service to the councils and the committees that serve them should be the department's primary function, with AFA's national magazine and monthly leadership bulletins also receiving top priority.

New Health Problems

The onset of desktop publishing significantly reduced the health and safety hazards we faced in our predesktop days. But desktop publishing brings its own set of concerns: eyestrain, backaches, headaches, carpal tunnel syndrome, poor ventilation, and even radiation from the monitors and printer.

Publications staffers work long, hard hours trying to meet deadlines and don't always take the breaks they should to reduce the strain on their eyes, backs, and wrists. All of us, as a result, feel the physical effects of a stressful sedentary job.

A year or so ago, AFA found itself negotiating with its staff union to provide screen covers to prevent eyestrain. We have also restricted smoking and tested the air quality in the AFA office. We have created more ergonomically improved workstations. And we encourage breaks. Eliminating all hazards on the job is difficult, but with education, sensitive observation, and enlightened management, even the less obvious dangers can be reduced.

Education and Training

Before we began desktop publishing, I was basically computer illiterate. As a writer, I wasn't eager to give up my yellow pads or depend on myself to set type, determine point size, leading, and fonts. But the desire to improve the efficiency of the department outweighed these concerns.

As I assure our local editors, I was able to learn our original desktop publishing software in just a few short training sessions. Tutorials were available with each software package and complemented the training programs. We learned quickly because, frankly, we had a magazine to get out and requests for services that had to be met.

In short, we learned the system by using it. Software is mastered by experience, just like everything else.

More Training

Never buy a desktop publishing system without intending to upgrade. That's a lesson we learned early.

The desktop publishing industry must have invented planned obsolescence. It seems that just when we master one software package, an upgrade comes out—and you can't upgrade a single piece of software because the new software will often function only with other upgraded software. You obtain that new software, and then you find you need more storage, so now you have to upgrade hardware.

At first I resented these continual upgrades because, like many people, I don't like change. But constant change makes the job more challenging, both to the staff and to the organization, and helps us improve the service we are able to provide.

Desktop Publishing Support for Staff and Field

Now that our United Council and the AFA PR department have their own desktop publishing systems, AFA Publications staff have become our union's unofficial desktop publishing consultants. Production coordinator Darlene Dobbs, originally hired to help the art director produce newsletters, can often be found on the phone advising editors and local leaders on which software to purchase or instructing PR how to use PageMaker.

When I recently upgraded my equipment, I transferred my original computers to another AFA department and to the editor of the large USAir Council. Now these staff and field workers call us for assistance.

The need for a desktop publishing computer expert on staff will continue to grow, and I recently found myself upgrading the production coordinator's job description and status to include this newly evolved responsibility. I cannot envision the department operating without someone who has the technical expertise on which the union has come to depend. All AFA Publications staff positions will now require computer experience.

Consulting Computer Experts

As the head of a new desktop publishing department, I am responsible for advising my union on making computer investment decisions with our members' dues dollars. I feel a tremendous responsibility to make the most informed decisions possible.

A number of good publications for desktop publishers exist, but these periodicals are often lengthy and technical, and I don't have time to read every issue. Today, fortunately, there are experienced computer consultants who can be hired for advice. When we recently purchased nearly $40,000 worth of upgrades and new equipment for the department, I met with two independent consultants and two dealers, as well as my own Publications staff, before finalizing a proposal for AFA's national officers.

Both consultants recommended that our union form a committee of staff and field leaders to construct a long-term plan for computerizing the union. As it is now, because so many of our union leaders are volunteers working from their own typewriters or computers, and because there has been little successful coordination between all the departments within the union, we have not been able to use technology to communicate with each other as efficiently as possible.

Seeking Outside Unionized Services

Desktop publishing has led to the proliferation of nonunionized cottage industries. At AFA, we are always seeking union shops because sometimes we still need to use outside services, to convert MS-DOS formatted documents, for instance, into files that can be brought into our Mac system without rekeyboarding. We also sometimes need to hire temps and free-lancers who specialize in desktop design as well.

Until these small shops are unionized, no one can guarantee that their staffers will have the skills we used to be able to count on when we worked with union typesetters, who had completed union apprenticeship and training programs. It's not easy to organize these small computer companies, but the numbers of organized workplaces are growing. Desktop publishing may be easy to set up and begin to use, but, like other skilled crafts, it needs hardworking, educated, and talented professionals who deserve fair pay and decent working conditions.

Desktop Publishing and the Future

In my eleven years of experience as a union journalist, I've watched labor journalism grow from yellow pads and wet slicks drying on bookcases to a cleaner, healthier, more productive union communication service.

Throughout AFA, we now communicate more often and in a more varied fashion, at a lower cost. We have added fixed assets to our union's net worth instead of wasting money on expensive outside services that have no long-term value to our members. We have revitalized a frustrated, overworked staff by creating constantly changing challenges, a healthier and more productive work environment, and exciting new career options. Most important, we have reduced the valuable time our volunteer local editors must donate to support their union.

Now our members can use time, their most precious commodity, in more efficient and productive ways.

Desktop publishing has revolutionized the world of labor journalism, both at the national and the local levels. As the Association of Flight Attendants' experience proves, desktop publishing has taken off, and it's here to stay. Welcome to the twenty-first century labor press.

"We Do the Work": A Step beyond Print

Daniel S. Beagle

Is television a viable medium for labor journalists who want to go beyond print to reach union members—and their neighbors?

Over the past four years, I've been involved in an effort that seeks to answer this question.

When we started, somewhere in the back of all of our minds was the line from the old movie where Mickey Rooney says to Judy Garland, "Hey, I know, we could put on our own show!"

Our show, "We Do the Work," was founded in late 1987 by a coalition of San Francisco labor unions, community groups, and media professionals. Since then, "We Do the Work" has emerged as the first and only nationally aired program on labor, widely recognized for its consistently high quality. Perhaps our most significant contribution has been our effort to become a "crossover" show—to be unabashedly union and yet to reach out to a broader audience.

The time was right for "We Do the Work" in 1987. The 1981 Machinists' study, described elsewhere in this volume, had sensitized many of us to how badly working people were treated in the media. And the PATCO and other disasters of the early 1980s had convinced everyone in the labor movement that we would be in even bigger trouble if we did not do a better job of explaining ourselves to the public.

In the mid-1980s, the landmark AFL-CIO report, *The Changing*

Daniel S. Beagle joined the staff of the International Longshoremen's and Warehousemen's Union in 1969 when he was hired as the assistant editor of the union's official newspaper, the Dispatcher. *In 1975, Beagle became editor of the* Dispatcher *and information director of the ILWU. In 1988, the ILWU officers asked Beagle to work with "We Do the Work" on behalf of the union. He's currently a member of the program's board of directors and chairs its outreach committee. Beagle works today as a trade union public relations consultant in San Francisco.*

Situation of Workers and Their Unions, sensitized the labor movement—at the highest levels—to the need for better communications. Some internationals were moving ahead on their own. Others were working closely with the AFL-CIO's new Labor Institute of Public Affairs, which appeared to have carte blanche to "do something" about the image of workers. By 1987 pioneering cultural outreach efforts like Local 1199's Bread and Roses Project in New York had begun to inspire and challenge the rest of us.

The San Francisco Bay Area was the right place to start the "We Do the Work" effort. For historical reasons, the Bay Area labor movement has been relatively cohesive and relatively independent. The split between the International Longshoremen's and Warehousemen's Union and the AFL-CIO on a national level had never damaged relationships at the Bay Area local level. The Teamsters, also unaffiliated with the AFL-CIO at the time we started "We Do the Work," were on good terms with most Bay Area unions, and the traditional distance between local building trades and industrial unions was minimal. We did have our jurisdictional and political conflicts in San Francisco, but we also shared a history of trust and civility, which made it possible to consider a project like "We Do the Work."

Other factors also helped us get our effort off the ground. The Bay Area's flagship public TV station, KQED-Channel 9, had been under pressure for many years to originate more local programming to serve the specific needs of the area with greater vigor. Station executives appeared ready to be responsive to a well-organized, institutionally sound effort to put working people on the air.

Finally, in the Bay Area we had something to build on. SEIU Local 790—a large union of public workers from all over the Bay Area—had sponsored a talk show on a small community college PBS station since 1984. Admittedly, Local 790 communications director Ed Herzog was flying by the seat of his pants. But over three years the show gradually began to look professional. The local—by its nature desperate for public support—backed the show financially and gave Ed the time to learn his way around the studio. The local ultimately purchased equipment that allowed Herzog to leave the studio and go out on job sites.

In the fall of 1987, Local 790 officers, who felt that their show could benefit from a broader base, invited Bay Area AFL-CIO labor councils, the state labor federation, and the then-unaffiliated ILWU and Teamsters to join in an effort to create a format that would highlight the perspectives of all workers. This fledgling labor group went on to invite community and church participation, and the resulting coalition became known as "California Working." The new show went on the air in January 1988 on three small Bay Area PBS stations.

The basic concepts, hammered out by the staff committee that took responsibility for the show, were relatively simple. We focused on affiliates of the Public Broadcasting System network simply because we believed PBS would enable us to reach a large and politically aware audience.

But access to PBS carried certain consequences, summed up in the word "balance," that often made us feel we were walking a tightrope. We had to conceive of our programming as broadly as possible. We couldn't be a commercial for unions. We couldn't be strident or ideological. We couldn't talk union shorthand, and we couldn't assume too much, either of our own members, whom we hoped would enjoy the show, or of the general public.

All this meant that we had to show at least two sides to every question. When we did our opening piece on the drive to restore Cal-OSHA—which had been blue-penciled by the governor—we asked for and were given an interview with a top administration spokesman. When we did a show on nonunion projects in the building trades, we gave a reasonable amount of time to the very mediagenic head of the nonunion contractors association. And so on. This approach was necessary to give us credibility with PBS. And, as it turned out, this approach was the right way to go.

Our new program needed to be both informative and entertaining. Our competition was "Entertainment Tonight" at worst, "60 Minutes" at best, not "Salt of the Earth," the classic labor movie.

Eventually, we evolved a basic approach, based on a fast-paced, professionally produced combination of investigative pieces, music, stories on labor's role in the community, interesting and unusual jobs, and comedy. We needed to be serious. But we didn't need to be dull.

Our shows have ranged from reports on the Pittston and Delta Pride strikes to a profile of former Dodger outfielder Gino Cimoli on his rounds as a United Parcel Service driver. We've produced segments on the working people who were the real heroes of the San Francisco earthquake, a history of flight attendants, and an in-depth look at the problems of the California workers' compensation system. One early favorite we did was a feature on the workers who cut the grass and maintain the grounds at the Oakland Coliseum. The piece featured

Dave Stewart and Mark McGwire, who discussed their own grounds-keeping needs as ball players.

Ratings available from our current outlets demonstrate a solid viewer base, which undoubtedly would be higher if we had more funds available for promotion. In the San Francisco Bay Area, viewers in some eighty thousand homes watch the show.

"We Do the Work" is produced by a nonprofit corporation, the California Working Group, Inc., which is affiliated with the Film Arts Foundation. The corporation's board of directors includes executive officers of Bay Area labor councils, as well as delegates from state and regional bodies of all major California unions. Community board members include representatives from religious and ethnic groups and even several corporate representatives. A group of academics, with expertise in labor and communications issues, fills out the board. The board meets quarterly. Day-to-day affairs are delegated to a working committee of board officers, committee chairs, and our two producers.

In June 1990, we contracted with the PBS Central Educational Network to place "We Do the Work" on satellite for acquisition by other PBS affiliates across the country. That effort brought "We Do the Work" to seventeen new stations across the country. "We Do the Work" currently airs in San Francisco, Los Angeles, San Mateo, Eureka, Santa Rosa, and San Diego in California as well as New York City and Buffalo, New York; Washington, D.C.; Indianapolis, Evansville, and Fort Wayne, Indiana; Nashville, Tennessee; Lincoln, Nebraska; Providence, Rhode Island; Charleston, West Virginia; and Flint, Michigan.

Television is an extremely expensive medium, but we remain committed to original, high-quality productions and to ongoing coverage of local events. We don't simply recycle material available at little or no cost that has been produced elsewhere.

Our current budget is approximately $300,000, a bare-bones budget made possible only by the payment of ridiculously low salaries to our staff and substantial in-kind contributions by Bay Area and other unions that cannot be sustained in the long run. The bulk of our funds have come from northern California unions, either through outright donations or a membership plan that, for $600 a year, provides each member union one videotape of the program every month. Several international unions have made substantial contributions. Every additional station that purchases the program also provides income to "We Do the Work," in an amount depending on the size of the market.

"We Do the Work" has also received several grants that, in the last year, totaled 10 percent of our receipts. Another 25 percent has come from corporate sources. Fund-raising in both areas is a top priority. Our annual Joady Awards dinner, which honors unions and media professionals who have worked to tell labor's story to the public, is another important source of funds.

The experience of "We Do the Work" has demonstrated that broadly based labor and community alliances can produce and find an audience for high-quality television programming on workers and the issues that concern them. "We Do the Work" gives labor its first regular exposure on PBS on a national scale.

But much more remains to be done. First, we need to get "We Do the Work" onto more stations. Second, we need to build our audience in the markets that already exist. Third, we need to continue to develop informative and entertaining programming. We've found a voice and a style. We need to get better at it. We need to maintain our base in the trade union movement, while maintaining the independence that makes the program credible to a broader audience.

Finally, we need to assure that we have the financial base to sustain the show over the long haul. Our efforts to raise funds inside and outside the trade union movement have met with increasing success. But if we are to stay on the air and build on the possibilities that have been created, we need dramatically increased support.

Part Four

Labor and Community

An Isolated Survivor: Racine Labor

Richard W. Olson

A few years ago, a contest judge for the UAW Local Union Press Association commented that "every community should have a community-based labor paper like the *Racine Labor*."

But few do. Today, in the United States, the local labor press has virtually disappeared. Yet the *Racine Labor*, after fifty years of publication, is still going strong. How has the *Racine Labor* survived financially and thrived as a strong advocate for social justice? The answer is worth exploring.

Racine is an industrial city of some eighty-five thousand people about thirty-five miles south of Milwaukee. It's a city where the social justice tradition runs deep. In the city's early labor days, nationally famous Milwaukee socialists such as Victor Berger exerted a strong influence on the Wisconsin labor movement.

When Loren Norman was hired in 1941 as the first editor of the *Racine Labor*, the head of the trades council was a socialist. And thirty years later, when I was hired to edit the *Racine Labor*, the president of the paper's board was an IBEW electrician named Earle Poulsen, a friend and backer of Frank Zeidler, the longtime socialist mayor of Milwaukee.

Milwaukee socialism, often disparaged by left critics as "sewer social-

A native of Iowa, Richard Olson was an anti–Vietnam War activist both at Dartmouth College and later in the U.S. Army. In 1972, after getting fired from his job as a cannery worker in Wisconsin during an organizing drive, Olson was hired as editor of the Racine Labor. *In 1979, Olson joined the Public Relations and Publications Department of the United Automobile, Aerospace and Agricultural Implement Workers of America. He is currently the managing editor of* UAW Ammo *and belongs to Local 22 of the Newspaper Guild in Detroit.*

ism," never tried to turn Milwaukee into a utopia, but it delivered progressive, honest government and social services for half a century. In spirit, this socialism was the social democracy that has created a comprehensive welfare state in Sweden and other countries: a mixture of private ownership, strong trade union involvement in government, and elaborate social benefits "from cradle to grave."

Racine workers, perhaps animated by this spirit, have long seen the need for a voice of their own. In the late nineteenth century, the town's printers published a daily labor paper after a lockout of union typographers. The paper, the *Racine Daily News*, gave labor extensive coverage in its early years, including a motion-by-motion account of the 1896 convention of the Wisconsin Federation of Labor, which was held in Racine. But the newspaper folded after several years.

From 1915 to 1927, a paper called the *Labor Advocate* offered Racine trade unionists a heavy dose of news from the national and international levels. But the paper lacked a real local focus and, without much public support, had to suspend publication.

The Depression brought renewed interest in unionism in Racine, and it was only natural that a paper would emerge to reflect the growing labor activity. In rapid succession, the Racine labor community supported weeklies called the *New Day*, the *Racine Day*, and, finally, the *Racine Labor*.

The *New Day*, radical in tone, lasted only a few years. The *Racine Day* and its successor, the *Racine Labor*, found a more successful formula. Clearly, for Depression Racine, a daily labor paper was too ambitious. A paper that just reprinted national and international news was too dull and irrelevant, and the tone of the *New Day* was too strident. By the time *Racine Labor* had survived its first year, Racine trade unionists had the paper they wanted: an activist weekly paper that would be community-oriented. Its politics would be left of center, but not too radical either for the times or the area.

Loren Norman, the first editor of the *Racine Labor*, got his start in labor journalism when Oscar Ameringer, editor of the *Illinois Miner*, offered him ten bucks for a story about the indignities of living off the welfare system. The topic was near to Norman's heart and close to his belly. He had worked off and on in the coal mines of central Illinois for four years.

Norman wrote for the *Illinois Miner*, then ended up studying at Brookwood Labor College in Katonah, New York, where he met his wife, Bette, in 1932. Norman eventually headed back to Illinois, where he helped edit a paper for a miners union challenging the United Mine Workers. He lost that job in a factional fight, then moved on to help organize unemployed workers' committees and the DuQuoin Miners Defense Committee, which sought a pardon for a group of young men charged with killing a young girl during the wars between the UMW and its rival, the Progressive Miners.

It was about this time that Norman learned that a weekly labor paper called the *Racine Day* was in trouble. So Norman headed to Racine to see Francis Wendt, an attorney who was the receiver for the paper and later the mayor of Racine. Wendt asked Norman if he was a communist. Norman replied that he was a socialist. Fine, Wendt replied, Racine was used to socialists, but "we don't want communists around."

Against the advice of a leading local trade unionist who feared that the paper could not survive, Norman accepted Wendt's offer to edit the *Racine Day*. The day he arrived in Racine to begin work, the printer cut off credit.

The *Racine Day* soon folded, and Norman emerged as the editor of the new *Racine Labor*. He quickly found himself under attack first from the left and then from the right.

The first conflict began after three local union presidents brought Norman a press release asserting that "the Yanks aren't coming," from a movement that opposed U.S. entry into World War II. Norman considered the group a communist front and refused to run the release. He had to defend that position before the autoworkers' council, but his opponents didn't get any support for their position, and that challenge quickly faded.

The next challenge came from the right and was more serious. The president of the board of the paper and the manager for the paper claimed the Racine police department had a dossier that labeled Norman a subversive.

The two had Norman fired. At the next meeting of the autoworkers council, one of the leaders of the largest UAW locals in Racine, and a socialist, got up to defend Norman. "Is he guilty of horse thievery?" the union leader asked, then announced that if Norman was fired, his local would pull its subscribers from the paper. With that threat in mind, the paper's board of directors asked Norman to return to work and paid him for the week he had lost.

In Norman's opinion, the paper's business manager and the president of the paper wanted a gossipy, friendly sort of paper—a pap sheet

OUTSIDE IT'S DELIGHTFUL

No one can say that the Wisconsin Supreme Court doesn't have fun.

Furthermore, the boys up there are becoming experts on the weather. They've discovered it changes frequently. But after all that's an advantage and a small price to pay for living in this heavenly climate blessed with snowfall and slippery conditions. If a pedestrian comes a cropper he should have been mindful of these advantages and stepped gingerly.

At least that seems to be the gist of a recent decision in a case involving Marvin Walley, 810 Park av. who sued for damages he charges were sustained as a result of injuries to his wife, Myrtle Ann Walley, in a fall on icy sidewalks at Eighth st. and College av. back on Jan. 1, 1951.

Mrs. Walley suffered two broken vertebrae in her spine and spent several months and several thousand of dollars in hospital and doctor bills while recuperating.

So Walley, a member of Case UAW Local 180, sued Mary Putake as an individual and as administratrix for the state of Rudolph Putake, charging negligence and a nuisance. (The Putakes owned the Eighth st. property).

The State Supreme Court on Jan. 19, 1956 upheld Circuit Judge Elmer D. Goodland's decision that the complaint did not state a cause of action in negligence but left a hint there might be a cause of action in nuisance. On Jan. 19, 1956, Richard Harvey, Jr., attorney for Walley, filed a proposed amended complaint. Judge Goodland upheld this and there was a second appeal to the State Supreme Court. Now the high court has thrown this out and directed the circuit court to dismiss the complaint.

I do not here attempt to pass upon the legal matter involved but as one who walks some 10 to 30 blocks through Racine's streets each day I am intrigued by the sage conclusions of the court about our weather.

The decision in this case, by Justice Grover Bradfoot, observes:

"Snowfall, with its attendant discomfort, is a small price to pay for the many advantages we enjoy as residents of this state. The only thing we can say with authority about Wisconsin weather is that it changes frequently. As a result, we will have many slippery conditions on sidewalks. Every pedestrian must be conscious of that fact and take due care for his own protection.

Here's a woman who suffered serious injuries as well as untold hardships and heavy expenses and 226 days after the accident she is informed that she should watch her step because the weather up here is changeable.

Shades of J. Howard Thompson, this flippant answer has me in stitches. In fact, it's enough to split a vertebra!

UAW Petitions At Insinkerator

The UAW has petitioned for a bargaining representation election at Insinkerator, Fourteenth and Racine streets, according to James Arena, UAW international representative. A hearing on the petition has been set for Feb. 19 at 10:30 a. m. at the company office. Members of the unit will meet Thursday night at Roma Lodge on Forest street. Employes at Insinkerator recently staged a brief sitdown strike and then came to the UAW for help. If a consent election is agreed upon or if the Board orders an election approximately 140 persons are expected to be eligible to vote.

Pawlik Resigns From Clerks Post

Dan Pawlik, jr. secretary-treasurer of State Council 14 of the Retail Clerks International Association, has announced his resignation from that post. Pawlik, who has worked in Racine recently, had held that post for the past several years.

RACINE LABOR
AFL ★★★ THE UNION NEWSPAPER ★★★ CIO
Reaching Racine's Greatest Consumer Market

Labor Calls For Probe

Rising Prices Blamed On Profit Gouge

MIAMI BEACH, Fla. — Laying the blame for the continued rise in the cost of living on "excessive profit margins" in industry, the AFL-CIO Executive Council has called for a sweeping government investigation of the relations between prices, profits, investments and wages.

Answering repeated attacks on union wage policies because of rising prices, the council emphatically declared that price increases "are overwhelmingly unrelated to wage increases."

"We firmly believe," the council said, "that excessive price increases in certain basic commodities have been unwarranted and ... have produced excessive profit margins in such key industries as auto and steel."

The 29-member Executive Council said "the American public

should be made aware of the fact that price rises for many basic goods have far outstripped wage costs. The price-profit policies of many major corporations in basic industries should be brought into the focus of public attention."

It urged Congress, through its Joint Economic Committee, to "conduct an investigation of the price-profit-investment-wage policies of the dominant price-leading corporations in basic industries."

Pointing to the fact that, in the 11 months between January and November 1956, the cost of living rose 2.8 per cent, as compared with an increase of only 1.4 per cent in the four years from January 1952 to December 1955, the council asserted:

"On the same day that Pres. Eisenhower delivered his State of the Union message, advising workers and unions to moderate their wage demands lest they supposedly create inflationary pressures, the newspapers simultaneously reported gasoline price increases and sharply rising inventories of gasoline and fuel oils." The council's statement said "the rise in output per manhour of

work and in output per unit of capital — along with increasing profit margins and substantial rates of return on investment — make possible both continuing improvements in wages, hours and fringe benefits and a relatively stable price level."

To underscore its contention that wage increases were not responsible for spiraling prices, the council pointed out that the 20-cent hourly package won by the United Steelworkers in 1956, "assuming no absorption out of increased productivity, translates into additional labor costs to U.S. Steel of $82 million. The corporation's price rise of $8.50 per ton increased its income . . . by approximately $230 million."

Thus, the Executive Council declared, "increased revenues from price rises exceeded labor 'costs' by an almost 3-to-1 ratio. This is evidently not enough for the industry because they are now agitating for further price increases."

The pattern, said the council, is substantially the same in the automobile, chemical, paper, aluminum, meat and food packaging industries.

AFL Aids Workshop, Students

The Racine Trades and Labor Council covered a lot of ground in its last meeting, contributing the sum of $145 to aid the Curative Workshop in obtaining a film explaining its role in the Community and adding its annual $25 bit for the Foreign Student Exchange program under which four students from other countries are now attending Racine high schools.

In addition, the council heard Dr. Sam Kachius, a candidate for school board, re-elected Gilbert Niesen to his ninth term as chairman of the executive board, approved Pres. William Kornwolf's appointment of a Committee on Political Education, voted to lend its assistance to the school janitors

NIESEN

and to the joint apprenticeship committee in seeking a meeting with the Vocational School Board and discussed a number of other important issues.

The council heard a report from George Lorenson, representative on the Curative Workshop Board, in which he pointed out that the Racine Building and Construction Trades Council had contributed $150 toward the purchase of "Three to Make Ready," a color movie about the Curative Workshop. He said the cost was $295, leaving another $145 outstanding. The delegates then adopted the executive board's recommendation that the council contribute that sum. The film will be shown to organizations in explaining the functions of the Workshop and the good it does for the community.

The council long has considered the student exchange program one of the best ways of creating mutual understanding among nations and renewed its usual contribution to the American Field Service committee which handles the program. H. E. Ross, 1534 Boyd av., is chairman of the pro-

Continued On Page Two

UAW Wins Poll At Young Radiator

Young Radiator UAW Local 37 won a bargaining representative election for time keepers, stockchasers and blue print crib attendants in an NLRB poll last Friday, according to Dennis Leankauph, president, and Warren Medienky, secretary of the local. The vote was 10 to 6 for representation by the UAW. Seventeen people were eligible to vote. The local will now be certified to the NLRB as representative of these employes and the officers then will meet with the company to negotiate for them. Harold Thompson, UAW international representative, said that "this is another example of how white collar workers are coming to realize more and more that their interests can best be served by a bona-fide union." He added that "with the national AFL-CIO drive for white collar workers getting under way we expect more such groups to be asking for our services."

Lithographers Local Officers Installed

OFFICERS of Lithographers Local 54 for the coming year were installed Saturday by the international president, George Canary, at a well-attended meeting in Roma Hall. Two former presidents of Local 54 who are now international representatives and an international vice president also were present. Shown together following the installation are seated, left to right, Paul Rosenquist, Local 54 president, and Canary. Standing, Oliver Mertz, international vice president; Giles Weisner, Local 54 vice president; Gus Petrakis, international representative; Cornelius Klorf, Local 54 secretary, and Leon Wickersham, international representative. Discussion of the 1957 contract was the main item of business at the meeting, which concluded with a refreshment hour.

Union Hails Kohler Ruling, Will Continue Its Boycott—

"We are gratified." That was the expression used this week by union leaders in describing the latest National Labor Relations Board ruling in the Kohler case.

By a unanimous vote, the full NLRB last week overruled trial examiner George A. Downing's recommendation that the union's unfair labor practice charges against the company be dismissed.

Effect of the decision is to order the trial examiner to render a decision based on the merits of the charges.

Downing has to assay 19,175 pages of testimony taken in hearings that dragged out more than a year in reaching his decision. Regardless of what it is, a further appeal is expected.

In Sheboygan, Pres. Allen Graskamp of the striking UAW Local 833 said:

"We predicted that the full board would reverse Downing and our prediction has come true. We now predict that the Kohler company will be found guilty as charged and that it will have to bear the full consequences of its act, just as in the Ertel case it finally had to settle and extend

to Edward Ertel — the worker whom it illegally fired for union activity — several thousands of dollars in back pay."

(Ertel was discharged for alleged unsatisfactory work by the Kohler Co. Oct. 4, 1951. The union contended that the discharge was due to Ertel's union activities. An attorney for the UAW said that Ertel

Continued on Page Eight

Union: scab preference the only key issue now

In a late-breaking development, Garment Workers Local 187 disclosed Thursday morning that the key remaining strike issue is Rainfair's insistence on super-seniority for "scab" replacement workers.

Recent discussions between the union and Rainfair indicated that agreements could be reached on the major economic issues, Local 187 President Oscar Rhone said. "But management insists that they have a 'moral obligation' to retain the strikebreakers, who have been working there for the past couple of months.

"Management is only offering the long-term Local 187 members any left-over jobs," Rhone stated. "Obviously, that is unacceptable.

"Up until now, the company has claimed that settling with the union would put Rainfair out of business," Rhone said. "Let's set the record straight: the problem is not economics, it's the company's refusal to rehire our members."

RACINE LABOR

Racine's voice of working people

Volume 51-Number 21   FRIDAY, October 25, 1991   .75

Serving labor since 1941   12 pages

UAW 642 takes its case to Mauston

Faced with outrage in Racine, Gov. Thompson's canceled his appearance last Friday at a groundbreaking ceremony for Dumore's new plant in Mauston.

Helped by $2.5 million in taxpayer-provided industrial revenue bonds, the Dumore Corp. will be shifting jobs from Racine to Mauston. At least 70 jobs will be eliminated here.

While Thompson stayed away, UAW Local 642 leaders and supporters decided to make an appearance of their own at the Mauston celebration. A delegation of nine people displayed protest signs at the ground-breaking and held a press conference.

"We made it clear that this is not a quarrel with the people of Mauston, because they are victims, too," related Dan Sharkozy, president of United Auto Workers Local 642. "We all need good-paying jobs that will support a family."

Sharkozy expressed hope that the press conference with a Mauston-area newspaper helped to alert the Mauston community to the destructiveness of competition between Wisconsin cities.

Sharkozy and others also used the press conference to stress the need for legislation to discourage the use of industrial revenue bonds for job shifting.

The Racine delegation to Mauston included UAW Local 642 Vice President Frank Roberts, Bargaining Committeeman Ron Olson, Wisconsin Action Coalition Co-Chair Phyllis Dressen and organizer Nancy Krifka, and two

Rainfair strikers.

Industrial revenue bonds are, in effect, low-interest loans to corporations. They pay below-market interest rates for the financing of new plants or expansions. Purchasers of the bonds pay no taxes.

Industrial revenue bonds are thus subsidized by taxpayers.

Dumore workers have expressed anger at the use of public funds to move their jobs from Racine.

Gov. Thompson's original plan to take part in the ground-breaking triggered had cries of outrage in Racine. "Gov. Thompson may
please turn to page 5

Fast appeals to Johnson family
United Farm Workers President Cesar Chavez kicked off a fast by Rainfair strikers at an Oct. 14 rally across from Johnson Wax on 14th St. From left to right were Maricruz Martinez, Verline Bedford, Bernice Wilson, John Friend, and Chavez. Not shown is Sylvia Guerrero.

Rainfair fast touches the heart of Racine

Before beginning a fast on Oct. 14, Rainfair striker Sylvia Guerrero said quietly, "I hope this touches people's hearts."

The fast is a traditional method of non-violent protesters like Gandhi used to express their spirit of sacrifice and self-discipline while making a moral statement.

That spirit seemed to be reaching the people of Racine as Garment Workers Local 187's strike headed into its fourth month this week.

Several clergy conducted fasts of their own in sympathy with the strikers.

The fast by Rainfair strikers is rallying community support at remarkable new levels, strike leaders say.

"Considering that this is a company town where the Johnsons (owners of SC Johnson & Son) are so prominent, the support we're getting is overwhelming," said Garment Workers Local 187 President Oscar Rhone.

In recent weeks, the Johnsons have become the focus of increasing attention. The union has called attention to the business links between the Johnson family and Rainfair, such as a Johnson executive serving on the Rainfair board and loans to Rainfair from Heritage Bank, which is Johnson-owned.

"The support is giving tremendous encouragement to our members who are fasting, and to all the strikers," he said. "We had wonderful spirit at our union meeting Monday night."

Five of the strikers have been fasting since Oct. 14. They are Verline Bedford, John Friend, Sylvia Guerrero, Norma Vela and Bernice Wilson. Joining in has been Ray Vela, Norma's husband.

The fasters have remained on a liquid-only diet developed by the World Health Organization to treat dehydration.

So far, the fasters have suffered from bouts of dizziness and diarrhea, but remain enthusiastic about the fast. One of the fasters, Norma Vela, had to receive treatment for a urinary-tract infection, but has remained on the fast.

Garment Workers spokeswoman Joanne Haupert reported, "Their health is good. The doctor did a thorough check-up and they were all okay."

Local chiropractor Kenneth
please turn to page 8

Service, vigil Sunday for Rainfair fasters

A prayer service with the fasting Rainfair strikers, followed by an all-night, candle-light vigil, will be held on Sunday, Oct. 27. The event will take place at the Cristo Rey Parish House, 800 8th St.

The prayer service will begin at 6 p.m. It is open to the public. The all-night vigil will follow the service.

October 25, 1991

Cesar Chavez contrasted against the Johnson Wax tower.

Local labor papers like the Racine Labor *used to be a common fixture of labor journalism. The* Racine Labor, *now over fifty years old, is the most prominent survivor.*

in Norman's view. But Racine unionists were after something very different, an active, socially conscious paper.

In some ways my history as editor of *Racine Labor* mirrors Norman's. Like Norman, I was an activist before I became editor of the *Racine Labor*, first in the movement that opposed the Vietnam War and then as a member of an alliance that wanted to pull together farmers, workers, and students in Wisconsin into a third party.

I was hired in 1972 and became the paper's second editor. I quickly learned that the *Racine Labor* is set up as a cooperative. Every local union that buys subscriptions gets proportional voting strength at the annual meeting at which a board of directors is elected. Most Racine unions subscribe for all their members.

The *Racine Labor* is not—and has never been—the official publication of any local central labor council. The absence of formal links between the paper and the council has clearly helped the paper weather the various splits and mergers within the labor movement. The *Racine Labor* has always worked to keep local unions united, no matter what their national affiliations. In the days before the AFL-CIO merger, for instance, editor Loren Norman convinced the paper's board of directors to adopt a policy that when disputes split the AFL and the CIO, he would either print both sides or none.

In 1970, when the UAW left the AFL-CIO, the *Racine Labor* would likely have disappeared if it had been an official AFL-CIO central labor body publication. The UAW has a strong presence in Racine, and the paper couldn't have survived if it had to publish without that support.

On the whole, the Racine labor movement has done a good job resisting pressures to split the labor movement. During the 1970s, for instance, when both the UAW and the Teamsters were outside the AFL-CIO, Racine unions formed an umbrella organization known as the Alliance for Labor, which included the AFL-CIO unions, the Teamsters, the UAW, and the Racine Education Association.

When I left the *Racine Labor* in 1979, about half the subscribers were UAW members and a third belonged to AFL-CIO unions. The Racine Education Association, the local affiliate of the National Education Association, which isn't affiliated with the AFL-CIO, started subscribing for its members in the mid-1970s, after a bitter strike, and continued that support until 1991.

During that hard-fought teacher walkout in the 1970s, the Racine daily, the *Journal Times*, lashed out stridently against the striking teachers right from the start. The *Journal Times* editor ran a front-page box every day to remind Racine exactly how many days the "illegal" strike had lasted. In response, the *Racine Labor* became the teachers' champion. When the teachers sat in at the school administration building, the *Racine Labor* was there. We were partisans, but we figured the daily paper was plenty partisan as well.

Outside of our dedicated subscribing unions, the *Racine Labor* has always had several hundred individual subscribers: people in the community, union retirees, and a few readers whom I suspect have been attracted by the paper's want ad policy. The paper offers free want ads to all subscribers, one per issue for many decades, but now once every other issue.

This policy has made the want ads a gold mine for bargain hunters. People who can't find anything else good to say about the paper always remark that they sure enjoy the want ads.

Paid subscriptions, either by unions or individuals, accounted for about half of the paper's income during my tenure as editor. The rest came from paid display ads. In the early years, the paper was packed with ads from local merchants. But by the time I became editor, the local merchants had been largely displaced by discount chains like K-Mart that would only advertise in the local daily. We received some advertising from the local banks and savings and loans, but gradually the banks became appendages to Milwaukee banks, and they had trouble finding Racine on the map.

Increasingly, the *Racine Labor* has had to turn to its local unions. In the 1970s, bulk subscription rates for local unions rose to $6 a year per member. Today the rates stand at $14.50. Even these higher rates aren't enough, alone, to keep the paper going. The paper has had to hold numerous fund-raisers. The ever-increasing postal rates, meanwhile, aren't helping any.

Still, the paper survives. The community needs it. The *Racine Labor* serves the community—in many ways.

Politically, for instance, the *Racine Labor* plays a role that goes beyond standard election endorsements and editorials. *Racine Labor*'s investigative journalism has sometimes exposed damaging information that other media have failed to uncover.

When I first came to town, Steve Olsen, a local union president who had served as an alderman for many years, was running for mayor. Racine had never elected a labor mayor, and many business leaders were worried.

Olsen (no relation to me) finished second in the primary. With the encouragement of local union leaders, I began digging into the financing of the front-runner, an insurance salesman who was running as the champion of the average citizen. Racine's big shots, it turned out, were financing the insurance salesman's campaign in a big way, and we had a good time exposing the salesman's campaign financing. On election day, Racine chose a union president as mayor. How big a role we played is hard to say. But Olsen's opponent gave us a good share of the blame for the turnaround between the primary and general election.

A few years after I left the *Racine Labor*, the paper took out after Terry Kohler, the Republican candidate for governor who was running on a program to bring "jobs, jobs, jobs" to Wisconsin. Kohler also happened to be president of the Vollrath Corporation, which was moving jobs *out* of Wisconsin to southern states and Mexico. *Racine Labor* editor Roger Bybee, my successor, interviewed workers at Vollrath's plant and checked out sources in the South who talked about the region's low wages. Tax records revealed that Vollrath had moved jobs out of Wisconsin despite considerable tax breaks from Wisconsin taxpayers.

The *Racine Labor* stories on Kohler were eventually picked up by a reporter for a Milwaukee daily. Later, an aide to Tony Earl, who went on to defeat Kohler, said the exposé in the *Racine Labor* marked a turning point in the gubernatorial campaign.

The *Racine Labor* keeps a constant eye out for stories that would never interest the commercial dailies. One example: A local barber, who had been elected alderman with labor support, pulled out of the barbers' union. The barbers' union brought the news to the labor paper, and we published it. Our story angered Racine's union community, and the alderman got the message. Not long after the article appeared, he dropped out of his reelection race, paving the way for the unopposed election of a progressive candidate.

Not every controversy is as clear-cut. In the mid-1970s, when local public employees and the mayor began to go at each other over the cost-of-living issue, the *Racine Labor* found itself in the middle of conflicting forces. The journalistic highlight of that conflict was our picture of the mayor, the former union president, driving a snowplow during the strike. Somehow, everything ended well. The workers got their cost-of-living increase, and the mayor was reelected with labor's endorsement.

The *Racine Labor* considers itself both a labor paper and a community paper, not just a labor paper for unionists or a community paper for citizens, but both.

During the 1970s, the *Racine Labor* took on an early savings and loan (S&L) crisis. In Racine, local S&Ls had been selling mortgages with an escalator clause that gave them the right to raise interest rates on already existing loans. People signed these loans never dreaming these clauses could be implemented, but in the mid-1970s, the S&Ls began giving their mortgage holders the bad news. Irate homeowners started picketing the S&Ls, talking to politicians, and complaining to the Racine daily newspaper. But despite the good visuals, the newspaper wasn't interested. Finally, some union members who were watching in horror as their mortgage rates were jacked up came to the *Racine Labor* to get coverage.

Their protests made front-page news in the *Racine Labor* for several weeks running. I wondered, at the time, what the effect would be on our advertising, since some of these same S&Ls took ads with us. We did lose some advertising from the S&Ls that were directly involved. But, ironically, the S&Ls that were more conservatively run and didn't need to escalate their mortgages started increasing their ads. I figured we broke even.

In 1990, the *Racine Labor*'s crusading helped restart bus service at a large mall. The mall's owner had banned the buses from the mall, and that ban was working real hardship on many elderly people, who had to wait outside the mall area to catch buses home. Editor Roger Bybee interviewed the bus patrons and generally kept hitting on this injustice issue after issue. Finally, Racine mayor Owen Davies ordered the restoration of the bus service.

Racine's daily did cover this story, but it never gave any editorial support to the suffering bus riders. The alliances between commercial dailies and their advertisers are very strong indeed.

Racine Labor's contributions have gone far beyond Racine's city limits. The widely admired labor cartoonist Gary Huck first began drawing for a union audience in the late 1970s for the *Racine Labor*. The *Racine Labor*'s role in providing a forum for Huck has helped labor editors across the country encapsulate the day's issues in wit.

So how is it that Racine has supported a paper like the *Racine Labor* for fifty years when so many other community-wide labor papers have folded?

I credit, first, the Racine labor community, the Racine trade unionists who every year give their support to the paper. When rough times set in during the 1980s, Racine trade unionists dug into their pockets at several fund-raisers to bail the paper out of its printing bills.

The survival of the *Racine Labor* also demonstrates the importance of having a strong editorial hand. If an editor is subordinate to the business manager, you'll get the "pap" that Loren Norman worried about in the early days of *Racine Labor*. A labor editor needs to have a strong commitment to the labor movement, an interest in labor history, the skill to stay in touch with the thinking of labor leaders and members, and the desire to put out a lively paper that the readers will want to read. The editor needs a gut-level interest in issues like minimum wage and trade and the future of the labor movement. Editing a labor paper can't be just a job.

But an editor can't simply regard a labor paper as his or her personal vehicle, because it's not. The editor of the *Racine Labor* has the same relationship to the paper's board of directors that the editor of a daily has to the publisher. A publisher who tries to call every shot will soon lose the editor. On the other hand, the publisher has the ultimate power to hire and fire.

The editor of the *Racine Labor* has traditionally had considerable latitude, but I once ran into trouble—and put my job as editor at risk—when I decided to get arrested with the public employees who were picketing outside the mayor's house to protest an ordinance banning residential picketing. And the current editor, Roger Bybee, once took an unscheduled "vacation" from writing his column for several weeks after writing a critical piece about Congressman Les Aspin.

Despite these episodes, over the course of fifty years, the Racine unions have never permanently tossed out an editor. That's a tribute to a relationship of trust on the part of the publisher-unions and good judgment on the part of the editors.

Down through the years, the *Racine Labor* has taken stands on international issues that ranged from supporting U.S. entry into World War II to opposing our involvement in Vietnam. Currently, the paper is opposing the proposed free trade agreement with Mexico. Loren Norman once said that the *Racine Labor* is a voice of sanity in a mad world. And, hopefully, it was and is.

But the editors have built support for the *Racine Labor* by covering the issues that hit closest to home: jobs and workplace issues. Over the years, the *Racine Labor* has helped the building trades in their fight against nonunion construction, the public employees in their battle for cost-of-living protection, the postal workers in their struggle for political rights, and the industrial unions in their campaign to keep good-paying jobs in the United States.

The *Racine Labor* has also reached out into the community with photos of ethnic festivals, features on canoeists reenacting historic explorations, reviews of Bruce Springsteen albums, interviews with religious leaders such as Archbishop Rembert Weakland, and a popular column by local writer Bette Norman that mixed gardening, grandkids, and sharp-witted political commentary. All in all, the *Racine Labor* has offered an eclectic mix.

Today, only a handful of cities have competing daily papers with differing editorial views. Racine once supported several dailies, today only one, the *Journal Times*, which belongs to Lee Enterprises, a small out-of-state newspaper chain.

For good reason, most labor leaders don't like the coverage their unions get in the daily press. But a community labor paper gives average workers a forum. The only catch is that it's not free. If the labor movement really wants its voice heard in the public debate, it has to be willing to pay the price. The Racine labor movement thinks the *Racine Labor* is worth the effort and the $14.50 per member per year. And that's why the *Racine Labor*, after fifty years, is still around, still advocating the cause of social justice.

A Labor Journalism Odyssey: The *Mill Hunk Herald* and Beyond

Larry Evans

The only way I know how to present the complicated lessons from my organizer's odyssey in alternative labor journalism is to lay before you my tumultuous trek from the mid-1970s into the early 1990s and hope that after reading it you can tell me what happened. I'm dying to know.

I'll unfurl first the fury of the wonderfully rebellious *Mill Hunk Herald* decade in Pittsburgh.

The Mill Hunk Years

> *When the rich concern themselves with the poor, that's called charity. When the poor concern themselves with the rich, that's called revolution.*
> —Bill Winpisinger

During the 1980s, in once mighty Pittsburgh, the *Mill Hunk Herald* magazine was a fast vehicle on blue-collar America's slow and hopelessly potholed road to working class solidarity. To understand the unusual success of this classic grassroots worker rag—sometimes a quarterly, sometimes biannual, sometimes never mind, but always "punchin' out"—you first have to understand the road conditions over

Larry Evans, a labor organizer and writer, has a resumé "that resembles a pizza with everything on it." The Baltimore-born Evans is a former steelworker who edited the Mill Hunk Herald *between 1978 and 1988. An anthology based on that experience,* Overtime: Punchin' Out With the Mill Hunk Herald, *won a 1991 American Book Award. In 1990, Evans coproduced* Perestroika from Below, *a documentary on Soviet coal miners.*

which it traveled and a little bit about the inspired drivers of this worker-writer–run express.

In the 1970s, while the Pepsi generation was busy eyeballing the PacMan revolution and the declining dollar and climbing interest and inflation rates began blowing America's blue collars out the trapdoor of their middle-class dreams, a confrontation of national proportions brewed. Rank-and-file organizations in steel (Steelworkers Fight Back), trucking (Teamsters for a Democratic Union), and coal (Miners for Democracy) began challenging the entrenched political machines of their international unions. Recognizing a good unfair fight when they saw one, organizers from all political persuasions and from all over the country "industrialized," joining the glorious struggle for democracy in the unions. I was one of them.

I remember attending a "Defend the Pressmen" rally for workers on strike against the *Washington Post* while living in Baltimore in 1975 and thinking how incredible it was to have helped bust up segregation, end a war, and unseat a president of the United States, yet feel powerless to help a few hundred strikers who were simply asking for a measly cut of Katharine Graham's bullish publishing empire. So I jumped into my '65 Dodge Dart (slant six, with a mere 168,000 miles on it) and migrated from my native Baltimore to Pittsburgh, the "Steel Center of the World." I began working in a mill my second day there. What can I say, they needed help.

Resistance from the Steelworkers union hierarchy to this creeping "new left" resurgence into union politics was predictably prompt. During the 1975–76 Steelworkers Fight Back reform candidacy of Eddie Sadlowski, when the principal issue was the democratic right of rank-and-file steelworkers to vote on their contracts, the campaign was opposed by an anonymous organization called SMART (Steelworker Members Against Radical Takeover). SMART's function was to put out red-baiting leaflets and physically bust up Sadlowski rallies. These were not a fun bunch of guys. A Pittsburgh district director even boasted to a young local union president of his complete cooperation with the federal government in "tracking down the Reds" in the union. The long litany of names included mine. That young union president, Tony Novosel, however, was a pal of mine, a soccer teammate, and would become one of the founders of the *Mill Hunk Herald*.

The international Steelworkers union also had some real-world advantages in its efforts to discredit the Sadlowski campaign. First, the industry, despite employers' encroachments on contract language, was still leading the world in pumping out the iron. Steelworkers were thus skeptical about our dire radical predictions of an "employers' offensive" looming on the horizon. Second, the union bureaucracy monopolized the means to reach the membership, via a press closed to all but mainstream opinions, bowling scores, and photos of officials squeezing fleshy palms aptly symbolizing tightly run conventions. Third, it was true that "outsiders"—liberal money, organizers, and the like—were "infiltrating" and bringing with them issues and some lunatic ideologies that the average steelworker felt cluttered his agenda. The radical message of the day was more often than not lost on the average worker anyway, much to the deflation of the self-importance of plant-gate rabble-rousers. I remember walking out of the mill after a graveyard shift with Willie, an older worker who pointed out to me the overnight appearance of twenty red posters of a cheerful Chairman Mao plastered across the plant-gate wall. Willie looked disgusted and said to me, "I don't know where that Reverend Moon gets all his money to put up them posters!"

Sadlowski lost the hotly contested election. More than 250 instances of voting irregularities were filed but later dismissed by the National Labor Relations Board as inconsequential to the outcome of the race.

In 1977, the United Mine Workers were facing a strike that would be a harbinger of the labor battles of the terrible 1980s. The Taft-Hartley Act, with its strike injunction power, was imposed and the miners retorted that "Taft can dig it, and Hartley can haul it, but I'm gonna leave it in the ground." Out of the dormant Sadlowski reform campaign in Pittsburgh arose the Committee of Concerned Unionists, which organized conferences and benefits for the miners—including a "Union Bowl" football marathon that involved a dozen different unions—and provided the germ for a cross-union publication, the *Mill Hunk Herald*.

The Committee of Concerned Unionists consisted mostly of steelworkers concerned about the state of democracy within the United Steelworkers of America (USWA). But our first discussions about the *Mill Hunk Herald* revealed motivations for initiating the paper that ran deeper, higher, and wider than I expected. Just how we would run the publication prompted the *Mill Hunk*'s first taste of left-wing fratricidal controversy. The Committee of Concerned Unionists' more orthodox, stick-in-the-mud members objected to both the *Mill Hunk* name (considered too flip) and its free-for-all, ultrademocratic editorial policy that gave everyone (writers, subscribers, semiconscious walk-ins off the street) equal say in determining what would be published. I'll never forget the showdown meeting when a disagreement developed between the more doctrinaire revolutionists and the rank-and-file rummies hanging out with me. In the heat of the passion, a former *comrade* called me a "Trotskyist." This didn't set well with a co-worker pal of mine, unaware of what the condemnation entailed but taking exception to the tone of delivery. The defending rank and filer, East Liberty (pronounced S'liberry) foundry worker Ron Hively, belted the comrade and laid him out flat. Hively possessed an unparalleled crap detector for classism and exercised it with equal frequency scrawling one-draft diatribes against company injustices and battling in barroom brawls. The *Hunk's* parent nonprofit "Piece of the Hunk Publishers" inaugural board meeting was held at Ron's favorite haunt—the Mellon Street Inn—and made the six o'clock news. "The only corporation ever to be conceived in a gritty back alley bar" was the broadcasted claim. Thus was our reputation unkindly soiled by the tag "a beer-sodden lot" as we commenced production on the first *Mill Hunk*, admittedly a little rough around the edges but beholden to no single point of view.

In the *Mill Hunk's* early days, I would "edit" the collective editing and layout sessions—sometimes while working a midnight-to-eight shift in the mill. We also used the facilities of the Labor Education Center at the local community college to polish up and churn out the first issue in February 1979. This first issue raised as many brows as its puny two thousand circulation could reach, delivered personally to picket lines (at the time Pittsburgh led the nation in strikes) and workplaces big and small. We got some instant reactions—for starters a certified letter notifying us that the college facility's support for us was a *misunderstanding*. This outraged another *Mill Hunk* founder, who had helped set up that Labor Center years before. Joey Muick was a Northside (Nor'side) pile driver and disco dancer and, in the heat of controversy, was also known to unfurl his rage. At a party, he pounded on the popular director of the Labor Ed Center.

The work of other early blue-collar contributors made sure our fledgling paper would survive. A typewriter liberated from some downtown corporate office was "donated" by a locked-out striking steelworker turned temporary janitor. An endless flow of office supplies was assured from a sympathetic graphics shop worker, as were promotional T-shirts from a boutique store owner. Various liquid refreshments would miraculously appear at meetings, compliments of a Teamster driver who would reroute his truck past our doorstep. Union locals on strike could call on us for some immediate picket line help,

You, the Working Class

Ron Hively
Pittsburgh, PA steelworker

"And what kind of work are you involved in?"

"Oh, I'm a steelworker (coal miner, factory worker, auto worker, etc.)."

"Oh...you mean you work with your hands. Excuse me, I must move on."

Has that ever happened to you? Through some strange circumstance you end up at a party or some other event that is out of your class, and when it is found out that you are from the working class, you can almost see the wall that separates you from the others— the professionals, the businessmen, the bosses, the politicians.

These "higher ups" don't want to associate with you because you're dirty, uneducated, uncouth, and basically not worth wasting time on. And, because they fear you.

The big thing is college. Every parent wants their child to go to college, so he or she can get a *good* job. In other words, go to college or get a job and mingle with the great unwashed. UGH!

Well, you're dirty because you work hard and sweat; dirt sticks to sweat.

You're uneducated because the system, the bosses, only allow a certain number of people from any generation to get a higher education. Preferably students from their own social class.

You are uncouth because you're environment is too busy surviving to take time out to teach the niceties of life.

That you are feared is something you should awaken to. The "higher ups" are justified in their fear. If *you* don't go into the coal mines, steel mills, factories, armed services...Who will?

If you don't drive the truck, walk the high steel, wash the dishes, do the welding, who will? In short: everything that is made, transported, serviced, or otherwise used by someone else is because of...You.

The working class, the dirty, uneducated, uncouth class, is actually responsible for every gain that the world has. Responsible yes, but you don't get the credit for it. The bosses, the professionals, the money men, they get the credit. They're considered to be real world shakers; dynamos. But they know without you, they would have nothing.

From MHH issue #1, February, 1979

Community Press Features

This essay from the Mill Hunk Herald's *very first issue in 1979 helped set the tone for the paper's decade of publication.*

and we regularly hosted meetings for radical unionists and cultural activists just passin' through. Some spent the night. One, an American Sioux Indian rights activist from North Dakota, spent the winter. Anonymous delegations of workers from downtown steel companies and international union headquarters would show up at our humble Nor'side basement office with collected donations. Anonymous phone calls pestered us with right-wing threats, and our mail was pilfered at just the worst times. In its early organizing stages, the *Mill Hunk* may not have always been a "class act," but it definitely was an act of class. The *Mill Hunk* believed that a good offense was the best defense. It would prove to be a popular and useful approach as events would soon turn Pittsburgh and the entire rustbelt on its head.

To swell the ranks of our writers, eventually numbering 741 over the *Mill Hunk*'s ten years, we took on the local press and union publications, boasting that we would be a democratically run publication for all working people, "not owned by anyone" or "operated from the top down" and not "ass kissing," as the original masthead proclaimed. We recruited from the rankled ranks of mainstream letters-to-the-editor writers who never seemed to get published frequently enough or in entirety. We clipped their letters and forwarded our invitation to write for us through the local papers. Of eighty folks approached in this way, some sixty-three sent us submissions. Some sent trunkloads. Glaring at this success, the editor of the *Pittsburgh Press* sent us a certified letter snooting that Pittsburgh's main daily would "cease to be a conduit for such solicitation." Interestingly, by comparison, the editor of the more liberal daily, the *Pittsburgh Post-Gazette*, sent an uncertified note praising our spunk.

Dryness always seems to afflict alternative presses looking to communicate to working class audiences. We sought to avoid that dryness. We asked graphic artists for approval to use their cartoons. Famed editorial cartoonists such as the *Washington Post*'s Herblock, the *Philadelphia Inquirer*'s Auth, and the then *Washington Star*'s Oliphant gave us encouraging nods. Even P. J. O'Rourke of the *National Lampoon* replied, "It's obvious to me that your new publication is a real troublemaker. Therefore feel free to use whatever you want from the National Lampoon. Give us a credit if you remember and when you are making tons of money, let us know so that we can bleed you white with lawsuits." Of course, the great talents of grassroots political cartoonists such as the United Electrical Workers' Fred Wright, Huck-Konopacki,

Carol*Simpson, Bülbül, and Nicole Hollander were also generous in meeting our needs.

Started and dominated early on by a group made up mainly of steelworkers, the *Mill Hunk* expanded to all trades and occupations as quickly as the mills shut down in the early 1980s. To the traditional editor, the *Mill Hunk*'s editorial process, in which every subscriber was welcome to come to editorial meetings to vote on manuscripts over an ample supply of beer and wine, might sound chaotic and unworkable. It was. But this chaos was our magic—our one claim to legitimacy—since nobody else in the labor movement, much less the known universe, operated that way. We imagined that our process would become an important blueprint for how all grassroots and union publications could operate.

Our meetings sometimes attracted upward of thirty to forty people. Sure we would occasionally have to endure a soapboxing radical fresh from the fringe or a right-wing conspiracy theorist telling us the KKK had us high on its list, but by night's end the high marks got published, leaving everyone feeling good and equally empowered. (It should be noted that writers' submissions to the *Mill Hunk* were never "edited." They were judged and printed whole or sent back to the authors for a rewrite.)

To keep the *Mill Hunk* going during the 1980s—an era of concessions and falling blast furnaces, the "Big Chill" of the working class—we organized massive public benefits: a *Mill Hunk* Ball, mixing a big band sound with new wave and reggae, attracting an incredible mix of Pittsburghers; a *Mill Hunk* Dunk swimming party; a *Mill Hunk* Junk flea market; a *Mill Hunk* Funk disco; a *Mill Hunk* Punk Reaganomics dance; A *Mill Hunk* Bunk pajama party; a *Mill Hunk* Haunt Halloween party; a *Mill Hunk* Munch dinner party (yes, we beat it to death).

We even took our progressive message to the working man's god—sports—and sponsored men's and women's softball teams, the *Mill Hunk* Funks and the Herald Angels, the only teams in the league that voted for their starting lineups. We organized a Kick in a Can (of food) Soccer Marathon for steelworker food banks and a Run of the Mill Race (10K) for mill shutdown victims and a Sister City Sprint (5K) and a Roberto Clemente Sports Fest for Nicaraguan children.

At community festivals, we operated a Reaganomics Obstacle Course where streams of people bobbed for Depression Apples, threw darts at Utility Balloons, and raced through Emergency Eviction Exercises. With the Pittsburgh Filmmakers, we hosted a Radical Humor Art Show and, with the Academy of Prison Arts, a series of poetry readings. We held a five-day Worker-Writer Conference that featured six wild writers and poets from England's Federation of Worker Writers and Community Publishers, and, later, we conducted six Worker-Writer Workshops for two hundred budding new Steel City novelists. Finally, we went to TV. We gained notoriety by publicly exposing first-person workplace alienation in living language and producing an experimental "Mill Hunk MTV."

Just as a protest group called the Denominational Ministry Strategy (DMS) was perking things up with pranks like putting dead fish in Mellon Bank safety deposit boxes, barricading activists in mill town churches, and skunk-bombing the Christmas parties of affluent parishes—perhaps making us seem practically mainstream by comparison—we became fundable. With our new-found "wealth," we conducted a Community Video Workshop for forty new neighborhood producers and we dominated the community channels with series entitled "Steelworkers Speak Out," "Mill Hunk Story Hour," "Her Show," and "Steel Valley Stories." We opened our doors to the flood of journalists, filmmakers, and academics wanting our opinions about the collapse of steel and looking for dramatic leads into the world of déclassé mill workers. Because the *Mill Hunk* was so outrageously bold and open, it became more than a magazine. It became a cultural movement—creating community, using the once derogatory *Mill Hunk* label as a rallying symbol for workers who wouldn't give up.

When we put out the first issue of the *Mill Hunk*, we laid out the following tidbit in our opening editorial: "There are three kinds of people in the world: Those that make things happen, Those that watch things happen and Those that wonder what happened." We were making serious jest here—hoping our limited audience in the mills and offices of a town brought to its knees might rise up and somehow, with us, create a new, just agenda. With those who did respond, we had a great time pricking society's conscience and blowing off steam. These were days of glory for the *Mill Hunk*—we won recognition from celebs like Studs Terkel, Kurt Vonnegut, and Pete Seeger and earned an "A. J. Muste journalism award" from the *Village Voice*'s Nat Hentoff—mainly because we provided refuge and expression for dissidents undemocratically flushed out of the mainstream labor movement, all the while letting willing workers speak their minds uncensored.

Many folks have asked me why the *Mill Hunk Herald* closed down. The front-page headline in the September 15, 1989, *Pittsburgh Post-*

Gazette offers perhaps the best answer: "*Mill Hunk Herald* follows mills and closes down."

Both objective and subjective factors led to the *Mill Hunk*'s demise. The numbers tell the bottom-line story. As Pittsburgh shrank from a town 100,000 steelworkers strong to 12,500, so did the *Mill Hunk Herald*'s subscription list. Over half of the hard-core editorial "staff" of our sixteen-member Hunk board of directors consisted of blue-collar couples. Four out of five of these couples broke up, mostly under the strain of economic disruption. They were "hip" to the shutdown, but not immune. Another two of our directors died, one by his own hand. Our editorial meetings became less social and more formalized. Attendance tailed off as the meeting sites shifted from homes to the back rooms of cafes. Fund-raising became more a frenzy and less a lofty, tongue-in-cheek pursuit. And I found myself wondering if I were piloting a sinking ship. Wise-ass friends would ask me when I was going to junk the rusted steelworker image and admit I was a writer. Finally, after my now ex-wife screamed at me for talking about myself in the third person, I knew I needed a sabbatical.

In 1989, the mighty *Mill Hunk* went down for the count. We made front page, for the first time, in the *Iron Age* industry journal.

The Ivory Tower/Blue-Collar Scholar Years

I became a good pitcher when I stopped trying to make them miss the ball and started trying to make them hit it.
—*Sandy Koufax*

After the *Mill Hunk*, I took my leave of Pittsburgh to begin a one-year graduate assistantship at the Rutgers Labor Studies Program—a fling at becoming a full-fledged "labor intellectual."

On my first day at Rutgers, the first assignment was to choose a famous labor leader and show how this person's life and decisions interact with your own. My first impulse was to scrap the long list of well-documented leaders offered by the prof as hopelessly out of reach of any interaction of mine.

Noticing my "*Mill Hunk*" funk, the professor offered me an alternative to pounding out the ten thousandth regurgitation on the life and eyebrows of John L. Lewis. "Ever hear of Clint Golden?" she asked. "Nope," I replied, and she handed me a book entitled *Clint: A Biography of a Labor Intellectual*. She challenged me to take this relatively obscure early union organizer and draw some lessons about my own experience.

I soon found that Clint and I went back a long way—in the common motivation our ancestors shared in leaving Europe to avoid Old World tyrannies. History never repeats itself exactly, but what I was able to come up with was a somewhat sketchy but fascinating interfacing of two similar periods—the 1920s and the 1980s—when Clint and I were both the same age.

As a thirty-year-old Philadelphia Machinist—a militant union that had elected a "socialist" as president in 1911—Clint was active in fighting for the mounting victims of the Immigration Act of 1918 and the later Palmer Raids. Russia had revolutionized and American capital saw red everywhere. Attorney General A. Mitchell Palmer "envisioned a national emergency, like a prairie fire, the blaze of revolution sweeping over every American institution of law and order." It was a time when society was off balance and workers were told that to strike was "un-American." In 1919, some 350,000 steelworker strikers were brutally repressed by a legion of company police and industrial spies. The forced labor peace of the "American Plan" cowed workers from the union shop and political dissent. It was a time of dislocation, with awkward shifts in the economy from production to service industries, from blue-collar to white-collar employment. Things were moving recklessly fast, and organized labor could hardly keep up the pace.

It was a time when unionists, liberals, and radicals unleashed creative support for union drives, through fund-raising, entertainment events, parades, rallies, producer/consumer banks, and cooperatives for building houses. A dozen labor colleges were begun in the 1920s, including two that Golden help found, the Philadelphia Labor College and the famous Brookwood. Golden lamented workers' ignorance of parliamentary procedure and lousy bookkeeping and correspondence skills and advocated "making knowledge a tool" and educating "workers towards the service of their fellow workers rather than away from them." Clint served on the national Worker's Education Board until the AFL took it over because it offered the labor movement too much self-criticism.

Brookwood was Clint's baby (just as the *Mill Hunk* was mine). A. J. Muste became chairman of the faculty, and its visiting lecturers included Norman Thomas, Sinclair Lewis, and Roger Baldwin. Blacks and women could be found among the students, as well as workers, mainly from the needle and coal industries. (Many of Brookwood's finest later helped organize the CIO.) These were Golden's kind of folks, "visionaries with a practical bent," stressing the "factual approach" over hot air. Students and faculty participated in chores and decision making equally. They made time for baseball and volleyball league play and built a magnificent swimming pool. The college churned out radio shows and published *Labor Age*, "a lodestone for liberals and radicals with an interest in the working class." From 1925 to 1930, Clint toured labor activity centers all over the country, pushing unions to develop scholarships for their most dedicated members. He sought to bring the best brains together collectively to sort out the collapse of labor during the "Terrible Twenties." In 1926, the editor of the *Journal of Electrical Workers and Operators* summed up Brookwood: "If you are discouraged about Labor's future, if you have lost hope, pay a visit to Brookwood Labor College . . . . You will be surprised. You will be thrilled . . . . It's a big place, a live place. It's not 'red.' It's not reactionary. It teaches facts—not theories; conditions—not propaganda . . . . Yes, it's quite refreshing . . . . It's the most hopeful spot in the American Labor World today."

Brookwood had its critics as well. The AFL withdrew its support because of the college's pro-CIO, pro-Soviet, and antireligious slant. The communists considered Brookwood "Social-Democratic" and accused the college of "Class Collaboration." Clint soon found himself in the middle of internal faculty strife. Eventually, Brookwood closed its doors in 1937. Lamented a disconsolate Clint on his way to starting a farm: "I have been in the Labor Movement for thirty years. In that time everything in industry has undergone a change. The organization of the workers has not made any corresponding change; in many instances they have gone backward."

When it came time to depart from my blue-collar scholar sabbatical at Rutgers and enter the job market of the 1990s, I was more convinced than ever that my decade with the *Mill Hunk Herald* was not wasted. Through my study of Golden and Brookwood, I felt somewhat validated. Perhaps Clint's experience and my experience many decades later offer lessons that labor still needs to learn.

Duty and Dilemma at the Labor Temple

> *If the people don't wanna come out to the park, nobody's goin' to stop them.*
> —*Yogi Berra*

Starting the new decade purporting to be an educated labor expert fresh out of Rutgers, I tried to sell my multi-disciplined talents (some say undisciplined is closer to the mark) to the most progressive bidder.

My first stop was a United Food and Commercial Workers local in Philadelphia. After I passionately presented my ivy-laced ideas on trade union democracy and sweeping rank-and-file reforms, the local president stopped me cold with a blunt appraisal: "Lookit Evans, you're young, intelligent, and good lookin'. That means right off the bat you're gonna threaten too many people around here!"

Washington, D.C., was next. I was called in by the Kamber Group, a state-of-the-art PR firm that handles labor accounts and other progressive causes and has been known to do straight commercial hype as well. At first, I was shocked to find that it's a common practice for some international unions to "contract out" all their "journalism" to PR firms. Would I feel comfortable editing the Laborers Union magazine, I was asked. I offered that the Laborers—one of three unions then under federal investigation for mob activity—might feel uneasy about my radical resumé, especially the part noting that I had supervised a student video team at Rutgers that explored the Laborers' highly publicized fight with the Jersey City Mailhandlers, who were busy breaking away from the Laborers "family." Still interested in harnessing my pluck, Kamber thought maybe I could sell video. That dream soured at the viewing of one of Kamber's more recent showcase pieces on behalf of the power plant allegedly responsible for polluting the Grand Canyon. I pictured myself at the OK Corral facing down Robert Redford's Rhinestone Cowboys. Asked if I could live with this, I answered, "Couldn't someone else handle that account?" In no time I was back out on K Street pounding leather.

I finally found myself at a headhunter's firm interviewing for a writer's position at the Service Employees International Union. Curious why a union was using a *corporate* manpower service, I was clued that it had something to do with the last SEIU editor lasting but sixteen days. The headhunter was my age, and we openly shared our baby-boom careers like old classmates might do at their twenty-fifth reunion. My next hurdle was Dave Sheridan, SEIU's new communications director. A more open communicator I'd never met—and with a wonderfully wry sense of humor (yes, he'd *need* this to hire me). Unsure if my freestyle, stream-of-consciousness editorial writing would squeeze into the necessary PR mold, Sheridan gave me a shot on SEIU's award-winning *Union* magazine.

For my first assignment, Dave challenged me to write a health care op-ed for the "best boss in the Labor Movement," SEIU president John Sweeney. I envisioned my first attempt at ghost writing as an invitation to spend precious moments getting to know the number one man's nuances and inflections so that I might capture the breadth of his commitment and personality. I pictured myself an occasional fixture in his plush office eavesdropping on newsbreaking strategies and nipping on his private liquor supply. What confidence they must have in my integrity and in the main man's indestructibility! I suggested to Dave that I might as well videotape John's oral history while we were sequestered away with each other pounding out his op-ed. "I'm afraid you don't get it," Dave replied. There would be no audience, no oral history, not even a lousy memo exchange. "Just write the op-ed from old speeches and news clips."

The other writers saw the humor in my naïveté and hastened to bring me and our new editor Susan Calhoun up to speed. At our first department potluck party to welcome Susan, fresh from a stint with *Foundation News* magazine, our spines were shivered by tales of SEIU's frequent staff turnovers. To survive, one must, of course, "get it"—the catchword for realizing that our foremost function is public relations, not journalism. Since the union's leadership scrutinizes *Union*'s every comma, the magazine is *theirs*, not ours, and not the membership's. Stories rolled on about how another previous editor, in a misguided moment of candor, had acknowledged to a dissident member that his mention in *Union* was disappeared by decree of the leadership. The editor found himself instantly on the carpet. Yikes!

My next big assignment came out of our first story budget meeting. The "Eyeopener" column would review *Roger and Me*, the blockbusting documentary about filmmaker Michael Moore's attempt to bring General Motors CEO Roger Smith face-to-face with the results of plant shutdowns in Flint. I developed the angle of asking trade unionists slugging it out in the trenches to go see the show and fantasize about how they'd use Mike Moore's camera to go after their bad bosses. I induced a Pittston miner, an Eastern baggage handler, and several SEIU organizers to let their creative and mischievous juices flow. For even-handedness, I put a call in to the United Auto Workers as well. Frank Joyce, a PR veteran from the UAW's famous Solidarity House, was on the line. "I hear you're aiding and abetting," popped Mr. Joyce. He was referring to my passing on Mike Moore's generous offer of assistance to the rank and filers I had contacted for the story. Since I had heard through the "do-lunch" grapevine that Frank was actually a great guy with a rabble-rousing background, I went to great lengths to tell him how my contact with Moore materialized. One late night at the office, I got a ring from movie mogul Mike himself. He suggested I come on over to his K Street office. He seemed to be wearing the same clothes that he so unfashionably modeled in the movie, and his office was an avalanche of moldy Chinese take-out containers and biodegrading pizza boxes. Over a six-pack, *Mike and Me* waxed philosophical about the good old alternative publishing days (Mike used to edit the *Michigan Voice* and *Mother Jones*) and tossed about ideas on how he could constructively spend his concessions money from Warner Brothers—a $3 million problem I was more than happy to help him with. He suggested I offer benefit showings of his popular flick to the struggling rank and filers I was interviewing. I added that "wouldn't it be nice" to do a sequel featuring some militant footage from these underpublicized frontier fights. Mike said, "Stay in touch," which I interpreted to mean, "Pass out my phone number to every union guy I'd meet with an idea for a better corporate mousetrap."

The *Roger and Me* piece I penned was predictably killed upstairs—inscribed with the red-penciled admonition "political minefield."

My only feature canned amid rancor from the top-floor censors and my Sweeney op-ed going nowhere after a second draft, I became increasingly pensive about how far out of my element I was dangling. I was only seeing routine PR assignments cross my desk and, as I'd cross paths with sympathizing pals in the building, I would be honored by a whistled bar of "Taps" or a graphically strung-up necktie. My *Mill Hunk* breakfast group back in Pittsburgh began a pool betting on how long I'd last.

In the final month of probation, just as I was beginning to feel closer to "getting it," a hot potato fell squarely into my lap. While I was interviewing a rank-and-file Hispanic member from one of the oldest locals in the union, my journalistic integrity was put squarely on the line. The member charged that building service companies and a union official were colluding to fire older Hispanic janitors so that the company could pay less to the fresh hires and the union could collect the new initiation dues. He challenged me to investigate. "That's the world out there for undocumented workers!" sighed the member. "We had to threaten to sue our own union before they'd back off [the practice]."

I got that sinking sensation again as I hung up the phone. I decided to spread the joy of my discovery to my fellow writers. Eyeballs rolled back, and hysterical mirth filled neighboring cubicles. I sat uncomfortably on it for about a week until I found myself loosening up at a cocktail party sponsored by SEIU for a liberal Pennsylvania politician I knew. President Sweeney was there, and I finally got to shake his hand. His recognition factor for me registered somewhere between zero and 0.5, so I refrained from asking him what he thought of my third draft or if he had yet taken in *Roger and Me*. Instead, clutching a rum-and-coke refill, I slithered away to a shadowy alcove of the reception, where lawyers were hanging out. After breaking the ice with a nifty dead-lawyers joke, I offered a three-men-in-a-boat morality scenario as an hors d'oeuvre to their meaty Marion Barry nosedive speculations. Without naming names, I filled the boat with a Hispanic union member, a union officer, and myself, a union journalist, and asked who should jump overboard with the aforementioned "hot potato." Suddenly I was reminded by "our" lawyer that one of the attorneys present was with none other than the Justice Department and that our internal union affairs might best first be discussed in private. I agreed and let the conversation move on to the less thorny abortion issue. The next day, "our lawyer" called me for lunch. I courageously explained away what I had heard from the janitor as vague rumor and declined—for the first time, mind you—a free trip to the trough.

If things could go further downhill from there, they did when I decided to publish pieces rejected by SEIU in outside and to-the-left publications. "Roger and Who?" appeared in *Z Magazine*, and a commentary about racism ran in *In These Times*. My friends in the halls would sarcastically quip, "So when are you going to start writing for us?" Thus it came to pass, by May 1, 1990, after four months of probation, my dreaded D-Day as a union staff new hire had arrived and I would no longer be a career writer for one of the fastest-growing international unions in America. Lifting my dead-meat spirits to the height of comes-around, goes-around irony, the UAW picked me to be a judge of its 1990 Journalistic Excellence contest! I was offered the chance to back out shortly after it was learned that I was no longer with SEIU, but, instead, I reconfirmed.

My actual departure from the handsome Service Employees headquarters was far less brutal than I reckoned might have been the case with, say, the Laborers Union. Thanks to the impeccable decency of Dave Sheridan, who compared me with Jack London, dubbing me the classic case of "the right man for the wrong job" and tracing my inability to write short and concise copy to having "too broad a vision," I did a "last lunch" and split feeling no animosity toward any individuals.

I learned a great deal from my stint in Washington, and I realized that my place was out there—organizing, writing at the local level, continuing the spirit and outreach approach of the *Mill Hunk Herald* in other situations. As John L. Lewis once put: "It's a pretty good rule to work with anyone who will work with you." I know that for me such work has to include writing, for two simple reasons: I can't keep my mouth shut and there's a mountain of education—the open, liberating, two-way kind—to be done out there!

Part Five

New Approaches

A "Trade Press" for Trade Unions: The Case for a National Labor Paper

Sam Pizzigati

The time: ten years from now. The place: any big city. You're at a corner newspaper stand, eyeing the dailies on the counter. The papers sit in neat stacks, the local daily next to America's "national" newspapers, the Wall Street Journal, *the* New York Times, USA Today, *and the brand-new national daily,* Working People, *the world's fastest-growing labor newspaper.*

Same time, the White House. A news conference is under way. The president has just finished explaining why the economy will do just fine in the second quarter. A correspondent rises. "Mr. President," she asks, "if the economy is doing so well, why are 12 million Americans still unemployed?" The president smiles wanly. His aides had warned him against recognizing any reporter from Working People, *the national labor daily.*

Same time, a high school classroom three thousand miles away from the nation's capital. A student is delivering a report on proposed California legislation that would raise the minimum wage. A higher minimum wage, says the student, quoting a Chamber of Commerce report, would throw teenagers out of work. "Hold on," says another student, "that's not what Working People *says!"*

A national labor daily. What a difference a daily paper by and for labor could make, in living rooms, in classrooms, in newsrooms across the United States. A labor daily could give working people everywhere a common point of reference—and force other media outlets to cover stories they would otherwise ignore. America's information dynamics would never be the same.

But is a national labor daily feasible? Is the American labor movement equipped to launch a daily paper that advances the labor agenda in communities big and small? Could the labor movement sustain a daily that would inspire union members, argue labor's case, and keep the rest of the media (relatively) honest?

These questions need not detain us very long. The simple answer to every one of these questions is no. At this point in American history, the labor movement can barely sustain itself, let alone a daily newspaper.

Forty years ago, one out of every three working Americans carried a union card. Today, that ratio is less than one in five, and hanging on at that meager level only because union membership has soared in the public sector. In the private sector, outside a few key industries, trade unionism barely exists. In such an environment, any talk about creating a daily labor paper that could act as a cultural and political counterweight to existing national daily newspapers is senseless, even ridiculous. Labor today lacks both the network that would be necessary to support a national daily and the vision necessary to animate it. Clearly, this is not a healthy situation. The labor movement needs a network, a broad national presence. And the labor movement needs vision. Without presence, without vision, stagnation is labor's only future.

So what should labor do? How can labor build a network, fashion a vision, avoid stagnation? What new strategic paths should labor follow? Don't expect an answer here. Nobody knows exactly how to cure what ails labor, and these pages are certainly not going to offer a sure-fire prescription for labor renewal.

But these pages will offer an observation about the renewal process. For any institution in trouble, the first step to renewal is understanding. To move forward, you need to understand where you are. And to understand where you are, you need to face facts. You need to compare interpretations. You need to be able to float and debate ideas.

Above all, any institution in trouble—or any institution that wants to stay *out* of trouble—needs a forum, a place where facts can be faced, interpretations contrasted, ideas debated. The labor movement today has no such forum. Indeed, the labor movement may be the only major community of interest in American society that lacks a serious national forum for discussion and debate. No other community of interest in American life with national pretensions communicates, within itself, as poorly as labor.

The reason is simple. Every other important community of interest within the United States today has something the labor movement does not: a trade press.

A trade press is a publication, or a collection of competing publications, that speaks directly to the men and women whose lives revolve around a particular industry or community of interest. Name the industry—auto, coal, finance, advertising—and you'll find a national *trade press*, publications that offer a meaningful forum for candid discussion and debate. Even the newest "trades"—the computer industry, for instance—quickly generate a trade press. Men and women who develop and market computer hardware and software for a living can choose between a wide variety of publications that chronicle their trade.

The best of these publications—weeklies like *Infoworld*—offer penetrating analyses that go behind the scenes to explain what's happening in the industry and why. These publications report and challenge the pronouncements of industry leaders. Dumb ideas are ridiculed, provocative ideas debated. You simply cannot function intelligently in the computer world unless you follow the computer trade press. Indeed, some might argue, the computer industry itself couldn't function without a trade press.

The best trade press publications routinely bruise the feelings of industry sacred cows. Trade papers are constantly second-guessing CEOs. But these papers thrive anyway because they're must-reads— and because they can afford to be independent. Trade press publications, if they're widely read by people in the trade, can always count on revenue from advertisers who want to reach the trade.

But a community of interest doesn't need to have deep-pocket advertisers to sustain a trade press. In the noncommercial world, for instance, some communities of interest have somehow managed to create vehicles for moving news, information, and candid commentary without income from major advertisers. In education, for instance, two different weekly newspapers, one for colleges and universities and the other for elementary and secondary schools, now offer education policy makers and officials news and appraisals. Foundation money helped launch both these ventures.

The labor movement does not have any comparable trade press publication. There is no publication within the labor movement that labor leaders, activists, and staffers feel they must read to know what's really happening and why.

The closest the labor movement comes to a national trade press is the *AFL-CIO News*, the weekly published by the AFL-CIO out of Washington, D.C. By reading the *AFL-CIO News*, you can track the issues and the initiatives AFL-CIO leaders consider significant. This information is useful and important. To be informed about what's happening in labor, you do need to know what AFL-CIO leaders are thinking and doing.

What the *AFL-CIO News* does not do is venture off the reservation. Issues that the AFL-CIO is not officially ready to pronounce upon do not get covered. Nor does the *AFL-CIO News* cover labor leaders who have provocative things to say or publish articles that are likely to discomfort AFL-CIO affiliates. In other words, the *AFL-CIO News*, the official publication of the House of Labor, is very much a house organ. The *AFL-CIO News* is safe and predictable, narrow and institutional.

The *AFL-CIO News* isn't the only nationally circulated publication that seeks a readership of men and women whose lives revolve around the labor movement. A handful of "insider" newsletters mostly regurgitate news releases from individual unions. The Bureau of National Affairs publishes much more serious newsletters "of record" that run straightforward news items on court cases, contract settlements, and a smattering of other material. Advocacy groups unhappy with labor's general drift also distribute various publications, of which *Labor Notes* is the most prominent example. But these advocacy publications appear monthly, at best, and only reach small audiences.

What's lacking is a national labor publication that serves the same role as *Infoworld* or *Advertising Age*, a publication that's read widely within the labor community of interest, a publication that talks straight about the concerns of labor people. In the absence of this sort of publication, the union movement communicates internally more like the preglasnost Soviet Union than a part of the U.S. body politic. Within the labor movement today, provocative ideas circulate in samizdat, as dog-eared photocopies of articles from obscure publications. Rumors and misinformation, meanwhile, flow ceaselessly because the official labor publications won't cover the stories that their readers most want to read about.

A case in point: the 1990 Indiana organizing battle between the American Federation of State, County and Municipal Employees, the United Auto Workers, and the American Federation of Teachers (AFT). This battle to win bargaining rights for Indiana state employees was, for months and months, a constant conversation piece within the labor movement, mainly because the Indiana campaign seemed to raise fundamental questions about labor's present and future. The battle pitted AFSCME, a union that represents government employees, against an alliance of UAW and AFT. In a series of representational elections, all three unions let out all the stops to win the votes of the more than twenty-five thousand Indiana state workers involved. Organizers flooded the state, as did dollars—over $30 million, according to some rumors—to buy television, radio, and print advertising.

The whole affair upset many labor people, both outside and inside the three competing unions. Indiana became a symbol for the internecine warfare that a declining labor movement can ill afford. Stories about the Indiana campaign, many wildly exaggerated, traveled via word of mouth all across the labor landscape. Labor leaders and staffers, in a thousand different conversations, debated who was to blame and wondered when such craziness would ever end.

But all this angst over Indiana never bubbled over into print, outside of a few articles in local or marginal publications with limited circulations. The debate within the labor movement over Indiana was never joined. Critics never made their case publicly. The unions involved never had the opportunity to justify their behavior. The movement, as a whole, never had an opportunity to consider ideas and proposals for making sure there would be no more Indianas—all because the national labor movement lacks a forum for straight news and straight talk.

But what if such a forum did exist? What if the labor movement had a true *trade press*, a weekly newspaper read by labor leaders, activists, and staffers at every level of the union movement?

This labor trade press weekly, if it had existed in 1990, would have covered the unfolding story of the Indiana representational election campaign, massive media budgets and all, in its news pages. The paper's op-ed pages would have seen a bristling debate on the appropriateness of the campaign, with plenty of opportunity for the accused to counter the charges against them. The paper editorially might have advanced some internal labor movement reforms that might help prevent fiascos like Indiana in the future.

Would this sort of coverage make a positive contribution to the labor movement? Probably. National labor trade press coverage of an episode like Indiana would likely make other unions think twice before launching opportunistic organizing forays onto turf where they don't belong. Unions might also rethink the advisability of extravagant, media-driven organizing campaigns if they knew whatever buys they made would be under the microscope of the entire union movement. And the AFL-CIO Executive Council would feel more pressure to take remedial action if a situation like Indiana had been openly discussed and debated in well-read trade press pages.

The labor movement, in other words, pays a price for *not* having a true trade press. Without a wide and open means of communication within labor, there can be no meaningful accountability, no opportunity for real debate, no outlet for frustrations that need to be expressed. In every other significant community of interest within American life, this means of communication exists. Why not within labor?

Some might wonder why the labor movement just doesn't simply revamp the *AFL-CIO News* and make it the true trade press the labor movement so desperately needs. But a revamped *AFL-CIO News* could never fit the trade press bill. The *AFL-CIO News* isn't broad enough. A trade press must cover the entire trade, and the AFL-CIO does not encompass the entire labor movement. America's largest union, the 2.1-million-member National Education Association (NEA), is not affiliated with the AFL-CIO. Neither is America's spunkiest union, the United Electrical Workers.

Even if the AFL-CIO did include the NEA and the UE, the *AFL-CIO News*, as the publication *of* the AFL-CIO, would still be inadequate as a trade press. A trade press, to serve the trade effectively, must be accountable to the trade but independent of it. This independence is the key to trade press effectiveness. Independence is what gives a trade press the latitude to question, to probe, to explore.

A trade press under the direct institutional control of a trade organization will not have this latitude. Institutional leaders have their own agenda, which they, appropriately, expect *their* press to move. A true trade press doesn't exist to move leadership agendas. A trade press instead lets leaders make the case for their agenda, lets skeptics question that agenda, and, through this process, helps build a consensus within the trade for a particular course of action.

This consensus-building process can get messy, even bruising. Labor leaders don't enjoy getting bruised. No one does, and, in an institutionally controlled press, even the best-intentioned leaders will seek to short-circuit the uncertainty and unpleasantness of consensus building. A well-intentioned leader, for instance, might ask that an article about a widely rumored problem in the union be delayed until the leader has had a chance to line up needed internal political support for a solution.

In and of itself, such a request is entirely reasonable. But the cumulative impact of acceding to such requests will inevitably undermine the effectiveness of a publication. A trade press cannot afford to meet such "reasonable" requests and remain credible. A trade press that does not cover events and issues that people in the trade are talking about will soon lose its usefulness to the trade. Only independence can guarantee this usefulness.

If independence is the key, then why don't some labor journalists simply go out on their own and start an independent newspaper for the labor movement? This is somewhat the approach taken by union organizer Thomas Deary, the publisher of the now defunct *New England Labor News & Commentary*, who has surveyed labor activists around the country on the prospects for launching a new independent labor paper.

Deary clearly sees his national paper as far more than a trade press that would target men and women already actively involved in the labor movement. "The audience we are reaching for," writes Deary, "includes millions of unorganized workers."

Deary's *New England Labor News & Commentary* had an equally broad vision. The *New England Labor News & Commentary* sought and gained support from New England local unions and regional labor bodies. But the paper was undercapitalized from the start. Editorially, the paper showed spirit, but the editors could never afford to create and publish an in-depth, quality product that had more than cheerleading appeal for labor activists. Along the way, Deary stepped on the toes of various AFL-CIO officials and, by the time the *New England Labor News & Commentary* ceased publication in July 1990, he faced the animosity of AFL-CIO officials and many labor editors.

Anyone hoping to build an independent national labor trade press cannot afford that hostility. A national labor paper, to serve the labor "trade" effectively, must be independent. But a national labor paper, to forge a serious national presence, must be able to count on some level of support from labor's institutional leadership.

Unlike the journalists in other trades, after all, journalists in the labor trade have only one source of start-up capital available: unions themselves. A would-be business trade publisher has much broader prospects. Every trade in industry—advertising, finance, auto—has vendors who sell to the trade, vendors who need a vehicle to reach their market. These vendors are potential advertisers in a trade paper. To obtain bank financing or venture capital, would-be trade publishers need only demonstrate that they can attract enough of these advertisers to make their publication profitable. Would-be trade publishers in a nonprofit environment like education don't have these same advertising opportunities. But they do have access to foundation support.

For the would-be labor trade press publisher, both these sources of capital are nonexistent. Only a limited number of vendors seek to sell to the union "trade," and banks and venture capitalists—even if they were friendly to labor, which, of course, they're not—would quickly see that a labor trade press would never offer much return on their investment.

Foundations, meanwhile, don't support large-scale labor union initiatives—partly because most foundations reflect the anti-union orientation of the corporate elite that begat them, partly because the more progressive foundations consider unions well enough endowed to support their own ambitious projects.

What about the eventual readership of a labor trade press—the local union officials, the shop stewards, the staff who would make up the vast bulk of the audience for a labor trade press? Couldn't this readership provide the financial wherewithal to launch a national labor trade press weekly?

Ultimately, of course, these grassroots readers are the only guarantor of the viability of a labor trade press. But it takes money—large amounts of initial capital—to reach potential grassroots readers. This capital needs to come from somewhere. That somewhere can only be unions themselves.

How might this union financing materialize? Here is one possible scenario.

First, a core group of national unions sets aside $150,000 to develop a prototype and business plan for a new national labor trade press publication. These unions take this step because they understand that, at this point in American history, labor desperately needs to regain the offensive. To figure out how, these unions realize, the men and women who consider unions the central focus of their work lives need a trade press, a source of information they can't find anywhere else, a forum for discussing the significance of that information, and a vehicle for debating strategies based on that information.

Second, a core group of labor journalists translates this vision of a labor trade press into a prototype for a national weekly labor newspaper that can be presented to a broad range of national union leadership bodies. In these presentations, the labor journalists ask individual unions to commit to one-year block subscriptions for their leadership—at all levels—and staff.

This target readership of national, regional, and local elected leaders, shop stewards, and staff could potentially reach half a million or more. The labor trade press core group would set its sight on a more reasonable total of fifty thousand.

The core group would ask unions to put on the table, up front, one-year subscriptions for these fifty thousand readers at a bulk rate of $25 each. For a million-member union, with a key leadership and staff list of five thousand, that up-front amount would be $125,000, a significant but by no means outrageously large sum for a major union.

Commitments for fifty thousand subscriptions would produce $1.25 million in start-up costs, enough to hire a high-quality staff and begin publication. Other subscription revenue would come from both interested union members who see the paper in the hands of local union leaders or people outside the labor movement—labor studies professors, for instance—who quickly see the publication as an indispensable source of information. Still other revenue would come from advertising—because there would be at least some vendors who would like to reach a labor national leadership audience. All these sources could bring the first-year revenue to more than $2 million, enough to cover the weekly's first-year costs.

At the end of the first year, the new national labor trade weekly would return to the national unions that made the initial bulk subscription commitments. One of two things would happen. One, the national unions might enthusiastically renew their bulk subscription commitments, believing that the new labor paper is indeed the trade press that the labor movement has so desperately needed. Two, the national unions might slam the door in the new labor paper's face, either because the paper has not proved to be the trade press the labor movement so desperately needs or because the paper has alienated union leaders by publishing articles that leadership found inappropriate or embarrassing.

If the national unions decide to continue their bulk subscriptions, the labor trade press weekly would be assured of another year's opportunity to grow and improve. But if the national unions chose to reject the paper and not resubscribe on a bulk basis, the paper would then have to approach the fifty thousand union men and women who received the publication free in the first year, thanks to the bulk subscriptions bought by their national unions. The labor weekly would have to ask these readers to resubscribe on an individual basis.

Would these readers take individual subscriptions—and keep the labor weekly alive? If the paper had truly failed to live up to its initial promise, these readers would not resubscribe. The paper would die a deserved death.

But if the new labor trade press weekly were doing its job, then readers would resubscribe on an individual basis, even if the paper had angered individual national labor leaders by occasionally publishing articles that those leaders would rather not have seen in print. Readers would resubscribe because the new labor paper would be delivering what trade union leaders, activists, and staff need and want: a candid and dependable source of news and views they can't find anywhere else.

In short, after the first year, the new labor weekly would survive only if it demonstrated its usefulness either to national labor decision makers or local-level leaders, activists, and staff.

The very idea of an independent national labor trade press weekly will, of course, make some labor leaders extremely uneasy. Some would undoubtedly worry about independent labor journalists getting carried away and airing soiled labor movement laundry in public. Such behavior, they would charge, would only give aid and comfort to the enemy, all in the name of journalistic intregrity.

This concern needs to be met. The last thing the labor movement needs is a rogue trade press slashing and burning its way through the lives of men and women working to build the labor movement. But if indeed a labor trade press weekly did go "too far," did go beyond the bounds of that great undefinable, "constructive criticism," the paper simply would not survive. Tens of thousands of union activists around the country are not going to resubscribe to a paper that's irresponsibly tearing down the cause that's near and dear to their hearts.

But, in the end, what gives aid and comfort to the enemy isn't the public exposure of dirty laundry. It's the silence that lets deadbeat leaders avoid scrutiny and dead-end policies go unchallenged. A labor movement that can't face up to its problems, learn from them, and move on is a labor movement going nowhere.

A new national labor weekly could speed this learning process along. In its pages, the men and women who lead and staff America's unions would find information and inspiration, the information they can't find in the commercial media and the inspiration that comes from knowing they're part of a broader movement of men and women who confront the same frustrations, the same uncertainties, the same hopes and fears that they do.

Eventually, through the discussion and debate that fill the pages of this new labor weekly, the men and women who make up the backbone of the American labor movement would come upon the strategies they need to reinvigorate American labor.

And if the readers of this labor trade press weekly do come upon the new approaches that new times demand, then the labor movement would start coming back as a mass, grassroots reality. If that happens, it may indeed become time to talk about taking bigger, more ambitious steps.

The time: ten years from now. You're at a corner newspaper stand, looking over the dailies on the counter. There, next to the neat piles of America's "national" papers—the Wall Street Journal, *the* New York Times, USA Today—*sits* Working People, *a brand-new national labor daily.*

The Case for a National Labor Paper: Rejoinder I

Karen Keiser

The 1990s don't appear to be the best of times to launch a new national publication. Declining ad revenues and smaller news holes are the norm at most daily newspapers. Television networks and local stations are cutting staffs and reducing air time for news and public affairs. In June 1991, a well-financed project to launch a national sports daily newspaper died a sudden death after eighteen months and losses of more than $100 million.

The 1990s also don't appear to be the best of times for the trade union movement in the United States. Membership continues to stagnate or decline in most areas. The political climate remains hostile. The many new labor initiatives of the 1980s offer no clear-cut path for renewal.

Despite these realities, a committed corps of labor journalists continues to harbor hopes that a national labor publication could be launched, survive, and eventually thrive. These hopes depend on two key elements that must be in place: financing that allows at least two years of publication and enough editorial independence to allow full debate and the expression of provocative opinions.

In his essay on the need for a national labor paper, Sam Pizzigati argues for a kind of academic debating society. He maintains that the labor movement needs a network, a vision, and a broad national presence. And he asserts that any institution in trouble needs a free forum for debate and discussion. The labor movement, Pizzigati contends, is the only major "community of interest" without this national forum.

Karen Keiser is the director of communications for the Washington State Labor Council and the president of the Western Labor Press Association. Before joining the council staff in 1981, Keiser worked as a news reporter and producer for KSTW-TV, where she also served as a shop steward for the American Federation of Television and Radio Artists.

His premise is faulty. Many other communities of interest—religious and minority communities, for instance—also lack a national forum for open debate. Communities under stress and attack do not naturally open themselves to unflinching self-criticism.

Yet the AFL-CIO's Committee on the Evolution of Work actually published a self-critical booklet in 1985. *The Changing Situation of Workers and Their Unions* opened some once-closed doors and made several rather astonishing recommendations. The report was widely discussed and debated. Many are disappointed that the committee has issued no follow-up reports, but the fact that the committee was able to publish such startling recommendations showed that the AFL-CIO was open to new ideas and programs and wasn't closed to honest appraisal.

Pizzigati's argument for a national trade press publication for labor is also premised on the "top-down" approach of influencing labor leaders and staffers. This "insiders" approach would produce a paper that would reach a very limited audience. The paper would have some potential to influence key people, but it would be unlikely to grow and expand into a true national labor publication.

National publications do not begin as specialized trade journals and grow into more popular versions. The mass media take an approach very different from the trade press. One does not develop into the other. *The choice is to decide which approach would be best for a national labor publication.*

Several national labor publications are already published every year. The house organs of the AFL-CIO and the international unions are often journals of record. Since no one else is telling labor's story, these house organs have an important function. That they avoid any bad news or divisive issues is understandable but doesn't help build much credibility. Two other nationally circulated labor publications—*Labor's Heritage*, from the George Meany Memorial Archives, and *Labor History*, published by the Tamiment Institute—are academic efforts to discuss labor history that do not market to a mass audience.

Attempts for an independent, topical national labor publication have had limited success. *Labor Notes* began publishing in 1979, and its monthly circulation has grown every year, to about eight thousand. Aimed at local officers and rank-and-file members, the publication often rankles labor leadership. Yet editor Jim Woodward says his publication's "influence has increased more than its circulation." Woodward also says his publication's goal remains to offer a free debate of ideas about the future of the labor movement. *Labor Notes* began with a foundation grant. It continues to grow with subscriptions, fund-raising appeals, and a profitable book-publishing side business.

A less ideological publication that is also finding some success is *Labor Research Review* from the Chicago-based Midwest Center for Labor Research. The center is independent, funded by foundations and fees for services. The *Labor Research Review*, published twice a year, is a substantial booklet that features articles and case studies focused on particular issues, sometimes with a pro-and-con debate. Past issues have covered both cutting-edge and traditional issues, with titles as varied as "Workers as Owners," "Up against the Open Shop: New Initiatives in the Building Trades," and "Privatization and Contracting Out." Circulation is growing. The journal's four thousand print run usually sells out. Marketing the publication more widely could increase its circulation substantially.

Other attempts at national labor publications have been less success-ful. An attempt in 1990 to launch a national publication entitled *Your Payday* folded after a couple of issues. A controversy over editorial control and advertising policies doomed the project. The *New England Labor News & Commentary* also ceased publication in 1990 after a grow-ing squabble over editorial control. Editorial control is the point of vulnerability for any labor publication.

If the goal is an independent, credible national labor publication that is not totally dependent on advertising, a large amount of working capital must be raised before the first issue is conceived. Pizzigati's financing scheme isn't strong enough. Two million dollars is a drop in the bucket for a national publication; fifty thousand subscriptions at $25 each isn't enough. The subscription rate must be increased, and the number of potential subscribers should be raised.

Very few unions would be wealthy, willing, or trusting enough to put up the necessary capital. (And it is a rare union that will give the names and addresses of its key leaders and local union officers to any outside agency.) A few unions might provide partial financing, but a full-scale search for foundation support would have to be undertaken. No pub-lication should be launched without at least $5 million in committed subscriptions for the first two years.

Advertising sales efforts—based on an advertising policy that ad-heres strictly to the International Labor Communications Association code of ethics—could be another avenue for financial support. Most advertisers probably wouldn't or couldn't advertise in a national labor publication, but the potential for some advertising revenue should not be completely rejected. Undercapitalization is a recipe for disaster. Every possible funding source and financial support would have to be in place before one word is published. Editorial independence cannot survive without financial independence.

Pizzigati is right to warn that the last thing the labor movement needs is a "rogue trade press slashing and burning its way through the lives of men and women working to build the labor movement." The labor movement has many critics. Labor leaders have to endure personal attacks and politically motivated critiques. More benign advice of "What labor should do" is often proffered but not often useful. Labor also has real enemies. Enemies can use devious tactics.

To be independent, but not a tool of some clique, political opponent, or ideological enemy, would be difficult but absolutely necessary. It would take a strong publisher to build credibility within and without the labor movement. It would require a clear statement of intent and purpose. The labor movement would be strengthened by an independent, credible, and financially healthy national publication. Past attempts—those that have failed as well as those that survive—offer guidance to those who would launch a new labor publication. Pizzigati's contention that after a year or two of bulk subscriptions, the publication would have to make a go of it independently with individual subscriptions is on the right track.

In the end, our members and friends would be the judge of whether such a national labor publication meets their needs and expectations. It would indeed be a worthy goal to put a national labor daily on the nation's newsstands in the next decade. With careful planning, adequate financing, and strong leadership, such a goal could be reached.

The Case for a National Labor Paper: Rejoinder II

Jo-Ann Mort

Does the labor movement need a national labor paper? Yes. Can it sustain a daily? Probably not. Can the labor movement afford not to intervene in some way, with a weekly—if not a daily—paper? I don't think so.

To use an out-of-fashion word, we in the labor movement need to establish hegemony. We need to change a media status quo that routinely ignores, dismisses, and contradicts the labor point of view. The media, of course, aren't supposed to shaft the trade union point of view. The media are supposed to be objective, and this objectivity remains a powerful myth. We in labor see this myth exposed on an everyday basis, perhaps most visibly in the collapse of the daily newspaper labor beat.

Historically, the labor beat reporter didn't just write about changes in union leadership or honorees at fund-raising dinners. More often than not, the labor reporter was someone sensitive to issues of concern to working people, issues ranging from health care to pensions to the economy. The collapse of labor beat reporting means that working people, in effect, have lost our eyes and ears on daily papers.

Now that newspaper business sections have proliferated, labor coverage has been relegated to business section reporters. These business reporters—even at the "best" newspapers—are usually unfamiliar with anything but the prevailing economic orthodoxy on the issues that affect working people. These reporters are profoundly unfamiliar with

Jo-Ann Mort is the director of communications for the Amalgamated Clothing and Textile Workers Union, but the views expressed here are her own. Mort is a member of the editorial boards of Dissent *and* Tikkun *magazines. Her articles have appeared in* Dissent, *the* Nation, Newsday, *the* New York Times Book Review, In These Times, Commonweal, *and other publications.*

left-of-center economists or with economic policies taken for granted in countries with large social democratic movements.

One painful recent example of this orthodoxy was the coverage of the debate over President George Bush's proposal for "fast-track authority" to negotiate a free trade agreement with Mexico. The media coverage hit hard on the theme that labor opposition to the Bush position was stifling "free trade." In newspaper editorials across the country, we in labor were killed.

The media coverage defined the free trade debate solely in terms set by the Bush administration. The coverage, for example, almost totally ignored the notion of a social charter, which many in the labor movement see as a viable alternative to the Bush approach to economic integration.

In Europe, where economic integration between nations is every bit as hot an issue as in the United States, the social charter concept is central to the debate. In the European Community, labor and its allies are taking a social charter approach to the problems of integrating low-wage and high-wage economies. The European social charter, for instance, is calling for a community-wide minimum wage that would discourage employers from shifting jobs from high- to low-wage nations and help improve the standard of living in low-wage countries.

If the United States were to integrate North America on the basis of the wage scale of Ontario, instead of Mexico, the labor movement in the United States would probably support a free trade agreement with Mexico and Canada wholeheartedly. The media never made this point in the coverage of the free trade issue. We in the labor movement were unable to get our central ideas into the debate. The available media outlets simply did not cover the full breadth of the economic spectrum.

The broader media problem here is the virtual lockout of labor from the op-ed pages of our nation's newspapers. This lockout doesn't just deny labor leaders meaningful access to op-ed space, particularly in comparison to business leaders. The lockout also extends to academics and other commentators who suggest a labor-oriented agenda.

This situation is changing slightly, but the exception still proves the rule. Economist Robert Kuttner comes to mind as one columnist who has broken through. Kuttner's column appears regularly in *Business Week* and the *Boston Globe*. Yet even the well-published Kuttner, who has written several critically acclaimed books, is not widely read or consulted by mainstream business reporters. Several different business writers from our nation's top newspapers have told me that they are totally unfamiliar with Kuttner's work.

All this brings us back to the need for a labor paper. I feel a sense of urgency on two counts. First, we need to provide a full range of information to union members and potential union members. Second—and equally important—we need a labor paper because writers and editors in the established media need an opportunity to learn about the world from a labor perspective.

A labor paper could change the tone of national political debate, especially on an issue like national health care. Today, we see no immediate solution to the health care mess on the horizon—no national leadership and, amazingly enough, no groundswell of protest. Why isn't there a revolt in the streets demanding access to health care? A national labor daily could perhaps begin to build a groundswell for health care in a variety of ways.

One would be by publicizing the misfortunes of worker-victims—not merely to the sixty thousand subscribers to the *AFL-CIO News*, most of whom are more knowledgeable about this issue than the average American, but to the tens of millions of potential allies whom we in the labor movement must reach to be able to generate national action on health care.

To fire up this debate, our new national daily would also have to cover the internal debate now raging within the AFL-CIO and in the rest of the labor movement around health care reform. Do we back a Canadian-style, single-payer, national insurance plan, or do we back a multi-payer plan similar to that of Germany? Instead of posing such a cutting-edge question as an internal matter for the leaders of organized labor to decide, we would take this debate to the pages of our national daily, where the goal wouldn't be to strengthen the hand of one side or another, but rather to inform and educate our members and all working people about the options.

Most Americans don't know what they're missing in health care because they don't know fully what the health care system is like in Canada or Great Britain or Germany. A national labor paper could broaden knowledge about health care options and help move health care to the forefront of the national agenda.

Other related issues like parental leave and child care could also be addressed in a newspaper that would give labor's legislative agenda full coverage. This coverage could influence a broad, voting public and help move labor's legislative program along.

What we don't need is another "trade" press. This is my fundamental disagreement with Sam Pizzigati's piece. The labor movement is not just another interest group or industry. The labor movement is—or should be—a social movement organized to fundamentally restructure society.

We in labor must formulate our own analysis of the economy, our own international perspective, our own agenda for the nation—in short, our own worldview. This requires a press with a class perspective and analysis. Either the labor movement sees itself as an agent of class struggle or it doesn't. I think we have to, if we want to survive. To wage this urgent battle, we need the tools. Our own media outlet would be a first step.

Even if we accept Sam's definition of a trade press—publications that speak "directly to the men and women whose lives revolve around a particular industry or community of interest"—I have to stress that a national labor daily would be much more than another trade publication because the labor movement must be more than another trade organization.

There is some minor precedent for the labor publication I have in mind. When eastern European immigrants made up the bulk of the needle trade unions, newspapers in Italian, Yiddish, and other languages proliferated. The Yiddish-language *Daily Forward*, for example, was the newspaper of the Socialist party wing of the needle trade unionists. This wing even had its own radio station in New York, WEVD, for Eugene Victor Debs. These media outlets were linked to specific political parties or tendencies and were not organs of the labor movement. But they did serve to inform and politicize a trade union constituency in an era of great militancy and fervor in the labor movement.

Such media outlets are essential. As George Orwell warned the British Labour government in 1946: "The most necessary step is . . . to raise the general level of political understanding . . . this business of publicising and explaining itself is not easy for a Labour Government, faced by a press which at bottom is mostly hostile."

Elsewhere in the world, explicitly ideological press outlets are commonplace. Newspapers in Europe are either identified with a social democratic or labor party, if they aren't identified with the right-wing party. In Israel, *Davar* is the newspaper of the labor movement. In France, *Le Monde*, that nation's equivalent of the *New York Times*, is considered close to the PS, the French Socialist party. In Spain, the leading newspaper supports the ruling Socialist party.

But, historically, the American labor movement has been less class conscious than its international counterparts. As a result, organized labor in this country has not developed a full-court cradle-to-grave strategy that would have to include a more aggressive press strategy.

Were we not victims of "American exceptionalism" as the world's only industrialized nation without a mass labor or socialist (I use "democratic socialist," "labor," "socialist," and "social democratic" interchangeably, and in the European context, for lack of a better shorthand) party, we would be more aggressive on the media front. We cannot undo history, but we can create a national labor daily, which would at least provide us with an outlet from which our ideas and agenda could percolate out to a broader public.

Who would write for such a paper? Unfortunately, there are too many excellent out-of-work labor reporters. These reporters could provide an immediate reporting and editing staff. Reporters, writers, and columnists could also be drawn from our membership. I agree with Sam that these reporters and editors must be independent artisans. As Sam points out, we're already set up on both a regional and national basis to assist in news gathering and distribution.

An independent labor daily would, no doubt, include squabbling points of view. My preference would be for a democratic socialist perspective similar to that of the mainstream European parties and the New Democratic party in Canada to emerge as the dominant perspective in such a newspaper.

In the 1990s, two priorities will be critical to labor's survival—and revival: organizing new members and changing the public climate about organized labor. Publicity and card signing go hand in hand. A broad-based labor paper would facilitate both.

Just as Sam daydreams of the reporter from our national labor daily asking a question at a White House briefing, I, too, have a fantasy. I imagine a small southern town where the textile mill owner also owns the sewer system, the school board, the newspaper, and the local cable TV operation. (That doesn't take much imagination!) I imagine that my union has just started an organizing campaign in this small southern town.

The lead article in the mill owner's evening newspaper—the equivalent of a captive audience meeting—alleges that unions are violent and strike-happy and demand high dues. But my union has its own media resource: the national labor daily. We take an ad out in the daily announcing the beginning of our campaign and asking all interested workers to be at the church on Main Street on Friday night to hear about the union campaign.

On the page opposite our ad is a story about what it's like to work in a unionized textile mill, where workers' pensions are protected. The labor daily compares this union mill to a nearby nonunion mill where the owner just shut down all operations and stole the pension fund as part of a leveraged buyout scheme.

Another page in the labor daily features a historical look at the Canadian health care system, charting the role the Canadian labor movement played in establishing it. Still another page spotlights a column written by a southern union member calling for the equalizing of funds for public education in the rural South.

Imagine if this labor daily newspaper appeared not only at the plant gates of the mill my union was trying to organize but also on sale at the gas station of the one union-friendly businessperson in town! What if this newspaper were sold in one gas station in every small southern town?

Imagine!

Concluding Thoughts

House Organs No More: Toward a New Labor Press

Sam Pizzigati and Fred J. Solowey

Not long ago, a local union official explained to us why he opposed any effort to start a publication in his local.

"Hardly anybody comes to union meetings now," said the local union leader. "If we started a newsletter, then nobody would come."

This offhand comment strikes us as a perfect place to begin these concluding observations on America's labor press because the assumptions behind this comment are widely shared within labor leadership ranks. And what are these assumptions? The first is obvious: that a newsletter could make no contribution toward getting members more involved in their organization. The second: that the only purpose of union publications—or union meetings, for that matter—is to pass *down* to members information held by union officials.

These two assumptions are part of a mind-set that blinds our local leader above from comprehending that a union publication or meeting might have a grander purpose than passing information down to members. This same mind-set is what drives even well-intentioned union leaders to pack their publications with articles about what they're doing and what they're thinking. For these labor leaders, union publications are one-way transmission belts for minutes, grievance reports, and exhortations. Officialdom passes information. Members receive it.

In effective organizations, of course, information is not a commodity that moves along one-way channels. A truly vital union—any truly vital institution—recognizes that the flow of information must be a two-way street. Union members, after all, aren't passive receptacles for information. They're men and women struggling to improve the quality of their lives.

These men and women need a forum, a place to exchange their thoughts with others, to learn from others, to test their ideas against others' ideas. Trade unions need to provide this forum by opening wide the channels through which information can flow, not just from leader to member, but from member to member, from member to leader.

Within the labor movement, the trade union publication offers what may be the single best forum for this absolutely essential exchange of information, which is why we believe that the debate over the role of the labor press must be joined by all labor, not just labor journalists.

We harbor no romantic illusions about the power of the labor press. No publications alone, no matter how vital, can overcome the social and economic pressures currently squeezing labor. But we deeply believe that a reinvigorated labor press can make a significant contribution to labor renewal. We deeply believe that labor papers can help people feel their unions belong to them. We deeply believe that labor journalism can help union members recognize the necessity of unity—and respect the value of diversity in an increasingly multicultural work environment.

The new labor press we envision is, as the contributions in this volume clearly demonstrate, now taking shape at every level of the labor movement. But this new labor press, even at its best, remains fettered by the habits of the past.

We have yet to break, for instance, the "good news" barrier. We labor journalists still hesitate to acknowledge our unions' internal shortcomings. We too often blame, almost by rote, all labor's problems on the "enemy." This isn't surprising. It's far easier for labor editors to place the blame on some external other than to make the case internally within our unions that faults ought to be admitted, that mistakes ought to be acknowledged.

Few leaders, of course, relish the idea of admitting failure. Few ever do. Indeed, has any union leader ever begun a president's column by acknowledging "I was wrong"?

Truly effective leaders, of course, don't fear candor. Effective leaders understand that candor—owning up to faults—can be an effective leadership strategy. Take the example of a male local union leader who decides to write a column denouncing sexual harassment in the workplace—but only after angry members charge that his local isn't doing enough for women who have been harassed. This column, if it followed the standard labor press formula, would solemnly condemn sexism and cite a long litany of union initiatives to advance equal rights for women.

What impact would this solemn declaration have on readers? Activists in the union would likely snicker at the hypocrisy of a union leader who only reluctantly took up the battle against sexual harassment. And what about those unreconstructed members of the local who can't understand why women are making such a "fuss" about "good, harmless fun"? Would the local leader's pious declaration against sexual harassment set these members thinking and maybe even change their behavior? Not likely. If pious sermons could change behavior, we wouldn't see any sinners sitting in churches.

But what if our local leader opened his column on sexism on a different note? What if he began by describing the sexist attitudes he himself used to hold? What if he admitted that his local union was slow to pick up on the fight against sexual harassment? What if he traced how his own personal thinking had changed over time? If the president's declaration took this more open approach, might not union members with wrongheaded attitudes about sexual harassment see in themselves the same attitudes that the local leader had overcome? Might not close-minded union members see the possibility of change in their own behavior?

Admitting error, of course, takes courage and flexibility on the part of leaders. But editors have to show courage and flexibility, too, for on them falls the responsibility for making the case for candor in an environment that regards candor as more a dangerous threat than a useful opportunity.

Editors, of course, must understand that theirs are political positions, that building allies and consensus for candid and meaningful labor journalism is a long and arduous process that cannot be short-circuited by fawning over union officials or grandstanding as crusaders. Editors, in short, need to develop the trust of their union's elected leaders. The more editors develop this trust—and win leadership support for an open, democratic approach to union publishing—the better their labor journalism will be.

All this, of course, is far easier to say than to do. We know, from a quarter century of labor journalism experience, just how difficult editing labor papers that really matter to members can be. Turn to our own publications, and you'll no doubt find much of what we criticize others for doing—or failing to do. We're not even certain that we can define, in every particular, just what the parameters of the new labor press we seek ought to be.

Should labor journalists, for instance, devote their scarce space to covering popular culture? Many decent activists within labor, including the union presidents in the roundtable that appeared earlier in this volume, consider cultural commentary a distraction from the labor business at hand. We tend to disagree. Why not review rock music or interview soap opera heroes? Looking at mass culture from a labor perspective might help people better understand where they stand in the world—and encourage union members to read their publications in the first place.

We hope this volume has raised a hundred other questions for you. But we're not offering any definitive answers. We don't intend to settle the debate opened here. In fact, we want to encourage more debate— more debate about what belongs in labor papers and what doesn't, more debate on who should call the editorial shots and why, more debate on what readers need and labor leaders want.

One of these leaders, AFL-CIO secretary-treasurer Tom Donahue, spoke at the November 1991 convention of the International Labor Communications Association in Detroit. Donahue was asked about his views on the labor press by a local union editor. He began by stressing that freedom of the press is a tough and complicated issue "for any publication or communication activity that is rooted in implementing the mission of an organization."

"I do think," Donahue continued, "that publications, some of which I see, which are pure vanity press are a waste of time." A publication that "tells you how grand the leader or leaders are," said Donahue, isn't going to impress the modern-day union member. Unions, Donahue went on to argue, ought to find appropriate mechanisms for "the presentation in union publications of the contrary position."

"We all believe that a free press is what makes democratic institutions thrive," concluded Donahue, "and a controlled house press is not a free press."

We hope labor leaders—and union members all across the country— will join Tom Donahue and, together, grapple with the issues that face the labor press. The future of the labor press, after all, isn't just a debate for labor journalists. It's a debate for all labor. Join it.

About the Editors

Sam Pizzigati currently directs the publishing program of America's largest union, the 2.1-million-member National Education Association. Before joining NEA in 1981, Pizzigati edited national publications for the American Federation of State, County and Municipal Employees (AFSCME), the Asbestos Workers, and the United Association of Plumbers and Pipefitters. He is the author of the 1992 book, *The Maximum Wage: A Common-Sense Prescription for Revitalizing America—by Taxing the Very Rich* (The Apex Press).

Fred J. Solowey is currently a communications coordinator with the International Brotherhood of Teamsters. From 1980 to May 1992, Solowey worked as an editor of the *Public Employee*, the 1.3-million-circulation journal of the American Federation of State, County and Municipal Employees (AFSCME). Solowey, winner of the prestigious Max Steinbock Award for labor journalism in 1985, also founded the AFSCME news service for local union editors. He is a vice-president of the International Labor Communications Association.

Index